HINDU LITERATURE

HINDU LITERATURE;

OR

THE ANCIENT BOOKS OF INDIA.

ELIZABETH A. REED

GYAN

Published by

Gyan Publishing House
5, Ansari Road
Daryaganj, New Delhi-110002
Phone: 011-47034999, 9811692060
E-mail: books@gyanbooks.com

Distribution Network
gyanbooks.com
India, USA, Canada, UK, Australia, France

ISBN: 978-81-212-8870-5 (PB)
First Published, 1891

2nd Impression 2023

Printed at: Gyan Press, Delhi.

HINDU LITERATURE
AUTHOR: ELIZABETH A. REED

HINDU LITERATURE;

OR

THE ANCIENT BOOKS OF INDIA.

BY

ELIZABETH A. REED,

MEMBER OF THE PHILOSOPHICAL SOCIETY OF GREAT BRITAIN.

CHICAGO:

SCOTT, FORESMAN AND CO.

1899.

TABLE OF CONTENTS.

HINDŪ LITERATURE; OR, THE ANCIENT BOOKS OF INDIA.

CHAPTER I.

HINDŪ LITERATURE.

CHAPTER II.

MYTHOLOGY OF THE VEDAS.

CHAPTER III.

MYTHOLOGY OF LATER HINDŪ WORKS.

CHAPTER IV.

THE VEDAS AND THE SUTTEE.

CHAPTER V.

THE BRĀHMAṆAS.

CHAPTER VI.

THE CODE OF MANU.

CHAPTER VII.

THE UPANISHADS.

CHAPTER VIII.

THE MONOTHEISM OF THE UPANISHADS.

CHAPTER IX.

COSMOGONY.

CHAPTER X.

THE ORIGIN OF MAN.

CHAPTER XI.

METEMPSYCHOSIS.

CHAPTER XII.

REWARDS AND PUNISHMENTS.

CHAPTER XIII.

THE RĀMĀYAṆA.

CHAPTER XIV.

THE STORY OF THE RĀMĀYAṆA.

CHAPTER XV.

THE STORY OF THE RĀMĀYAṆA, CONTINUED.

CHAPTER XVI.

THE STORY OF THE RĀMĀYAṆA, CONCLUDED.

CHAPTER XVII.

THE MAHĀ-BHĀRATA.

CHAPTER XVIII.

LEGENDS OF THE MAHĀ-BHĀRATA—THE GREAT WAR.

CHAPTER XIX.

LEGENDS OF THE MAHĀ-BHĀRATA—THE GREAT WAR, CONCLUDED.

CHAPTER XX.

LEGENDS OF THE MAHĀ-BHĀRATA, CONCLUDED. SĀVITRĪ AND SATYAVĀN.

CHAPTER XXI.

THE BHAGAVAD-GĪTĀ.

CHAPTER XXII.

THE PURĀṆAS.

CHAPTER XXIII.

KṚISHṆA.

CHAPTER XXIV.

CONCLUSION.

PREFACE.

THE ancient books of India comprise such an enormous mass of literature that the labor of a single lifetime would not suffice for the mastery of their contents and a solution of the problems which they present; yet such has been the progress of Oriental philology during the last decade, that an intelligent survey of this great field of research is quite possible to the student.

A careful study of the Purāṇas alone in the original Sanskṛit would occupy half a century, but a valuable series of extracts and analyses can be found in twenty-six large folio volumes of manuscripts in the library of the Asiatic Society of Calcutta, and a year of patient work devoted to Professor Wilson's translations gives one an intelligible idea of their contents.

Colonel Colin Mackenzie occupied his leisure time for years in collecting and arranging thirty-four large folio volumes of manuscripts, and his careful methods were of great value to scholars who came after him.

Historical students have also been greatly aided by the pioneer work of those who have examined and compared genealogical lists, deciphered inscriptions, and discovered the sites of ancient cities. The Vedas themselves have been carefully copied and translated, and, indeed, all of the most important portions of Indian lore are now available to the English reader. Still, the books themselves, with their commentaries and the works connected with their history and philology, constitute so large a library that the busy people of modern times cannot afford to spend their years in sifting the contents of these colossal works in order to find the gems of thought which they may contain.

In a field so vast it is only by a division of labor that satisfactory results can be accomplished, and hence an effort has been made in the present volume, to give the chronology of these ancient books, showing where they belong in the world's history, together with a résumé of their teachings and specimens of their literary style. The work has been done as briefly as was consistent with accuracy, in the belief that an intelligible idea of Hindū literature in a condensed form would be acceptable to many readers.

Beginning with the earliest composition of the Āryan race, the current of Brāhmanic thought has been traced down through their most important works, which have been considered in chronological order from the earliest songs of the Ṛig-veda to the fanciful conceits of the latest Purāṇas.

The primary object of the work has been accuracy of statement; therefore the quotations from Hindū works have been carefully chosen from the best available translations, and no historical or chronological statement has been made without the concurrence of the highest authorities.

It is a pleasure to acknowledge one's indebtedness to such rare scholars as Professor F. Max Müller, the late Horace Hayman Wilson, a distinguished foreign member of the French Academy, and of the Imperial Academy of St. Petersburg, and Sir M. Monier-Williams, K. C. I. E., the Boden Professor of Sanskṛit at Oxford University, who has devoted fifty years of his life to the study of Sanskṛit literature and to a solution of the problems of India.

Although many other Orientalists have been consulted, and credit duly given where the quotations are made, yet the author is especially indebted to Professor F. Max Müller and Sir M. Monier-Williams, for assistance derived from their personal letters, and particularly desires to acknowledge their great kindness in examining portions of the work.

The manuscript of the chapter entitled "Kṛishṇa" has been carefully revised by Sir M. Monier-Williams, who has also added valuable foot-notes, while other portions of the copy have been revised by Professor F. Max Müller.

In giving a brief synopsis of the great Indian Epics, the main lines of thought and incident in the original poems as given by Wheeler, Griffiths, and others, have been carefully followed. It has been deemed best, however, to present these classic gems in simpler forms of narration and description than can be found in literal translation.

The work has been prepared in the hope that it may attract the attention of the general reader to the beauties of Hindū literature, and be of real service to careful students in this field of thought. To their interests it is commended by

THE AUTHOR.

PRONUNCIATION.

A LITTLE attention to the diacritical points will enable the reader to pronounce correctly the musical names of the Hindūs.

In the present volume Sir M. Monier-Williams' method of transliteration, as presented in his Sanskṛit Grammar, has been chiefly used; the nasal *m*, however, is represented here as in the works of Prof. Max Müller by the italic letter; *n*, as pronounced in "singe," is also indicated by the italic.

Diacritical points are omitted from the foot-notes, the system of pronunciation being clearly presented in the body of the work.

A—a is pronounced as in rur*a*l.
Ā—ā " " t*a*r, f*a*ther, etc.
I—i " " f*i*ll.
Ī—ī " " pol*i*ce.
U—u " " f*u*ll.
Ū—ū " " r*u*de.
Ṛi—ṛi " " mer*ri*ly.
Ṛī—ṛī " " ma*ri*ne.
E—e " " pr*e*y.
Ai—ai " " *ai*sle.
Au—au " " H*au*s (German).
N̲—n̲ sounded like *n* in the French mo*n*.
Ṇ—ṇ " as in *none* (ṇuṇ).
m (italic) has a nasal sound.
ḥ is a Visarga, or a distinctly audible aspirate.

Kh—kh sounded like *ch* in *church.*

Kh—kh	pronounced as in		in*kh*orn.
G—g	"	"	*g*un or do*g*.
Gh—gh	"	"	lo*g*-*h*ut.
Ć—ć	"	"	dolće (in music)=English ch in *ch*ur*ch*.
Ćh—ćh	"	"	churc*hh*ill.
Ṭ—ṭ	"	"	*t*rue.
Ṭh—ṭh	"	"	an*t* *h*ill.
Ḍ—ḍ	"	"	*d*rum.
Ḍh—ḍh	"	"	re*dh*aired (reḍ *h*aired).
Th—th	"	"	nu*th*ook, though more dental.
Dh—dh	"	"	a*dh*ere, though more dental.
Ś—ś	"	"	*s*ure, se*ss*ions.
S—s	"	"	*s*ir or mi*ss*.

THE ANCIENT BOOKS OF INDIA.

CHAPTER I.

HINDŪ LITERATURE.

WHAT IS THE VEDA — THE AGE OF THE VEDAS — WHEN WRITTEN — THE ṚIG-VEDA.

A MOST fascinating field for research is to be found in the ancient literary productions of the Hindūs. These gems of antiquity belong to that region where the peaks of the Himālayas lift their icy brows to the morning light, and where in the groves at their feet were chanted the early Vedic hymns.

India is the land of the cocoanut and the palm, of the feathery tamarind and the stately mango tree. The brightest birds from the southern isles come to feast in her spicy groves and linger among her flowers. Her sacred Ganges is indeed "the gift of heaven." Finding a birthplace in the snow fields between the mountain peaks, the pure current rushes down the rocky pathway in a long cascade, bringing life and hope to the green valleys below.

The literature born in this dream-land of beauty and fragrance bears within its bosom the eloquence of poetry and the rhythm of song; but India's ancient books are so colossal in their proportions that European scholars looked upon them for years in dismay. Life is too short to enable any one student to obtain a complete knowledge of Oriental philology, language, and history.

The late Horace Hayman Wilson devoted his vast learning and many years of arduous labor to the translation of a portion of the ancient books of India, while Prof. Max Müller has given twenty of the best years of his life to the Veda alone.

It was not until our own generation that Indian literature was properly classified and published, even in the Sanskṛit tongue. Hitherto the veil of antiquity and mysticism had hidden these works from investigation. The Vedas were chanted for ages before they were ever written, being handed down orally from one generation to the next. The years which were devoted to education by the better class of Hindūs were largely occupied in learning the Veda from the lips of the teacher.[1] The fact that these books for a long time existed only in the living volumes of memory gave them a weird influence over the European as well as the Hindū, and when we consider that the Veda occupies nearly the same position in Sanskṛit that the Old Testament holds in Hebrew literature, that it is as sacred to the Hindū as our own Scriptures are to the Christian, we cannot wonder that it has attracted the attention of scholars and antiquarians in every part of the world.

After a time the Veda was committed to writing, but still it existed only in manuscript, and when the directors of the East India Company invited the

1 Origin and Growth of Religion, page 148.

Pandits, or Hindū professors, to publish a complete edition of their own sacred books, it became apparent that there was not a single Brāhman in Bengal who could edit or supervise such an edition. The work therefore devolved entirely upon European scholars, and bravely they have accomplished their formidable task. Prof. Max Müller patiently copied the entire text of the Ṛig-Veda and also the commentary upon it. And thus it came to pass that the whole of the work was first published, not on the banks of the sacred Ganges, but under the shadow of an English university. In restoring these old manuscripts and placing their thoughts in permanent form, our scholars have preserved relics more ancient than the ruins of Nineveh and Babylon; more fascinating to the student of literature than the foundation stones of Thebes or Memphis.

The Sanskṛit edition was translated by the indefatigable Wilson, and this ancient literary monument of India became the property of the English-speaking world. The work of restoring and translating Hindū works was greatly facilitated by Colin Mackenzie, the enthusiastic collector of Indian MSS.; but to such men as Sir William Jones, H. T. Colebrook, Horace Wilson, and Max Müller, the world owes a debt which it can never pay.

Orientalists were at first unable to resist the temptation of giving to the public the gems only, which they recovered from masses of almost worthless literature, and it is evident that much harm has been done by this partial work at the hands of enthusiastic translators who have given us, unintentionally, no doubt, far more exalted ideas of the general character of these books than are justified by impartial views of even one complete section. The time has come when the Vedas must be treated with more candor, even though with less enthusiasm; when they must receive honest criticism and impartial representation at the hands of scholars. Later translators, feeling that fancy must yield to fact, and imagination give place to fair investigation, have sought to make their task a faithful one. Paragraphs which are too gross for translation have been appended in the original text, so that the critical historian may decipher even these if necessary. A fair estimate of these books can, of course, be obtained only from complete translations, and one of the grandest results of the life-work of Max Müller is the service he has rendered in the translation of these large volumes of The Sacred Books of the East into the English tongue. He has been assisted in this arduous and discouraging work by such distinguished scholars as Beal, West, Bühler, Palmer. Cowell, Darmesteter, Rhys Davids, Eggeling, Jacobi, Jolly, Kern, Legge, Oldenberg, each one of whom is found in the front rank of his own special department of Oriental literature.

The scholarship and character of these men place the integrity of their translations beyond question, and they have opened before us a most fascinating field for investigation. When we add to this valuable series, the Ṛig-veda Saṇhitā, the Vishṇu Purāṇa and other translations by Prof. Wilson, the Rāmāyaṇa by Griffiths, the digest of the two great epics by J. Talboys Wheeler, and the various partial translations of the Mahā-bhārata by different scholars, besides a multitude of translations from Hindū drama and romance, the collection of Indian works now available to the English reader is a very extensive one.

According to Max Müller, the Pandits were seriously opposed to the publication of the Veda in Sanskṛit by English scholars, for although they are honest enough to admit that the edition is complete and authentic, its publication has taken from them their principal weapon against Christian missionaries. In former times the Brāhmans claimed that there was no commandment in the Old Testament, no precept in the New, which had not been anticipated in the Veda, and if the incredulous missionary called for the manuscript he was coolly informed that so sacred a book must not be profaned by the touch of an unbeliever. But Hindū assumptions are now discredited by the publication of the Veda in both Sanskṛit and English. It was also claimed that the Veda was thousands of years older than the Old Testament, and that the historic portions of the Hebrew Scriptures were borrowed largely from Hindū sources. Many honest men, and even scholars, who should have been more careful in their statements, indorsed this theory, the novice with loud and confident assertion—in which some of them still indulge—the scholar with more reserve.

Lieut. Wilford, who was an honest enthusiast, determined, with praiseworthy zeal, to find out the truth of the statements which were being freely made by a certain class of critics. With this object in view, he interviewed Hindū scholars, but without obtaining any information. Becoming more explicit, he related the stories of Adam and Eve, of Abraham and Sarah, and assured them that they would find these narratives in their sacred books. To stimulate their zeal, he offered ample rewards if they would find in their ancient manuscripts the stories he had told them. The reserve of the Pandits was fully conquered by the hope of gain, and ere long Lieut. Wilford was delighted to have placed in his hands Sanskṛit manuscripts containing the very proofs he sought. Great was the enthusiasm in Calcutta, London, Paris, and throughout the universities of Germany when these manuscripts were pronounced genuine by such experts as Sir William Jones and others. At last, however, the coincidences became so numerous, and the supply corresponded so exactly to the financial reward, that the manuscripts were again carefully examined, when it was found that clever forgeries had been committed; that leaves had been carefully inserted in ancient manuscripts, and on them had been written in Sanskṛit the Bible stories which the Hindūs had learned from the lips of the enthusiastic Wilford.

Lieut. Wilford, to his honor be it said, did not for a moment hesitate to acknowledge that he had been imposed upon.[1] But in the meantime, his essays had been widely read, and they are still quoted by men who have never heard of his public confession.

The literature of the Vedas is not logical in its construction. There is no page of lucid reasoning or convincing argument in all its ancient lore. It is not scientific; its theories of cosmogony and anthropology

[1] Chips, Vol. V., pp. 102-109.

are wild and fanciful in the extreme, and though of great historic value in many ways, it is in no sense whatever the production of historians. The dreamy sons of the Southland had very little taste for historic facts, and much of the literary value of their writings is found in their poetry. It is true that many of their hymns and songs are childish or vulgar—in the language of Max Müller, they are "tedious, low and commonplace." But amidst masses of literary rubbish we find poetic gems which are worthy of any age or clime.

Some of the songs of the Veda are entitled to high rank, and in many points the great epics of India will compare favorably with the immortal productions of Homer. The imagination of the Hindū is as luxuriant as his own tropical forests. His mighty rivers come pouring down from the grandest mountain ranges of the world, where amid the lightnings that flash around their peaks, Sublimity holds her court. Poetry lives in the very atmosphere of the Himālayas—it haunts the rich verdure at their feet, and kisses their snowy brows in the crimson light of the setting sun. The romance of India's people is as irresistible as the current of her Indus or the musical waves of her Ganges.

The exploration of this labyrinth of thought is like wandering through a tropical forest, where the grandeur of towering trees alternates with sunny glades of vine-wreathed beauty and fragrant flowers; but the student must not gather the roses of romance and avoid the sterner work of careful analysis; it is the province of fair investigation to examine every tree and floral vine in this wilderness of literature, and to keep carefully along the path of honest criticism even in the Indian land of enchantment.

WHAT IS THE VEDA?

The word Veda means knowledge and is the term applied to divine unwritten knowledge. In the Hindū world it is not only the earliest literary production, but the acknowledged standard of authority referred to in all their important works, both sacred and profane. The Veda is quoted or alluded to in philosophical, grammatical, lexicographical and metrical, as well as theological treatises. Indeed, this important work may be said to form the background of the whole literary world of India, and upon all subjects it is considered the best and highest authority, from which there is no appeal.

The name Veda is applied by the Brāhmans to the whole body of their sacred writings. The earliest collection of Vedic literature may be classed in three grand divisions:

1. MANTRA, or the Hymns of Prayer and Praise, as found in the Ṛig-veda. By this is meant the collection of hymns and invocations, which were doubtless composed by a succession of poets in very early times, and which, while they are of unequal poetical merit and contain many foolish repetitions, are still important as embodying the earliest forms of religious conception known in the history of this strange people.

2. THE BRĀHMAṆA, or the ritualistic precepts and illustrations which are intended to direct the priests in the performance of their religious ceremonies. They

also give long and tedious explanations of the origin and meaning of the sacrifices themselves.

3. THE UPANISHADS, which are supposed to teach the doctrines of the Vedas, although it would be a difficult task to deduce any system either of faith or practice from this labyrinth of confused philosophy and fanciful conceits.

The later important divisions of Hindū literature are:

1. The Rāmāyaṇa and the Mahā-bhārata. These colossal epic poems[1] of themselves form a grand division of literature and reflect the romance and poetry of the Hindū people. They present the most brilliant pictures of Oriental coloring, and the most gorgeous scenes of Eastern magnificence to be found upon the pages of fancy.

2. The Purāṇas, which are confessedly the latest of all productions in Hindū sacred literature; they claim to have been written by a generous sage in order to simplify the doctrines of the Veda for the benefit of women and others who might not aspire to the reading or comprehension of the earlier works. Although they do not, critically speaking, belong to the Vedic age, they contain Vedic legends which have been worked up in more modern form, showing that these works were finally given to the world at a time when "the world of the Veda," in its strictest sense, was living only in tradition.

The Vedas proper are only four in number, viz.: the Ṛig-veda, which is the book of praise, and of whose

[1] Prof. Williams speaks of the great epics as being "the bible of the mythological phase of Brahmanism."

hymns there is but one genuine collection. The Sāma-veda is merely an extract from the older work; the Yajur-veda is another manual of extracts intended for the use of the priests; and the fourth, or Atharva-veda,[1] is of much later origin, and of inferior literary value. Therefore the Ṛig-veda is the primary work of its class, and the only one of importance.

Each of the Vedas is an unarranged and promiscuous mass of hymns, prayers, exhortations, and dogmas, without either system or harmony.

According to the teaching of the Hindū priests, the Vedas were coeval with the creation, being simultaneous with the first breath of Brahmā—the creative power—or, at all events, Brahmā was their author and they were among the first things created.

In the Ćhāndogya Upanishad, 17th *Kh*anda and 4th Prapâ*th*aka, it is said of the productions of the Vedas, "Pra*g*âpati (*the Creator*) brooded over the worlds, and from them, thus brooded on, he squeezed out the essences, Agni (fire) from the earth, Vāyu (air) from the sky, Āditya (the sun) from heaven.

"He brooded over these three deities, and from them, thus brooded over, he squeezed out the essences—the

[1] The Atharva-veda, which has been ably edited by Professors Roth and Whitney, is confessedly the most modern of the four, and was not recognized as a fourth Veda until a much later period, according to some authorities, not until after Manu.

Says Prof. Whitney, "The most prominent characteristic feature of the Atharvan is the multitude of incantations which it contains; . . they are directed to the procuring of the greatest variety of desirable ends; most frequently, perhaps, long life or recovery from grievous sickness is the object sought; in that case a talisman, such as a necklace, is sometimes given, or in numerous instances, some plant endowed with marvelous virtues is to be the immediate external means of cure; further, the attainment of wealth or power is aimed at, the downfall of enemies, success in love or in play, the removal of petty pests, and so on, even down to the growth of hair on a bald pate."—*Oriental and Lin. Studies, Vol. 1, page 20.*

Ṛik verses from Agni; the Yagus verses from Vāyu; the Sāman verses from Āditya.

"He brooded over the three-fold knowledge (the three Vedas), and from it, thus brooded over, he squeezed out the essences, the sacred interjection Bhûs from the Ṛik verses, the sacred interjection Bhûvas from the Yagus verses, and the sacred interjection Svar from the Sāman verses."

Each Vedic hymn is said to have its Ṛishi—the sage or philosopher by whom it was first communicated—some of whom were members of the military, and others of the Brāhmanical order. Each Veda consists of two parts, called the Mantra and the Brāhmana, or prayers and precepts. The complete collection of hymns, prayers, and invocations belonging to one Veda is called its Saṉhitā.

AGE OF THE VEDAS.

The Sanskṛit language is antique in form and perfect in structure; it has the refinement of the Greek and the fluency of the Latin, while it bears a strong affinity to both. This classical language of the Hindūs held the same position in India which was accorded to the Greek at Alexandria, and its importance was equal to that of the Latin during the Middle Ages. But the Sanskṛit tongue does not disclose the origin of the races that first spoke it,[1] and the power of historic narration is entirely wanting in its earliest writers.

Klaproth, Kennedy, and others, claim that at a remote period the tribes which were descended from Japheth, the third son of Noah, came from the northwest

[1] It had ceased to be a spoken language at least 300 B. C.—*Sci. of Lang.*, *p. 147.*

and settled in the plains of Hindūstān, bringing with them their own language, which was the stock of the Sanskṛit. This position is apparently endorsed by Adelung,[1] but the data concerning the first peopling of India is not entirely satisfactory. The Sanskṛit furnishes no key with which to unlock the vaults of its own historic treasures. From the first hymn of the Vedas to the last fable of the Purāṇas—a period extending over three thousand years—there is no page of clear historic fact; no biographical account that is not so mixed with legend as to make it unintelligible.[2]

The Vedas are confessedly the oldest of the Hindū scriptures. But their age has been greatly overestimated. It has been customary for a certain class of writers to ascribe to them an antiquity greater by thousands of years than they can justly claim. So long as the question of their age was purely guess-work and the wish was father to the thought, a few thousands, or even a million of years could be added without scruple, and as Sir William Jones remarked, "The comprehensive mind of an Indian chronologist has no limits." History, however, is taking the place of speculation in this, as well as other departments. Says Max Müller, "It will be difficult to settle whether the Veda is the oldest of books, and whether some portions of the Old Testament may not be traced back to the same, or even an earlier date than the oldest hymns of the

1 Hist. Sans. Lit., p. 1.

2 The one reliable date which we have for Indian history before Christ is the mention by Greek historians of an Indian prince (Sandrokottos). He was a contemporary of the early successors of Alexander. . . . He was the founder of a new dynasty upon the Ganges, and his grandson Asoka was the Constantine of Buddhism.—*Whitney.*

Veda."[1] We have no Vedic manuscripts which extend back further than 1200 or 1500 years after Christ, but their contents have been handed down orally from the time of their earliest composition until they were committed to writing, at a comparatively modern date.

In the face of these facts it is no wonder that the eminent Orientalist remarks that "It is not very easy to bridge over this gulf of three thousand years." And again, "It is by no means certain that a further study of Sanskṛit will not deprive many a book of its claims to any high antiquity. Certain portions of the Veda even, which, as far as our knowledge goes at present, we are perfectly justified in referring to the tenth or twelfth century before our era, may dwindle down from their high estate, and those who have believed in their extreme antiquity will then be held up to blame or ridicule."[2]

There is very little historic data on which to form an opinion concerning the time when the Veda began to be written. Max Müller says, "We shall not be able to trace the Indian alphabet much beyond Alexander's invasion. It existed, however, before Alexander." And again, "The Sanskṛit alphabet has always been suspected of being derived from a Semitic source and has not certainly been traced back to a Greek source."[3] He argues that while the alphabet itself existed earlier, the practice of writing came in "toward the latter part of the Sūtra period," and was probably at that time applied to the preservation of the Vedic hymns and other forms of Brāhmanic literature. The Mahā-

[1] Chips, Vol. 1, p. 5.
[2] Int. Sci. of Rel., p. 301.
[3] Hist. Sans. Lit., pp. 516 and 521.

bhārata says, however, that "Those who sell the Vedas, and even those who write them, shall go to hell," showing that although writing was in use at the time of the compilation of the Mahā-bhārata, it was by no means popular as the medium of communication for the Vedas. The fact that there are no Brāhmanic inscriptions earlier than the third century before Christ shows the comparatively late date of the art of writing in India, and Max Müller maintains that until the latter part of the Sūtra period "the collection of hymns and the immense mass of Brāhmanic literature were preserved by means of oral tradition only."[1]

The Sūtra period here alluded to was about 500 B. C.; it was an era of remarkable activity in the intellectual world. In India it marked the formulation of Brāhmanism by her priesthood as shown in her system of jurisprudence collated by Manu, and witnessed the reformation of Buddha, who led the reaction against her recognized code. It is looked upon, too, as the approximate date for the beginnings of her great epics. Greece had then her Pythagoras, and according to Mitford, "no Grecian state had its laws put into writing until about the same period"[2] (the reign of Cyrus, king of Persia.) Persia at this important epoch had not only her Cyrus, but also her Zoroaster. The Hebrews had their Daniel, and China's intellectual horizon was illumined by her Confucius.

Vedic literature is classified by Prof. Max Müller in four strata:

1st. Sūtra Period, 500 B. C.

2d. Brāhmaṇa Period, 600–800 B. C.

[1] Hist. Sans. Lit., p. 524. [2] Hist. of Greece, Vol. I., p. 129.

3d. Mantra Period, 800–1000 B. C. (To this period he ascribes the collection and systematic arrangement of the Vedic hymns and formulas.)

4th. *Kh*andas Period, 1000 B. C. ("Representing the free growth of sacred poetry.") There are but few hymns, however, belonging to the earliest or *Kh*andas period.

Close investigation has greatly reduced the supposed antiquity of the Vedas, and is very likely to reduce it still further. But in the light of their present knowledge, Prof. Max Müller and Sir Monier Williams agree in assigning the original composition of the early hymns to the time between 1000 and 1500 B. C.[1] Kennedy places the period "at which they began to be composed" at 1100 to 1200 B. C. Stevenson, Wilson, Wheeler, and Barthélemy St. Hilaire express similar opinions. Thus it will be seen that the ablest Orientalists assign to these books an origin which is far this side of Abraham; indeed, the extreme limit sanctioned by modern scholars scarcely reaches back to the birth of Moses.

The Vedas furnish no chronology save their fabulous millions of years. In the whole of their literature there is not a single reliable date by which any event or series of events may be assigned to its proper place in the world's chronology.

Still, the fact remains that these early hymns and songs are hoary with the frost of centuries. Reaching back in the world's history almost to the birth of Moses, they were chanted in the sacred groves of India long before the Persian conqueror crossed the Indus.

[1] Chips, Vol. I., p. 18; also Brah. and Hin., p. 7.

Since their musical numbers were first breathed upon the air, cities have risen and fallen, and the earth has been swept by successive storms of conquest. The palaces of Nineveh and the temples of Babylon have slept for ages in the long night of time, but the simple hymns of the Veda still live in the hearts of men. They belong to the realm of song, and thought must live though monarchs die and thrones decay.

THE ṚIG-VEDA.

This is by far the most important, as well as the most primitive of the collection, the others comprising little more than extracts from it, together with a variety of incantations, charms, and formulas for different ceremonies. The Ṛig-veda means the hymns of praise, or hymns to celebrate praises. Some of them are written in metre, and others in prose. They are dedicated to a variety of gods, and some of them are beautiful compositions. The gods are constantly invoked to protect their worshipers, to grant them food, large flocks, large families, and a long life, for all of which they are to be rewarded with praises and sacrifices, offered day after day, or at certain seasons of the year.

Sanskṛit literature without this book would be like Greek without the works of Homer. The Ṛig-veda belongs to universal history as well as to the history of India, and fills a place in the Āryan world of letters that can be supplied by no other book. This venerable work, which is the fountain head of Vedic literature, is composed of about one thousand and twenty-eight hymns, each hymn containing an average of ten verses each. In the language of Müller, "Large numbers of the Vedic hymns are childish in the extreme." Translations of these compositions, even when enriched by all the graces of modern scholarship, are often marked with tedious repetitions and offensive epithets. They sometimes pass abruptly from sound wisdom to childish foolishness, and from high culture to the lowest grade of morality, while sudden transitions from the sublime to the ridiculous are not at all infrequent.[1] The Ṛig-veda does not teach idolatry, although there is no doubt that multitudes of the Brāhman devotees are now veritable idol worshipers. The worship of images is declared to be an act of inferior merit, and it is claimed that in reality even the idolators worship only one God, who is manifested in various forms, and that their images of stone and clay are used merely to represent him. This is done upon the principle that the ignorant classes cannot raise their conceptions to abstract deity, but need some tangible object to which their devotions may be addressed. It is said that "The vulgar look for their gods in the water; men of more extended knowledge, in the celestial bodies: the ignorant, in wood, brick, and stone." Another theory is that in the beginning there was only one God—but that he made many others, and hence all the phenomena of nature were personified and worshiped. The greater number of the prayers and invocations are mythological and unmeaning, some of them claiming that the gods are all equal, as in the stanza, "Among you, O gods, there are none that are

1 Sir Monier Williams says, "Although the majority of the Hindus believe that the four Vedas contain all that is good, great and divine, yet these compositions will be found, when taken as a whole, to abound more in puerile ideas than in lofty conceptions."—*Brah. and Hin.*, *p. 18.*

small, none that are young—you are all great indeed." Still, the hymns addressed to individual deities are very liable to claim supremacy for the god addressed, while others claim that there is but one, as in the following:

"In the beginning there arose a golden child;
He was the one born Lord of all that is;
He established the earth and this sky,
Who is the God to whom we offer sacrifices.

"He who gives life, he who gives strength,
Whose command all the bright gods revere;
Whose shadow is immortality, whose shadow is death,
Who is the God to whom we shall offer our sacrifice.

"He whose greatness these snowy mountains,
Whose greatness the sea proclaims with the distant river,
He whose these regions are, as it were his two arms,
Who is the God to whom we shall offer our sacrifice.

"He to whom heaven and earth, standing firm by his will,
Look up tremblingly, inwardly,
He over whom the rising sun stands forth,
Who is the God to whom we shall offer sacrifices.

"He who by his might looked even over the water clouds—
The clouds which gave strength and lit the sacrifice,
He who alone is God, above all gods,
Who is the God to whom we shall offer sacrifice."[1]

[1] R.-v., 10-12, Müller's trans.

But what we sometimes regard as monotheism is in reality pantheism, or the belief that the creation and Creator are identical with each other. Brahman in the neuter form means simply infinite being—the only eternal essence, which, when it passes into actual manifested existence, is called Brahmā, and develops itself in various forms. The creed of many of the Hindūs at the present day asserts that there is only one real being in existence, and that he constitutes the universe. While some of the hymns seem to teach monotheism, there are allusions in the Ṛig-veda to thirty-three gods.[1]

One hymn assigns all the phenomena of nature to one first cause, while another attributes them to several causes operating independently, and still another argues that the whole visible creation is animated by one universal, all-pervading spirit.

As the Semitic races relapsed occasionally into polytheism, so the Hindūs have sometimes returned to monotheism, but says Prof. Müller, "In both cases these changes were not the result of a gradual and regular progress, but of individual impulses and peculiar influences. The mere occurrence of monotheistic ideas is not sufficient to stamp any class of hymns as of modern date."[2] The religion of the Ṛig-veda was either polytheism, monotheism, tritheism, or pantheism, according to the individual preference of the worshiper, but it was not yet idolatry. The forces of nature were spoken of as being under the control of divine personages, but

[1] Max Müller says, "No doubt if we must employ technical terms, the religion of the Veda is polytheism, not monotheism."—*Chips, Vol. 1, p. 27.*

[2] Hist. Sans. Lit., p. 559.

they were not as yet represented by images and worshiped.

A beautiful hymn in the Veda is addressed to the sky god, Varuṇa, as follows:

"The mighty Varuṇa who rules above, looks down
Upon the worlds, his kingdom, as if close at hand.
When men imagine they do aught by stealth, he knows it.
No one can stand, or walk, or softly glide along,
Or hide in dark recesses, or lurk in secret cell,
But Varuṇa detects him, and his movements spies;
Two persons may devise some plot, together sitting,
And think themselves alone; but he, the king, is there,
A third, and sees it all. . . . His messengers descend
Countless from his abode, forever traversing
This world, and scanning with a thousand eyes its inmates,
Whate'er within this earth and all within the sky;
Yea, all that is beyond, King Varuṇa perceives.
The winkings of men's eyes are numbered all by him;
He wields the universe as gamesters handle dice."[1]

Another gem is found in the hymn of adoration to the sun god (Sūrya):

"Behold, the rays of dawn like heralds lead on high
The Sun, that men may see the great, all-knowing God.
The stars slink off like thieves in company with Night,
Before the all-seeing eyes whose beams reveal his presence,
Gleaming like brilliant flames, to nation after nation.

[1] Atharva-veda, IV., 16, Williams' trans.

Sūrya, with flaming locks, clear-sighted god of day,
Thy seven ruddy mares bear on thy rushing car.
With these thy self-yoked steeds, seven daughters of
thy chariot,
Onward thou dost advance. To thy refulgent orb
Beyond this lower gloom, and upward to the light,
Would we ascend, O Sun, thou god among the gods."[1]

These are representatives of the finest poetry of early Vedic literature. There are others like the following "Purusha hymn of the Ṛig-veda," which is remarkable for its peculiar theological combination, and seems to teach monotheism and polytheism, as well as pantheism and the institution of caste, which has been the bane of India for more than two thousand years:

"The embodied spirit has a thousand heads,
A thousand eyes, a thousand feet, around
On every side enveloping the earth,
Yet filling space no larger than a span.
He is himself this very universe;
He is whatever is, has been, and shall be;
He is the Lord of immortality.
All creatures are one-fourth of him, three-fourths
Are that which is immortal in the sky.
From him called Purusha was born Virāj,
And from Virāj was Purusha produced,
Whom gods and holy men made their oblation.
With Purusha as victim, they performed
A sacrifice. When they divided him,
How did they cut him up? What was his mouth?

[1] Williams' trans.

What were his arms? and what his thighs and feet?
The Brāhman was his mouth, the kingly soldier
Was made his arms, the husbandman his thighs,
The servile Śūdra issued from his feet."[1]

Virāj was a secondary creator, considered sometimes of the feminine and sometimes of the masculine gender. Manu says that Purusha, the first male, was called Brahmā and was produced from the supreme self-existent spirit.

It is easy to see how the system of caste was fostered by a hymn which declares that the priestly class issued from Purusha's mouth, the soldier from his arms, the husbandman from his thighs, and the slave from his feet.

The hymns of the Veda too often descend to bacchanalian songs in honor of the god Soma,[2] the Bacchus of India, and the whole of the ninth book of the Ṛig-veda is devoted to his praise. The soma is a plant said to have been brought "by a fair winged falcon from afar" and planted in India. It is a creeper with succulent leafless stems, bearing the botanical name of Asclepias Acida. The juice, after being expressed by stones and mixed with milk or barley juice, became a strong intoxicant with whose exhilarating properties the Āryans were so infatuated that they supposed it was endowed with its wonderful powers by a god. The soma became to them the king of plants, and its juice was largely used in offerings to their gods, some of whom were supposed to have a peculiar weakness for

[1] R.-v. (Man. 10-90), Williams' trans.

[2] In later times the name of Soma was also applied to the moon.

the intoxicating draught. Therefore not only the one hundred and fourteen hymns of the ninth book of the Ṛig-veda are devoted to the praise of the Hindū Bacchus, but there are many others in different parts of the work, as well as frequent references to his favorite beverage in those songs which are not entirely devoted to its glory. The following is a sample of the hymns to Soma:

"Oh, soma drunk by us, be bliss to our hearts as a father is indulgent to a son. May these glory-conferring, protecting soma streams knit together my joints as cows draw together a chariot falling in pieces; may they keep us from a loosely knit worship;[1] may they deliver me from sickness."[2]

The various gods to whom the soma juice is offered in sacrifice are represented as partaking of it even to drunkenness. For instance, "When bright Maruts (the storm gods) you harness to your car over the mountain, then you exhilarate yourselves with the soma juice."[3] And again, "Drinker of the pure soma, Vāyu, come to us. I offer thee the exhilarating food of which thou hast the prior drinking."[4] Also the following, to be chanted when offering soma to Mitra and Varuṇa, both names being often applied to the sun, although Varuṇa is generally spoken of as the god of the firmament, or sky god:

[1] When the soma is drunk the worship becomes consolidated.

[2] R.-v. San. Vol. V. p. 93, Wilson's trans. In a recent letter to the author Prof. Max Müller says of Wilson's translation, "It professes to give the traditional rendering of the hymns according to Sayaṇa's commentary, and as such it will always retain a place of honor."

[3] Vol. VI., p. 249. [4] Ibid, Vol. IV., p. 185.

"May this soma libation be gratifying to Mitra and Varuṇa, to be enjoyed by them as they drink of it inclining downwards. A divine beverage, fit to be enjoyed by the gods, may all the gods well pleased to-day accept it."[1]

The intoxicating liquid was presented in ladles to the deities invoked, and in all cases, says Wilson, "the residue of the liquor was taken by the assistants." The condition of the worshipers after the rites were accomplished may be better imagined than described.

One of the favorite gods of the Ṛig-veda was Indra, who was the Jupiter of the Āryan race. He is repeatedly referred to as the "rain god," "the air-born Indra," "the thunderer." In the earliest age he is represented as inhabiting the sky between the earth and the sun, riding upon the clouds and pouring forth the rain, hurling the forked lightning upon the earth, and speaking to men in the awful tones of thunder. But Indra's special weakness is for soma juice, which he quaffs in fabulous quantities, and thus invigorated becomes invincible, and hastens away to vanquish the hostile powers of the atmosphere which are withholding the rain from the parched earth.

"Indra, animated by the soma juice, thou didst engage in battle. . . Exhilarated by the soma, thou hast expelled the waters from the clouds. . . In thee, Indra, is all vigor fully concentrated. Thy will delights to drink the soma juice."[3]

1 Vol. II., p. 53.
2 Indra will be treated more fully in the following chapter.
3 R.-v., San., Vol. 1., p. 137.

Again he is addressed as follows:

"Lord of steeds! Thou art exhilarated when the sacred soma juice has been imbibed by thee. . . It is exhilarating, inebriating, invigorating, and the yielder of delight, satisfying as food, and the giver of a thousand pleasures. May the soma libation reach you, for it is exhilarating, invigorating, inebriating, most precious. It is companionable, Indra, enjoyable, the overthrower of hosts—immortal. Thine inebriety is most intense, nevertheless thine acts are most beneficent. Thou desirest, bountiful giver of horses, that both thy inebriety and thy beneficence should be the means of destroying enemies and distributing riches."[1]

Indra is also repeatedly invoked as "Voracious drinker of the soma," "Indra with the handsome chin . . . drinker of the soma, showerer of blessings," etc. He is also repeatedly hymned as "Handsome-jawed Indra," and it is said "The exhilarating soma juices flew toward the shining Indra as milch kine hasten to their calves,"[2] and again, "The stomach of Indra is as capacious a receptacle of soma as a lake, for he has partaken of it at many sacrifices, and inasmuch as he has eaten the first viands he has been the slayer of Vṛitra and has shared the soma juice with the gods."[3] The condition of the inferior deities who shared Indra's generosity is perhaps best illustrated in the following verse:

"Swift is the excessive and girth-distending inebriation of Yajāta and Mayin. By drinking these juices

[1] Vol. II., p. 170. [2] R.-v. San., Vol. V., p. 307. [3] Vol. III., p. 60.

they urge one another to drink. They find the copious draught the prompt giver of intoxication."[1]

The hymn from which the above is an extract also represents the wife of a great sage as joining in the convivialities of the occasion, while at another festive scene the gods and sages are represented as "screaming like swans" when exhilarated by the flowing bowl.

The doctrine of metempsychosis, or transmigration of souls, which afterward became a cardinal doctrine of Hindū faith, finds no place in the Ṛig-veda, which is also free from the crime of child marriage, the barbarous customs of caste, and the idolatry of modern times. The people were then rich in flocks and herds; they practiced the art of agriculture, and to a certain extent that of architecture. Polygamy existed, but was not the rule of life. They killed animals and ate animal food, not even objecting to the flesh of cows. Their vices were sensuality and gambling, as well as drunkenness.

Hymns of a still more indelicate nature than the foregoing might be cited, but it is pleasanter to close these extracts from the Ṛig-veda with the following beautiful "Hymn to Ushas" (the Dawn).

1. "She shines upon us like a young wife, rousing every living being to go to his work. When the fire had to be kindled by men, she made the light by striking down darkness.

2. "She rose up spreading far and wide, and moving everywhere. She grew in brightness wearing her bril-

[1] Ibid, Vol. III., p. 311.

liant garment. The mother of the cows (the mornings), the leader of the days, she shone gold-colored, lovely to behold.

3. "She, the fortunate who brings the eye of the gods, who leads the white and lovely steeds (of the sun), the Dawn, was seen revealed by her rays, with brilliant treasures following every one.

4. "Thou art a blessing where thou art near. Drive far away the unfriendly; make the pasture wide; give us safety! Scatter the enemy, bring riches! Raise up wealth to the worshiper, thou mighty Dawn."[1]

This vision of the dawn personified as a pure and lovely woman is fair enough to atone for many a sin against rhythm and measure. Wearing her garments of silver and tinted pearl, she comes leading the white steeds of the sun. With her fair brow flushed with the gold and crimson light of the morning, she appears as the "leader of the days," and marshals her host in golden splendor before the sons of men. Wearing the hallowed crown of maternity, she becomes in Sanskṛit poetry "the mother of the mornings," and the infant days begin the journey of life amidst the tinted clouds of rose and amber that float around the morning sun.

The Ṛig-veda is a book of startling contrasts. Amidst coarse bacchanalian songs we find such poetic gems as "The Golden Child," the eloquent pleas to Varuṇa and Agni, and this Vedic vision of the morning, with many others of equal beauty.

[1] R.-v., 7, 77, Müller's trans.

CHAPTER II.

MYTHOLOGY OF THE VEDAS.

RESEMBLANCE BETWEEN THE MYTHOLOGIES OF INDIA AND GREECE — AGNI — SŪRYA — VARUṆA — YAMA — USHAS — MARUTS — HYMNS OF EXECRATION — INCONSISTENT THEORIES — INDRA — SIMILARITY OF NORTHERN MYTHS.

THE mythology of India is as fascinating as that of Greece. The storm-swept peaks of her Himālayas are grander than the heights of Olympus, and the golden eagle that floats on burnished wing beneath her solemn sky is dearer to the hearts of her people than was the imperial bird of Jove to the dwellers by the Ægean sea.

India is the home of the beryl and the amethyst; her sunlight flashes in her diamonds, and her moonlight gleams amidst her pearls. Hence, her dreamy sons have invested the heavens of their gods with the splendor of her gems and the fragrance of her roses. Their loveliest flowers are said to bloom only in Paradise, and Vishṇu sits upon a throne of lotus blossoms, while the pillars of Indra's heaven are enwreathed with rose-colored flowers.[1]

The many striking similarities between the gods of the Hindū and Grecian mythology suggest the common

[1] The Camalata or Love's Creeper.

origin of these early myths. It is a well-attested historic fact that in the early days of the Āryan races they dwelt together in a common country. The various tribes which left this central home to settle in different parts of the world carried with them a language which was the stock of their later tongues,[1] and also a common mythology. In India, Greece, Persia, and even in Northern Europe, the similarities between the various myths are so striking that they continually remind the reader of the common origin of the Āryan nations. The character of Indra, especially, so strongly resembles that of Jove that the similarity cannot be considered accidental.

In the earliest Vedic hymns there appears to be no regular system either of religion or mythology. The worship which they prescribe is generally of a domestic nature, consisting of oblations to fire, prayers to the god of fire, of the firmament, of the winds, of the seasons, or to the sun and the moon. The Brāhman who offers the sacrifice, or the priest who offers it for those who are not Brāhmans, invites these deities to be present and accept the offering, which often consists of melted butter or the juice of the soma. In return for these gifts the gods are supplicated to confer life, wealth, and prosperity upon the worshiper. The myths exhibit no settled genealogy, the same name being sometimes used as an adjective, and sometimes as a noun. The same goddess is addressed in one hymn as the mother, in another as the wife. The brother is

[1] Says Max Müller, "English, together with all the Teutonic dialects of the Continent, belongs to that large family of speech which comprises besides the Teutonic, the Latin, Greek, Slavonic, Celtic, and the Oriental languages of India and Persia." (*See Chips, Vol. II., p. 221.*)

spoken of now as husband and again as son, while each god in his turn is supplicated and praised as superior to all the others.

The most prominent and sacred deities of the early Hindūs are Agni, Sūrya, Indra, Varuṇa, Yama, Ushas, and Maruts.

AGNI,

the god of fire, is addressed as the supreme god who created all things; he is represented by the light of the sun, the flashing lightning, and the clear flame of the domestic hearthstone. He is the guardian of the home, the minister of the sacrifice, and comprehends within himself a multitude of other deities, as the circumference of a wheel embraces its spokes. He is one of the eight guardians of the world, his special province being the southeast quarter.

As the protector of mankind and the guardian of the home, his presence is invoked at the nuptial ceremony, and indeed upon all solemn domestic occasions.

From his body[1] issue seven streams of glory, and in his right hand he holds a spear, while a tongue of forked fire issues from his mouth. As a symbol of social union and the guardian of the domestic hearthstone, his mission is almost identical with that of the Grecian goddess Hestia, who was the daughter of Saturn and Rhea. In the Prytaneum of every Grecian city stood the hearth on which the sacred fire flamed, and where the offerings were made to Hestia. In like

[1] He is usually described as having two faces, three legs and seven arms, and riding upon a sheep. But he is sometimes represented as a corpulent man of ruddy complexion, with eyes, eyebrows, and hair of a tawny color, and appears riding on a goat.—*See Garrett's Clas. Dic. Ind., page 15.*

manner the sacred fire was kept alive in every Hindū home, and oblations of butter and rice were offered to the god of the flames. It will also be remembered that the early Romans worshiped at the shrine of Vesta, who like the Greek Hestia presided over the public and private hearths. A sacred fire, watched over by six virgin priestesses called Vestals, burned in her temple at Rome, and upon the continual preservation of this fire the safety of the city depended. If it went out it must be lighted only from the sun, the great fountain of light. Among the Hindūs, Agni is invoked as father, mother, brother, and son. He presides at the marriage service, receives the offerings upon the domestic altar, and at the death of his worshipers, takes their bodies to his bosom, and bears the "unborn part" away to the unseen world.

HYMN TO AGNI.

1. "Agni, accept this log which I am about to offer thee, accept this my service, listen well to these my songs.

2. "With this log, O Agni, may we worship thee, thou son of strength, conqueror of horses; and with this hymn, thou high born.

3. "May we thy servants serve thee with songs, O granter of riches, thou who lovest songs and delightest in riches.

4. "Thou Lord of wealth and giver of wealth, be thou wise and powerful, drive away from us the enemies.

5. "He gives us rain from heaven. He gives us invincible strength, he gives food a thousand-fold.

6. "Youngest of the gods, their messenger, their invoker most deserving of worship, come at our praise to him who worships thee and longs for thy help.

7. "For thou, O sage, goest wisely between these two creations (heaven and earth, gods and men) like a friendly messenger between two hamlets.

8. "Thou art wise, and thou hast been pleased; perform, thou intelligent Agni, the sacrifice without interruption."[1]

SŪRYA, THE SUN.

One of the first objects to attract the Vedic worshiper was the god of day. He was adored under various names, being addressed sometimes as Arvat, or even Varuṇa, and again as Āditya or Mitra. Coming out of the chambers of the east, with their draperies of scarlet and purple, this monarch of the day received the early oblation of his worshipers. As his golden chariot swept across the heavens they fancied they saw the milk-white steeds that drew the car of the king. At evening as he rolled away in a sea of splendor, leaving his crimson mantle upon the mountain peaks, the devotee knelt again to receive his parting blessing. After a time, when the pearly tints of morning again announced his coming, he was hailed with joyous songs:

TO SŪRYA.

1. "The wonderful host of rays has risen; the eye of Mitra, Varuṇa, and Agni the sun, the soul of all that moves or is immovable, has filled (with his glory) the heaven, the earth, and the firmament.

[1] R.-v., 2-6, Müller's trans.

2. "The sun follows the divine and brilliant Ushas as a man follows a young and elegant woman, at which season pious men perform the ceremonies established for ages, worshiping the auspicious sun for the sake of good reward.

3. "The auspicious, swift horses of the sun, well-limbed, road-traversing, who merit to be pleased with praise, reverenced by us, have ascended to the summits of the sky, and quickly circumambulate earth and heaven.

4. "Such is the divinity, such is the majesty of the sun that, when he has set, he has withdrawn (into himself) the diffused (light which had been shed) upon the unfinished task. When he has unyoked his coursers from the car, then night extends the veiling darkness over all.

5. "The sun in the sight of Mitra and Varuṇa displays his form (of brightness) in the middle of the heavens, and his rays extend, on one hand, his infinite and brilliant power, or on the other (by their departure), bring on the blackness of night.

6. "This day, gods, with the rising of the sun, deliver us from heinous sin! and may Mitra, Varuṇa, Āditya, ocean, earth, and heaven, be favorable to this our prayer."[1]

VARUṆA, THE GOD OF THE FIRMAMENT AND OF THE OCEAN.

Varuṇa is derived from the root Var (to cover). In the Veda it is used as a name for the firmament, but only in connection with the night, being opposed

[1] R.-v., Vol. I., page 304, Wilson's trans.

to Mitra (the day). It will be remembered that Hesiod uses the name of Uranos for the sky, and it is repeatedly said that Uranos, or Ouranos, covers everything, and that when he brings the night he is stretched out everywhere embracing the earth. But the Indian Varuṇa is the god of the sky, as well as the sky itself. It is said that "Varuṇa stemmed asunder the wide firmaments; he lifted on high the bright and glorious heaven; he stretched out apart the starry sky and the earth."[1] Like the other gods, Varuṇa is hymned as the Supreme Being:

"Thou art lord of all, of heaven and earth; thou art the king of all, of those who are gods and of those who are men."

He dwells in all worlds as their sovereign; he made the sun to shine in the firmament, and the moaning winds are but his breath. He formed the channels of the rivers which flow by his command into the sea which they can never fill. He knows the pathway of the birds through the blue ether, and the trackless course of the ships upon the wide ocean. He witnesses the truth or falsehood of men, and nothing escapes his countless eyes.

The two oceans (aërial and terrestrial) are Varuṇa's stomachs, and the stars of night are his all-seeing eyes.

Varuṇa is not only the Uranos, or Ouranos, of the Greeks, but he is their Neptune as well, being the "god of the raging main" and "monarch of the deep." It was Varuṇa who supplied the sage Ricika

[1] R.-v., 7, 861, Müller's trans.

with a thousand fleet horses, an allusion which is suggestive of the production of the horse by Neptune in his fabled contest with Minerva for the right of naming the city of Athens. Indeed, the horse in Greek mythology was sacred to Neptune and the rivers, and Homer represents the "monarch of the watery main" as whirling over the crystal chambers of the deep in his chariot drawn by "brass-hoofed steeds," while

"The parting waves before his coursers fly,
The wondering waters leave his axle dry."

Even so Varuṇa rides upon the waters or hides in caves beneath a rocky strand; but he also fills the halls of night with his presence and draws near to his worshiper in the cooling touch of evening, and when the veil of darkness covers them he comes to the hearts of men with the blessed peace and calm of evening rest.

YAMA

Is the king of death and the judge of the dead. He is the Pluto of Hindū mythology, and like him he is the lord of the world from whose dominion there is no return. The regions of Pluto were guarded by the three-headed dog Cerberus,[1] who watched at the entrance, but Yama has two terrible dogs of the "four-

[1] There is a diversity of expression among classic authors in relation to the famous dog of hades. The first mention of him is by Hesiod, who describes the furious creature as having fifty heads. Sophocles, however, speaks of him as the three-headed dog of Pluto, and the Latin poets generally agree with this author. Horace, however, calls the dog hundred-headed. Champollion traces a strong analogy between the Egyptian and Grecian mythology in relation to the dog of hades.—(*See Anthon's Clas. Dict.*)

eyed tawny breed of Saramã." This "King of Death" is the first of men who died, and he guides the spirits of other men to their destination in heaven or hell. In the later mythology he is represented as the judge of the dead, but not in the Vedas. The region over which Pluto presides is represented in the Iliad and in Hesiod's Theogony as being within the earth, while in the Odyssey it is placed in the dark region beyond the stream of ocean.[1] But Yama himself dwells in celestial light, and in one place he is represented as taking part with other gods in a festive scene beneath a tree.

The following fine poetic tribute is paid to the King of Death in the Ṛig-veda:

HYMN TO YAMA.

"To Yama, mighty king, be gifts and homage paid.
He was the first of men that died; the first to brave
Death's rapid rushing stream, the first to point the road
To heaven, and welcome others to that bright abode.
No power can rob us of the home thus won by thee;
Oh king, we come! the born must die, must tread the path
That thou hast trod—the path by which each race of men
In long succession, and our fathers too, have passed.
Soul of the dead! depart; fear not to take the road—
The ancient road—by which thy ancestors have gone;
Ascend to meet the god—to meet thy happy fathers,
Who dwell in bliss with him. Fear not to pass the guards—

[1] Od. 10, 508.

The four-eyed brindled dogs—that watch for the departed.
Return unto thy home, O soul! Thy sin and shame
Leave thou behind on earth; assume a shining form—
Thy ancient shape—refined and from all taint set free."[1]

USHAS.

Perhaps the most beautiful and poetic of all the Vedic deities is Ushas, the dawn. This radiant goddess is the Aurora, or Eos, of the Greeks.

> "Now fair Aurora lifts her golden ray,
> And all the ruddy Orient flames with day."

Even so does the Hindū goddess light up the eastern sky with the tints of opal and morning gray. She lives in their poetry as a beautiful woman pursued by her devoted lover, the sun, who at length overwhelms her with his ardent kisses. She is borne onward through the sky in a gleaming chariot drawn by ruddy horses, dispelling darkness, waking the birds, and illumining the world. Sometimes she is hymned as a beautiful maiden, sometimes adored as a wife and mother (see page 27); sometimes she is pictured as desolate and deserted by the sun, who disappears in the western skies, leaving only the clouds of crimson and gold to comfort his dying bride. But she is always young, for she is born every morning with the crown of immortal youth. Like Aurora, she wears a golden robe and comes out of her cloud-curtained palace to ascend her triumphal car The gates of the morning

[1] Williams' trans. [2] Odyssey, Bk. 8, 1.

are opened by her rosy fingers, and her fair brow is crowned with the morning star. She is addressed as the "daughter of the sky," the "kinswoman of Varuṇa."

In one passage the moon is said to be born again, and ever new to go before Ushas as the herald of the day. In the Ṛig-veda the early morn is saluted thus:

"Hail, Ushas, daughter of the sky,
  Who, borne upon thy shining car
  By ruddy steeds from realms afar
And ever lightening, drawest nigh—
Thou sweetly smilest, goddess fair,
  Disclosing all thy youthful grace,
  Thy bosom fair, thy radiant face,
And luster of thy golden hair.

"So shines the fond and winning bride
  Who robes her form in brilliant guise,
  And to her lord's admiring eyes
Displays her charms with conscious pride,
Or virgin by her mother decked,
  Who, glorying in her beauty, shows
  In every glance her power; she knows
All eyes to fix, all hearts subject.

"But closely by the amorous sun
  Pursued and vanquished in the race,
  Thou soon art locked in his embrace,
And with him blendest into one.
Fair Ushas! though through years untold
  Thou hast lived on, yet thou art born
  Anew on each succeeding morn,
And so thou art both young and old."[1]

[1] Dr. Muir's trans.

MARUTS OR RUDRAS.

Maruts or Rudras is the god, or, rather, the gods, of wind and storm, to whom the people prayed for protection for themselves, and for the destruction of their enemies. They were addressed as "shakers of the earth," and besought to tear in pieces whatever fiends might be aroused to attack the people. They dash through the heavens in chariots drawn by dappled deer; they are termed "worshipful and wise," and implored to come with their whole help "as quickly as lightnings come after rain." Rudra was afterwards the god of destruction—Śiva, the world dissolver.

The following hymn in praise of the storm gods is one of the most vivid conceptions of Hindū poetry that can be found upon the pages of the Ṛig-veda. It is radiant with life and strength through all its eloquent periods :

HYMN TO THE MARUTS.

1. "The active, the strong, the singers, the never flinching, the immovable, the wild, the most beloved and most manly, they have shown themselves with their glittering ornaments, a few only like the heavens with the stars.

2. "When you see your way through the clefts, you are like birds, O Maruts, on whatever road it be. The clouds drop (rain) on your chariots everywhere, pour out the honey like fat for him who praises you.

3. "At their ravings the earth shakes as if broken, when on the (heavenly) paths they harness their deer for victory. They the sportive, the roaring, with

bright spears, the shakers of the clouds, have themselves praised their greatness.

4. "That youthful company (of the Maruts) with their spotted horses, moves by itself, hence it exercises lordship and is invested with powers. . . . Therefore thou the strong hast, and thou wilt cherish this prayer.

5. "We speak after the kind of our old father; our tongue goes forth at the sight of the soma; when the shouting Maruts had joined Indra in the work, then only they received sacrificial honors.

6. "For their glory these well-equipped Maruts obtained splendors; they obtained rays and men to praise them; nay, these well-armed, nimble, and fearless beings found the beloved home of the Maruts. On your bodies there are daggers for beauty; may they stir up our minds as they stir up the forests.

7. "For your sake, O well-born Maruts, you who are full of vigor, they have shaken the stone for distilling soma. Days went round you and came back, O Maruts, back to this prayer, and to this sacred rite—the Gotamas making prayer with songs have pushed up the lid of the well (the cloud) to drink.

8. "No such hymn was ever known as this which Gotama sounded for you, O Maruts, when he saw you on golden wheels—wild boars, rushing about with iron tusks. This refreshing draught of soma rushes toward you like the voice of a suppliant—it rushes freely from our hands, as these libations are wont to do."[1]

The hymns of the Veda are not all of them hymns of praise. The denunciations of their priests were

[1] R.-v., Vol. I., pp. 148-158, Müller's trans.

poured out upon the people, and even upon each other, in the breath of these poets. For instance:

"No, by heaven! no, by earth! I do not approve of this; no, by the sacrifice! No, by these rites! May the mighty mountains crush him! May the priest of Atiyâga perish!"

"Whosoever, O Maruts, weans himself above us, or scoffs at the prayer (Brahma) which we have made, may hot plagues come upon him; may the sky burn up that hater of Brāhmans."

"Did they not call thee Soma, the guardian of Brāhmans? Did they not say that thou didst shield us against curses? Why dost thou look on when we are scoffed at? Hurl against the hater of the Brāhmans the fiery spear."[1]

And again, "Indra and Soma, burn the devils; destroy them; throw them down, ye two bulls, the people that groan in darkness! Hew down the madmen, suffocate them, kill them; hurl them away, and slay the voracious. Indra and Soma, up together against the cursing demon! May he burn and hiss like an oblation in the fire! Put your everlasting hatred upon the villain who hates the Brāhman, who eats flesh, and whose look is abominable. Indra and Soma, hurl the evil-doer into the pit, even into unfathomable darkness! May your strength be full of wrath to hold out that no one may come out again."[2]

The numerous deities are fully described and multiplied to a certain extent, even in the early songs;

[1] R.-v., VI., 52. [2] Müller's trans.

for instance, instead of the one god of storms, we have many. Yet, although hymns and prayers to the various gods abound in the Vedas, it is declared in some texts that there are but three deities—the air, the sun, and fire—and their places are the earth, the middle region (between heaven and earth), and heaven. There are also repeated texts which claim that there is but one deity—the supreme spirit. "He who from the universal world proceeds, who is Lord of the earth, and whose work is the universe, is the Supreme Being."[1]

It is fortunate that our translators have not undertaken the task of reconciling the Vedas with themselves. They have simply tried to give us a faithful reproduction of these books, with all their contradictions and inconsistencies. Although the pages of the Ṛig-veda abound with incongruities and absurdities, they are free from the grosser immoralities which pollute the later literature of the Brāhmans. There is no account in the Ṛig-veda of such characters as Śiva and Kali; no trace of the miraculous stories concerning Vishṇu. These, with the descriptions of the licentious Kṛishṇa, were reserved for the later fables of that romantic clime.

INDRA.

This was, perhaps, the most popular of all the early Vedic deities. Like Agni, his brother, he is hymned as the Supreme Being, superior to all the other gods of the pantheon. Though sometimes called the sunlight, he is looked upon as the watery atmosphere, ever seeking to dispense his dewy treasures (indu), and

[1] Religion of Hin., Vol. II., p. 51.

constantly opposed by a spirit of evil called Vṛitra. He is also styled the "thunder-bearer," or god of battles. He was the Hindū ideal of a hero, who was always fighting and was never conquered. He was the Jove of early Indian mythology, and the favorite deity of a people who were fighting for new homes and rich herds of cattle. Hence the great number of prayers and hymns addressed to him. He is represented as "the king of heaven," as "the showerer of blessings," and as "the thunderer." Many passages suggest the scene upon Olympus

"Where far apart the Thunderer fills his throne,
O'er all the gods superior and alone."

Like Jove, he has supreme control of the elements; he rides upon the storm cloud and flashes his lightnings across the darkened sky. He is the archer who uses the rainbow as his weapon, whose quiver is filled with lightnings, while his wrath is like that of the Grecian god to whose will Vulcan counsels submission,

"Lest roused to rage he shake the bless'd abodes,
Launch the red lightning and dethrone the gods."

Indra, the wielder of the thunderbolt, may also be compared to the German Donar, the Saxon Thunar, and the Thor of the ancient Norseman.

Indra is the king of the Devas, or millions of celestials who belong especially to his own Paradise. He is represented with four arms and hands, with two of which he holds a lance, while a third carries a thunderbolt. His reign is to continue one hundred years of the gods, after which another may, by great sacrifices, usurp his position. One hundred successful Aśvamedhas, or horse sacrifices, are said to qualify the devotee for becoming the successor of Indra, therefore the god usually sends one of his celestial attendants to steal away the horse before the sacrifice can be performed.

The reign of this popular deity extends from the early Vedic period down to the Purāṇic age, when his star declines before the supremacy of more modern gods. Still, he is a chieftain among inferior deities and is always at war with the giants and demons, by whom he was at one time deposed. Indra's partiality for the intoxicating draught has been discussed in the previous chapter, and in this, too, he resembles the Grecian Jove, as well as Bacchus. It will be remembered that in the First Book of the Iliad Vulcan stayed the quarrel between Jove and his angry queen by counseling his "goddess mother" to submit to the imperial will, and then

> "Rising with a bound
> The double bowl with sparkling nectar crowned,"

he passed to all the deities in the assembled conclave, and they drank freely of its contents, while

> "Vulcan with awkward grace his office plies,
> And unextinguished laughter shakes the skies."

The frequent offerings of the intoxicating beverage made to Indra in the Vedic age were accompanied by the chanting of hymns urging him to drink, that he might become "invigorated" and able to cope with his enemies. These copious offerings of soma so frequently made to the "king of heaven" suggest that classic scene where the Greek and Trojan powers were feasting through the night, the troops of Greece upon the field, and those of Troy within her towers:

"But Jove adverse, the signs of wrath displayed,
And shot red lightnings through the gloomy shade.
Humbled they stood, pale horror seized on all,
While the deep thunder shook the aërial hall.
Each poured to Jove before the bowl was crowned,
And large libations drenched the thirsty ground."

The heroes of northern mythology also share in this weakness of the Indian and Grecian deities. Odin, the chieftain of the North and the father of Thor, lived exclusively upon wine or beer, giving the food which was set before him to the two wolves that lay at his feet.

Indra is represented as swiftly obeying the summons of his worshipers when the soma is poured out in floods for the gratification of his palate and the exhilaration of his whole being. It is claimed that he receives strength from this beverage to such an extent that he not only vanquishes his foes, but supports the earth and sky. Heaven and earth tremble with fear at the crash of his thunder; his enemies are pierced and shattered by his arrows of lightning, and the waters descend in torrents to the earth, filling the rivers which rush in rolling floods toward the sea.

The following hymn to Indra is a sample of the songs which are chanted in his praise:

"Let no one, not even those who worship thee, delay thee far from us! Even from afar come to our feast! Or, if thou art here, listen to us. For these here who make prayers to thee sit together near the libation, like flies round the honey. The worshipers anxious for wealth have placed their desire upon Indra, as we put our foot upon a chariot. Desirous of riches, I call him who holds the thunderbolt with his arm, and who is a good giver, like as a son calls his father. These libations of soma mixed with milk have been prepared for Indra. Thou, armed with the thunderbolt, come with the steeds and drink of them for thy delight—come to the house . . .

"He who prepares for thee, O Vṛitra killer, deep libations and pours them out before thee, that hero thrives with Indra, never scorned of men. . . .

"Offer soma to the drinker of soma—to Indra, the lord of the thunderbolt; roast roasts; make him to protect us. Indra, the giver, is a blessing to him who gives oblations.

. . . .

"Do not grudge, ye givers of soma; give strength to the great god, make him to give wealth. He who alone preserves, conquers, abides, and flourishes; the gods are not to be trifled with.

"No one surrounds the chariot of the liberal worshiper, no one stops it. He whom Indra protects and the Maruts, he will come with stables full of cattle. . . .

"A mortal does not get riches by scant praise—no wealth comes to the grudger.

"The strong man it is, O mighty! who in the day

of battle is a precious gift to thee like as to me. We call to thee, O hero, like cows that have not been milked; we praise thee as ruler of all that moves, O Indra—as ruler of all that is immovable.

"There is no one like thee in heaven or earth; he is not now and will not be born. O mighty Indra! we call upon thee as we go fighting for cows and horses. Let not evil-disposed wretches and unhallowed tread us down. Through thy help, O hero, let us step over the rushing eternal waters."[1]

Food is provided for the horses of Indra by the worshiper who pours out libations of soma to the master, for "the king of heaven" is repeatedly represented as driving furiously through the sky in his chariot drawn by tawny steeds. So in Book Eighth of the Iliad the sire of the gods

"Called his coursers, and his chariot took.
The steadfast firmament beneath them shook;
Rapt by the ethereal steeds the chariot roll'd,
Brass were their hoofs, their curling manes of gold."

His fleet-footed horses rush along between the extended earth and sky until they reach the top of Mount Ida, when

"From his radiant car the sacred sire
Of gods and men released the steeds of fire."

These numerous and startling coincidences between the early Vedic deities and the gods of Greece point

[1] R.-v., II., 32, Wilson's trans.

to the common origin of these Āryan myths, especially in view of the fact that the Iliad itself has been traced by Grote and Buckley to 776 B. C. Herodotus gives still earlier dates, for he places Homer with Hesiod, 400 years before his own time. The figures given by Herodotus (who wrote 444 B. C.) are corroborated by the arguments of Wood[1] and Haller,[2] and also of Mitford, who makes a strong argument for the historic value of Homer's works.[3] These authorities place Homer about the middle of the ninth century B. C., while the Arundelian marbles assign him to 907 B. C. When we consider that the myths of Greece existed long before her epic poems, we must refer them back almost to the early songs of the Veda.

The mythology of Northern Europe also bears unmistakable evidence of having been brought from the common home of the Āryan race, although it has been developed in harmony with the temperament of the Northern people. Even amidst these rugged rocks and icebergs we find almost a counterpart of Indra and of Jove in the descriptions of the gigantic Thor, before whom the mountains burst and the earth blazed. Sleipnir, the fleet-footed horse of Odin, compares favorably with the "tawny steeds" of Indra, or the flying coursers of Jove. If Neptune's "brass-hoof'd steeds" were

"Fleet as the winds and deck'd with golden manes,"

the famous horse of the Northern god cleared the gates

[1] Essay on the Original Genius of Homer.
[2] Heyne, Excurs. 4 ad. Il., 24. [3] History of Greece, pp. 81 and 139.

of Hel[1] at a single bound, while his speed rivaled that of the winds, and the golden bridge of Gyöll trembled more beneath his tread than when five bands of dead men rode over its solemn arches. Ty, or Tyr, the son of Odin, is the god of war—the Mars of Northern Europe—who rides fearlessly into the thickest of the fight. Gerd, the beautiful maiden with shining arms, resisting the advances of Frey, the god of rain and sunshine, represents Ushas, the fair goddess of the morning, fleeing from the kisses of the sun. Œgir is the storm god of the ocean—the Neptune of the Northern seas—before whose trident the angry billows roll upon the helpless shore.

Loki, the god of fire, bears to the Northmen the relation that Agni holds to India. His servants are the subterranean forces which, even though chained in darkness, throw from throbbing mountains their burning breath and liquid fires.

These are only a few of the many parallels which might be cited. The Persian myths could also be shown to belong to the same common stock; but the illustrations already given are sufficient to prove that it was in the early days of the Āryan race, when the people dwelt in a common home and used a common language, that their myths were either born from the realms of fancy or builded upon the fragments of history.

[1] Hel is derived from *at helja*, signifying to hide. It is used in the Edda to denote the kingdom of death, and all who died, whether saints or sinners, hastened to this dark region, or concealed place—the world of the tomb. It is said that Hermod, or Hermôdhr, the son of Odin, rode the fleet horse Sleipnir for nine days and nights before he came to the barred gates of Hel, hoping to recover his brother Balder.

CHAPTER III.

MYTHOLOGY OF LATER HINDŪ WORKS.

MULTIPLICATION OF DEITIES—ANALOGY BETWEEN INDIAN AND GREEK GODS—MODERN DEITIES—BRAHMĀ, VISHṆU AND ŚIVA—INCARNATIONS OF VISHṆU—GARUḌA—RECOVERY OF THE LOST NECTAR OF THE GODS—ŚIVA.

FROM the foregoing examination of the early Vedic deities it has been seen that Vedism was little more than reverent love for the forces of nature, and a desire to propitiate them in order to receive temporal blessings at their hands. No one can examine the Vedic hymns without being struck with the great number of prayers offered for cattle and horses, for rain and abundant food, as well as for vengeance upon enemies. The gods were at first few in number and simple in form, but these early deities were soon multiplied a thousand-fold, and at length the Hindū pantheon contained three hundred and thirty millions of gods. Out of this vast number it is impossible to do more than glance at the most promiuent characters of Indian mythology. Strong points of analogy might also be shown between the Grecian deities and the later forms of Hindū myth. For instance, the goddess Durgā, the wife of Śiva, may be said to represent Juno, the imperious queen of Jove. Śrī might also be compared with the Latin Ceres—

"As when on Ceres' sacred floor, the swain
Spreads the wide fan to clean the golden grain,
And the light chaff before the breezes borne,
Ascends in clouds from off the heapy corn."[1]

Sarasvatī, the goddess of speech and of the arts, represents Minerva, who was born from the head of Jove, and who taught Epeus to frame the wooden horse which caused the downfall of Troy. Kāma, the god of love, is the Cupid of the Hindūs, while Rati, his wife, may be compared to "the silver-footed dame" of the Iliad. Kārttikeya, the god of war, was, like Mars,

"With slaughter red, and raging round the field."

Nārada was the inventor of the lute in Indian mythology, while Mercury of the Greeks invented the lyre. Vāyu, the god of the wind, represents the Grecian Æolus, who tied up all the winds (except Zephyrus) in a bag of ox-hide for the benefit of Ulysses, that he might have a favorable passage homeward. Gaṇeśa, who presided over the beginning of all undertakings, represents Janus, the two-faced deity of the Latins, who was invoked at "the commencement of campaigns."

BRAHMĀ, VISHṆU, AND ŚIVA

are the most popular deities in modern times. In the Middle Ages bitter rivalries sprang up between the advocates of the various theological systems, the Purāṇas being divided in their allegiance to these gods. But at the present time a more tolerant spirit prevails, and the names of Brahmā Vishṇu, and Śiva, are by many

[1] Iliad, V., 500.

regarded merely as manifestations of one Supreme Being. Brahmā is confessedly the most difficult deity in the Hindū pantheon to locate intelligently. The difficulty arises from the fact that the word brahman originally meant force, will, or wish; it was impersonal, but came to be considered as the creative force in the universe, even before it was endowed with personality, and while it existed only in a neuter form. Brahman (neuter) in the sense of a creative principle does not occur in the Ṛig-veda. It does occur, however, in the later productions, the earliest of which is the Atharva-veda. In the Brāhmaṇas this Brahman is called "the first-born, the self-existing, the best of the gods," etc. The word Brāhmaṇa is derived from Brahman, which is afterward developed into a personal deity. In Manu (whose code dates from about 500 B. C.) Brahman is represented as evolving his essence in the form of Brahmā, the creator. In one of the Upanishads there is an account of the creation of all things by this deity, which will be examined in a future chapter, under the head of Cosmogony. The word Brahma is the nominative case, of the neuter Brahman. When Brahma decided to create the universe he assumed the quality of activity and became a male deity, Brahmā. He also willed to invest himself with preserving power, and thus became Vishṇu, the preserver; then wishing to obtain the destructive power, he became also Śiva, the destroyer. This doctrine of the triple development of the previously neuter form does not occur, however, until we reach the Brāhmanized version of the Indian Epics. These three manifestations of Brahmā, Vishṇu and Śiva exhibit the principal forms of Hindūism as expressed in the epic poems, and stronger still in the later Purāṇas.[1] And yet Brahmā, who in his later form is the creator of all things, is said to have been born in the lotus blossom that sprang from Vishṇu, and is described as having four faces. In the Vishṇu-purāṇa, which dates from about the eleventh century of the Christian era, Brahmā is said to live one hundred years, each day of which consists of 4,320,000,000 of the years of mortals. During the nights of Brahmā the universe ceases to exist, but it is reproduced at the beginning of the next day. Like other prominent gods of the Hindūs, he is repeatedly praised as the Supreme Being and the creator of all the others. But the myth grew slowly, for in the Mahā-bhārata, a work hundreds of years subsequent to the Atharva-veda, Mahā-deva is represented as the creator of Brahmā. "From his right side he produced Brahmā, the originator of worlds; from his left side, Vishṇu, the preserver of the universe, and when the end of the age had arrived the mighty god created Rudra" (afterward Śiva).[2]

VISHṆU.

There is mention of a god Vishṇu in the Ṛig-veda, but he is there spoken of as a manifestation of solar energy, or rather as a form of the sun. He is represented as stepping over the heavens in three paces, symbolizing the sun's rising, his passage across the meridian, and his setting. Afterwards Vishṇu takes his place among the twelve Ādityas, or twelve phases of the sun during the twelve months of the year. Later,

[1] Ind. Wis., pp. 324-327. [2] Muir's Sans. Texts, pp. 156-162.

in the Brāhmaṇas, he is identified with sacrifice. It was the Vedic Vishṇu who afterward became the world preserver, while Rudra (connected with Indra and the Maruts), the god of tempests, became the world dissolver, Śiva. There is no trace of Vishṇu in the Institutes of Manu, unless the allusions to inferior gods may apply to him. In the Mahā-bhārata he is sometimes regarded as the most exalted deity, and again he is represented as paying homage to Śiva and recognizing the superiority of that deity over himself. He is quite prominent in the Rāmāyaṇa, but it is in the Purāṇas that the most wonderful exploits and the greatest glory are assigned to him. From the beginning of the Christian era to the Purāṇas there were from six to eight centuries, during which Vishṇu was growing in importance, till in the 11th century A. D. he was glorified in the most extravagant terms in the voluminous Vishṇu-purāṇa. The writer of this work exhausts the resources of language in extolling the deity who has reached the zenith of his popularity only in mediæval times. No exploit is too great, no descriptions too wild, no mythology too fabulous to be applied to the god who is here claimed to be the conqueror of Indra and the creator of Brahmā. He is alluded to in various forms in these later books (the Purāṇas), as it is claimed that he had ten avatars, or incarnations.

The doctrine of the avatars of Vishṇu is not fully developed until we come down to the Purāṇas, about the middle of the Christian era. It is true that the legends of the fish, the boar, and the tortoise are found in the Śatapatha-brāhmaṇa, but it is only in the much later Purāṇas that they are described as incarnations of Vishṇu.[1]

1. MATSYA, or fish,[2] in which character he saved the seventh man, the progenitor of the human race, from the delnge. (This story is graphically told in the Śatapatha-brāhmaṇa, and is repeated in the Mahābhārata.)

2. KŪRMA, the tortoise, In this form he descended to aid in recovering certain valuable articles lost in the deluge.

3. VARĀHA, the boar. Having assumed this form, he descended to deliver the world from the power of the golden-eyed demon, who had seized it and carried it down to the depths of the sea. Vishṇn as a boar dived into the abyss, and after a contest of a thousand years he slew the monster and raised the earth. In other legends the universe is represented as a mass of water, and the earth, being snbmerged, was upheaved by the tusks of the divine boar. "It is a noticeable fact," says Sir Monier Williams, "that the first three incarnations of Vishṇu are all connected with the tradition of a universal deluge."

4. NARA-SIṈHA, the man lion. He assumed this shape to deliver the world from the tyranny of a demon, who had obtained from Brahmā the promise that he shonld not be slain either by a god, a man, or an animal. (These four incarnations are said to

[1] Trans. Vic. Inst., Vol. XXI., p. 167.

[2] The first incarnation of this god as a fish is suggestive of Janus, the two-faced deity of Roman mythology, who, with his wife and his sister Camasane is often represented as half fish and half human. Compare also the avatar as a fish with the Babylonian legend of Oannes and the Syrian goddess Atergatis, who was worshiped at Hierapolis, having a woman's figure, the lower part of which was a fish.

have taken place in the Satya, or first age of the world.)

5. VĀMANA, the dwarf, which character he assumed to deprive the demon Bali of the dominion of the three worlds. Vishṇu presented himself as a very diminutive man, and solicited as much land as he could step over in three paces. When this request was granted he strided over heaven and earth, but in compassion to the demon he left hell in his possession.

6. PARASU-RĀMA, Rāma with the ax; in this character Vishṇu is said to have cleared the earth twenty-one times of the Kshatriya, or military class.

7. RĀMA-ĆANDRA, hero of the epic poem Rāmāyaṇa.

8. KṚISHṆA, the dark god, which form he assumes at the end of the Dāvāpara, or third age of the world. Kṛishṇa was the younger brother of Bala-rāma, "the strong Rāma," who has sometimes been called the eighth avatar of Vishṇu. But in later times Kṛishṇa appears to have supplanted his brother as the eighth incarnation.[1] As Kṛishṇa worship is nowhere mentioned in the early Vedic writings, this god will be treated in connection with the later forms of Hindū literature, where he chronologically belongs.[2]

9. BUDDHA. According to the Brāhmans, Vishṇu assumed this form to delude the demons into neglecting the worship of the gods, and thus exposing themselves to destruction.

It appears that Buddha was canonized, so to speak, by receiving the rank of the ninth avatar of Vishṇu after the expulsion of Buddhism as a sect from India.

[1] Trans. Vic. Inst., Vol. XXI., p. 177. [2] Chap. 23.

10. KALKI, or KALKIN, who is yet to appear at the close of the fourth age, when the world has become wholly depraved, for the final destruction of the wicked, the re-establishment of righteousness upon the earth, the renovation of all the earth, and the return to a new age of purity. According to some, he will be seen in the sky, seated on a white horse, with a drawn sword in his hand, blazing like a comet. This last picture—taken in connection with the well-established fact of the modern character of the Purāṇas—seems to have been drawn from Revelation xix: 11 and 15: "And I saw heaven opened, and behold a white horse, and he that sat upon him was called Faithful and True, and in righteousness he doth judge and make war. . . . And out of his mouth goeth a sharp sword, that with it he should smite the nations, and he shall rule them with a rod of iron. And he treadeth the wine-press of the fierceness and wrath of Almighty God."

Some works give twenty-four avatars, and some call them numberless, but the generally received mythology accords to Vishṇu only the ten which are here spoken of.

Vishṇu is represented as riding upon Garuḍa, a creature which is half man and half eagle. This is the king of birds and the fearless enemy of the serpent tribe. The intrepid Garuḍa of the Hindūs is represented in Persia by the Simurgh,[1] that ancient bird which has seen the

[1] The golden-pinioned Simurgh is a fabulous bird that is said to live in the Caucasian mountains, and Prof. Eastwick supposes that the idea was derived from the Jewish tradition of a huge bird mentioned in the Talmud under the name of Yukhush. A picture of the Simurgh, which was taken from a Persian drawing, represents him as flying with an elephant in his beak and another in each of his talons.

great cycle of seven thousand years twelve times, and twelve times beheld an unpeopled earth. He finds a parallel in the fabled Anka of Arabia which is said to be "known in name and unknown in body," the Eorosh of the Zend, and the Kerkes of the Turks. The Japanese also have their Kirni, while China rejoices in her nondescript dragon, a combination of bird and reptile.

The Hindū Garuḍa suggests, too, the Griffin of Chivalry,[1] the fabulous monster, half bird and half lion, that protected the gold of the Hyperborean regions from the one-eyed Arimaspians, and the Phœnix of Egyptian fable—the bird of gold and crimson plumage that is burned upon her nest of spices every thousand years, and as often springs to life from her ashes. To these wonderful parallels we might add the ancient bird in Scandinavian mythology which sits in the branches of Yggdrasil, the great ash tree, which is the most sacred place of the gods, and where they daily sit in judgment.[2]

1 In the Second Book of "Paradise Lost" Milton makes a comparison with the Griffin as follows:

"As when a Gryphon through the wilderness
With winged course, o'er hill and moory dale,
Pursues the Arimaspian who by stealth
Hath from his wakeful custody purloined
His guarded gold," etc.

2 The branches of the Yggdrasil spread themselves over the whole world and tower far above the heavens. It has three roots, and various theories are given as to their exact location; but according to the prose Edda, the first root reaches to the middle of the world; the second to the frost giants, and the third is constantly gnawed by the great serpent Nidhogg. Under the first root is the sacred fountain of Urd, where the gods sit in judgment, and a fair hall, from which go forth three maidens, the past, the present, and the future. In the branches of the tree sits an eagle that knows many things. Between his eyes sits the hawk. The squirrel runs up and down the tree and carries bitter messages between the eagle and the serpent, while four harts run among the boughs and bite the buds of the tree.

RECOVERY OF THE LOST NECTAR OF THE GODS.

One of the most interesting exploits of Vishṇu is his recovery of the lost nectar of the gods. In this beautiful legend the gods are represented as having been conquered in battle by demons and robbed of their strength, whereupon Vishṇu gives orders to have the ocean churned into a nectar for the gods, declaring that this nectar will at once restore their supernatural power and enable them to destroy their enemies. For this purpose the gods are ordered to collect all plants and herbs and cast them into the sea, taking the mountain Mandara for a churning stick and Vāsuki, the serpent, for a rope, while Vishṇu himself, in the form of a tortoise, becomes a resting-place for the mountain. Then they churn the ocean until they have produced the ambrosial food of immortality.

"Straightway they gathered herbs, and cast them
Into the waters; then they took the mountain
To serve as a churning staff, and next the snake
To serve as cord, and in the ocean's midst
Hari (Vishṇu) himself present, in tortoise form,
Became a pivot for the churning staff.
Then they did churn the sea of milk,[1] and first
Out of the waters rose the sacred cow,
God-worshiped Surabhi—eternal fountain
Of milk and offerings of butter; next, . . .
With eyes all rolling, Vāruṇī uprose,
Goddess of wine. Then from the whirlpool sprang
Fair Pārijāta, tree of Paradise, delight
Of heavenly maidens, with its fragrant blossoms
Perfuming the whole world.

[1] The sixth circumambient ocean of the world, according to Indian cosmogony.

". . . Then seated on a lotus
Beauty's bright goddess, peerless Śrī,[1] arose
Out of the waves; and with her, robed in white,
Came forth Dhanvantari, the gods' physician.
High in his hand he bore the cup of nectar—
Life-giving draught—longed for by gods and demons.
Then had the demons forcibly borne off
And drained the precious beverage,
Had not the mighty Vishṇu interposed.
Bewildering them, he gave it to the gods;
Whereat incensed, the demon troops assailed
The hosts of heaven. But they with strength renewed
Quaffing the draught, struck down their foes, who fell
Headlong through space to lowest depths of hell."

This poetic legend is given in the beautiful translation of Sir Monier Williams. The dark and turbid waters of Oriental literature became gradually purified as they flowed through the poetical natures of some of our translators. The vulgarity and meaningless repetition which we often find in the works of native scholars gives place in other hands to expressions of high poetic beauty. Their own literary style is so refined that, unconsciously perhaps to themselves, English scholars have elevated Hindū poetry to a rank which it never could have occupied without them. The contrast is never more forcible than when comparing their work with the translations of the Pandits. Boldness then gives place to beauty; vulgarity yields to refine-

[1] According to Hesiod Venus was born from the foam of the sea (Hes. Theog. 188 seq.) and Homer speaks of Thetis as rising from the ocean:

"When like the morning mist in early day
Rose from the flood the daughter of the sea."

ment and delicacy; while crude ideas are so clad in the graceful drapery of language as to seem like the masterpieces of thought.

The modern triad of Hindū theology is completed by

ŚIVA, THE GOD OF DESTRUCTION.

Says Max Müller, "The stories of Śiva, Kālī, Kṛishṇa, etc., are of late growth, indigenous to India, and full of wild and fanciful conceptions."

In the form of Śiva, Brahmā is supposed to pass from the work of creation and preservation to that of destruction. Even the god of dissolution was represented by the human form. Hence, he was said to be living in the Himālaya Mountains, together with his wife Pārvatī, the daughter of the mountain. She was worshiped in Bengal under the name of Durgā.

The name Śiva means "auspicious;" like the other deities, he is represented as the Supreme God, though having over a thousand names, such as "The Lord of the Universe," "The Destroyer," "The Reproducer," "The Conqueror of Life and Death," etc., etc. His especial worshipers are called Śaivas, who exalt him to the highest place in the heavens; he is represented as Time, Justice, Fire, Water, The Sun, as also the Creator and the Destroyer. His personal appearance must be rather striking, as his throat is dark blue and his hair light red, thickly matted together on the top of his head. He is well supplied with hands, the number varying with different authorities from four to eight or ten. He has five faces, in one of which is a third eye situated in the centre of the forehead, and pointing up and down. These three eyes are said to denote his view of the three divisions of time—past, present, and future. He holds a trident in his hand, to denote that the three great attributes of Creator, Destroyer, and Regenerator are combined in him.

He wears a tiger's skin for a garment, while his neck is encircled with two necklaces, one made of human skulls and the other of serpents, which twist their horrid forms around his body and neck. The shield of Jove is described as

"Dire, black, tremendous! Round the margin roll'd
A fringe of serpents, hissing, guards the gold."

In like manner this Hindū deity bristles everywhere with snakes. They are bound in his hair, they twine around his neck, their slimy forms encircle his wrists, his arms, and his legs. He wears them as rings about his fingers; they hang like mammoth pendants from his ears, until he is like

"Gorgon rising from the infernal lakes,
With horrors armed, and curls of hissing snakes."

According to Wilson, Śveta (white), Śvetāśva (white-horsed), Śveta-śikha (white-haired), and Śveta-lohita (white-blooded), were the names of four disciples of Śiva. Prof. Weber thinks that this form of myth has grown from the teachings of Syrian Christians, and claims that both the Upanishad and the Gītā—the latter especially—may have borrowed ideas from Christianity.

The ideal Hindū deity taxes the imaginative mind of the worshiper to the utmost, and the grotesque is everywhere mingled with the beautiful. For instance, Indra is represented as having a thousand eyes, and Agni two faces, three legs and seven arms, with eyes, eyebrows, and hair of a tawny color. He is sometimes represented as riding a ram, and again he appears on the back of a goat, and still later in a gleaming chariot drawn by "tawny steeds." Varuṇa has two stomachs, each of which contains an ocean. Ushas, the beautiful woman who personifies the dawn, is said to be the "mother of cows or mornings."

Kārttikeya, the god of war, and also the god of thieves, is a handsome young man with six faces.

Rāvaṇa, the demon king of Ceylon, has ten heads, twenty arms, copper-colored eyes, and a heavy beard composed of the shining bodies of black serpents. Brahmā is described as having four faces, golden tusks, and wonderfully complicated feet. Gaṇeśa has the body of a man and the head of an elephant, on which he wears a crown. His ears are adorned with jewels and his forehead is sprinkled with sacred ashes. He has four arms, two of which being elevated hold a rope and an elephant goad; the other two grasp respectively an elephant's tooth and a pancake. He is said to be very fond of pancakes, and his image stands in almost every house, where he is worshiped by men and women at the beginning of any important event. Indeed, the whole pantheon teems with horrible and grotesque creations, half man and half god.

In the Indian Epics, troops of deities and semi-divine personages are constantly appearing, while gods, animals, and men keep changing places. The gods often look to mortals for their daily sustenance. They are represented as actually living on the sacrifices which are offered them by human beings, and are supposed to gather in hungry troops at every sacrificial ceremony to feed on the oblations. It is supposed that the gods would starve to death but for these offerings.

They are also represented as being dependent upon animals and plants for the means of conveyance. Brahmā is carried on a swan, sometimes on a lotus. Lakshmī is seated on a lotus, or carries one in her hand. Śiva rides a white bull, which is his companion. Kārttikeya, the god of war and of thieves, appears astride a peacock. Indra is borne on an elephant; Yama, the god of death, appears mounted on a buffalo. Kāma, the god of love, rides either a parrot or a fish. Gaṇeśa is associated with a rat, a symbol of great sagacity; Varuṇa with a fish. Durgā, the wife of Śiva, rides a tiger, though she is sometimes represented as being on the bull with Śiva and his countless serpents.

Vishṇu is represented as the Supreme Being sleeping on a thousand-headed serpent called Śesha, and Śesha in his turn is the chief of a race of Nāgas, or semi-divine beings, half serpents and half men, their heads being human, and their bodies snake-like.[1] The simple faith of the Hindū accepts the most incongruous fiction without a doubt or a question. There is apparently no demand for history in their literature. The Oriental imagination craves the most impossible creations, and worships with simple devotion at the shrine of the most repulsive combinations.

It has been shown that the Āryan people at one

[1] Ind. Wis., p. 429.

time shared a common home, and that when the various families migrated to different countries they carried with them a language which became the stock of the modern languages of Europe, and also the germs of their later mythologies. But in those early days when their worship was simple adoration of the forces of nature, their faith was purer and their lives consequently better than when in later centuries their pantheon contained millions of deities, and the worship of painted idols was mingled with the adoration of the host of heaven.

CHAPTER IV.

THE VEDAS AND THE SUTTEE.

LITERARY IMPORTANCE — DISCUSSIONS BETWEEN EUROPEAN AND NATIVE SCHOLARS — COLEBROOKE'S TRANSLATION OF DISPUTED TEXT — MUTILATION OF THE TEXT — TESTIMONY OF RAJA RADHAKANT DEB — THE RITE NOT ADVOCATED IN THE ṚIG-VEDA — DISGRACE OF AVOIDING THE SUTTEE — INSTANCE OF ESCAPE — ENTHUSIASM OF NATIVE POETS — LORD WILLIAM BENTINCK.

AN examination of the historic suttee is peculiarly interesting in connection with the teaching of the Vedas, as the question became purely a literary one. The English government had pledged itself not to interfere with Hindū religion; therefore, if the Vedas proper, really sanctioned the horrible crime of burning a living woman with her dead husband, the government would be powerless to prevent it.

For many years an animated discussion was carried on between our own scholars and natives of high position and learning in relation to the teaching of the Vedas upon this subject.[1] When the English government proposed to prohibit the terrible custom the natives appealed at once to the official pledge that they

[1] While this question was being discussed the number of women burned alive varied from three hundred to eight hundred per year.

should not be deterred from the exercise of their religious rites. For a time the country was threatened with a fanatical rebellion in consequence of the agitation of this question. Raghu-nandana and other learned natives quoted the Ṛig-veda in support of their claim for the suttee, and H. T. Colebrooke, a Sanskṛit scholar of world-wide fame, translated this passage in harmony with their views:

"Om: Let these women not be widowed, good wives adorned with collyrium, holding clarified butter, consign themselves to the fire. Immortal, not childless, not husbandless, well adorned with gems, let them pass into the fire, whose original element is water." It has been claimed that the natives mutilated this text by changing the word "agre" into "agneh," but no one was then able to detect this literary outrage, and women continued to be offered as living sacrifices upon the dead bodies of their husbands. In India, where human life was so lightly esteemed, these human sacrifices failed to inspire the horror that they would have aroused in the early history of the Jewish people, whose laws were so emphatically against such practices.

The first Oriental scholar to discover the imposition which had been practiced upon the people by the corruption of the text, was Prof. Horace Hayman Wilson, who makes an elaborate argument to prove that the Ṛig-veda teaches no such thing as the natives claim. Max Müller stands faithfully by Wilson, and claims that the true rendering of the mutilated passage should be: "May these women who are not widows, but have good husbands, draw near with oil and butter. Those who are mothers may go up first to the altar without tears, without sorrow, but decked with fine jewels." He also claims that the verse which the Brāhmans have mutilated in the support of their claim is followed by these words, which are addressed to the wife of the dead man: "Rise, woman, come to the world of life; thou sleepest nigh unto him whose life is gone. Come to us, thus hast thou fulfilled thy duties of a wife to the husband who once took thee by the hand and made thee a mother."[1] In J. H. Bushby's valuable work on this subject, he claims that the weight of evidence, from both native and European Orientalists, is in favor of the humane exposition of the Veda. But on the other side we have the testimony of the most distinguished scholar of Calcutta, Raja Radhakant Deb, who occupied a foremost place amongst the Sanskṛit scholars of the world, and whose literary encyclopedia of the Sanskṛit language in seven quarto volumes occupies a prominent place in Europe, as well as India.

Prof. Wilson says that "any opinion coming from him on subjects connected with the ancient literature of this country is entitled to the greatest deference." His views in relation to the suttee were fully expressed to his friend, Dr. Wilson, in a cordial letter. This communication was written after the abolition of the hideous practice in the Indian territories belonging to the English government. The question having been legally settled, its discussion was looked upon by the learned Hindū as being of interest to the historian only, and that merely from a literary point of view. This being the case, his most strenuous opponents could hardly accuse him of literary dishonesty or misrepresentation.

[1] Chips, Vol. II., pp. 33-37.

It is a noteworthy fact that he does not base his opinion upon the text, which, Prof. Wilson confidently stated, had been mutilated by the natives. Raja Radhakant Deb claimed that the most explicit authority for the burning of a widow with her deceased husband was to be found in one of the Upanishads, and he gave the following literal translation of the extract:

1. "O Agni, of all Vratas,[1] thou art the Vratapati,[2] I will observe the vow (Vrata) of following the husband. Do thou enable me to accomplish it.

2. "Here (in this rite) to thee, O Agni, I offer salutation: I enter into thee: (wherefore) this day satisfied with the clarified butter (offered by me) inspire me with courage, and take me to my lord." "Agreeably to this Vaidic instruction, the Sūtrakāras direct that the widow, like the sacrificial utensils, should be made to lie upon the funeral pile of her husband. To the widow placed beside the lifeless body of her husband, a certain part of the Mantras are to be addressed by her husband's brother or fellow student."[3] This eminent authority also cites extracts from various sacred books, from which the rules and directions of the cruel rite have been derived.

Radhakant Deb admits that there is some variance among the sacred works upon this subject, and says: "Where there are two authorities of a contradictory character, but of equal cogency, an alternative must be supposed to be allowed. The Sūtrakāras upon the Vedic authority above set forth direct that the widow as well as the sacrificial utensils of the deceased Brāh-

[1] Vowed or voluntary observances. [2] Lord of Vratras.

[3] Works of H. H. Wilson, Vol. II., p. 296.

man be placed upon his funeral pile; but as the widow has a will of her own, she cannot be disposed of like the inert utensils. The Ṛig-veda, therefore, gives her the option of sacrificing herself or not, according as she may or may not, have courage. When the widow lies on the funeral pile, it is presumed that she is inclined to immolate herself, and a verse is then addressed to her, which is designed to test her resolution, and to induce her to retire if she will." It is also declared, in view of such a contingency, that although the Satī who retires from the funeral pile commits a highly sinful act, it may nevertheless be expiated by performing the Prājāpatya penance—that is, she must for three days eat only in the morning; for three days only in the evening; for three days she must partake of food which is given unsolicited, and during the last three days she must eat nothing at all.

It is true that the Hindū woman was allowed to choose between being burned alive and leading the life of a widow, but if she chose the latter, she was considered a dishonor to her relatives, and the disgraced family lost no opportunity of visiting penalties upon the cause of their reproach. They made her life so intolerable that in most instances the woman preferred to be burned alive rather than lead a life of continual torture and disgrace. Instances are also on record where women, horribly burned, have been driven by their agonies from the funeral pile, only to be captured and thrown back again by their loving (?) relatives. Dr. Massie relates several instances of this kind. In one case the poor victim was driven by her sufferings from the flames, upon which some gentlemen who were spectators immediately plunged her into the river. She retained her senses, and complained that the funeral pile was so badly constructed that it burned slowly, and with wonderful heroism expressed her willingness to go back into the flames if they would change its construction, so that her sufferings would be sooner at an end. This the cruel natives refused to do, and taking their suffering relative by the head and feet they held her in the fire until driven away themselves by the heat, when they threw her into the blazing pile; but she again made her escape, and going toward the river, ran into the arms of a European gentleman, and cried to him to save her. The writer says: "I arrived at the grounds as they (the natives) were bringing her a second time from the river, and I cannot describe to you the horror I felt on seeing the mangled condition she was in." (Here follows a description too revolting for repetition.) She was rescued by the Europeans, lingered in agony about twenty hours, and then died.[1]

Men who had kept at a safe distance from the fire were sometimes very eloquent on the beauties (?) of this ceremony. Boyses translates from a poet of about two thousand years ago the following eulogy upon the horrible custom, and the extract is quoted by Raja Radhakant Deb in his celebrated letter to Dr. Wilson:

"Happy the laws that in those climes obtain,
Where the bright morning reddens all the main.
There whensoe'er the happy husband dies,
And on the funeral couch extended lies,

[1] Uncivilized Races, p. 1409.

His faithful wives around the scene appear,
With pompous dress and with triumphant air,
For partnership in death ambitious strive,
And dread the shameful fortune to survive.
Adorned with flowers the lovely victims stand,
With smiles ascend the pile and light the brand,
Grasp their dear partners with unaltered faith,
And yield exulting to the fragrant death."

Raja Radhakant Deb also argues with great force that the custom must be derived from Vedic authority, from the fact of its having prevailed in India in very remote times—when Vedic rites only were in vogue. He claims that it was practiced during the lives of their early kings and sages, who were imbued with Vedic learning and devoted to the observance of Vedic rituals. It appears, therefore, from the evidence of the best Orientalists, both European and native, that although the early mythological songs of the Ṛig-veda do not teach that a living woman must be burned upon the dead body of her husband, the Vedic teachers have not prevented it. The Ṛig-veda is not a ritual; the directions for performing this horrible rite of human sacrifice and self-immolation are found, however, in other ancient and sacred books of the Hindūs—all of which are classed by the Brāhmans under the general name of Vedas. Certain it is that this terrible custom prevailed in India for more than two thousand years, and it would doubtless be practiced even now if that country had not been penetrated by the advancing light of Christian civilization.

At the close of the 18th century seventy widows were

burned alive with the body of one of the rajas. When Lord Wm. Bentinck was appointed Governor-General of India, he determined that this terrible crime should cease, and the Hindū dignitaries were astonished by a sudden decree, which they found it impossible to repeal or modify. Under the wise administration of Lord Bentinck the suttee was abolished in 1830, and the venerated Ganges flowed to the sea with her waves unstained with blood.

Marshman accuses Prof. Wilson of being an advocate of non-interference with this barbarous rite, but we must remember that we are indebted to this very scholar for the detection of the mutilated text, by the aid of which the natives long held the English government at bay, under the promise of the latter that their religion was not to be interfered with. Lord Bentinck and others who have been brought into daily contact with the practical cruelty of this people are far less enthusiastic over the race than is the European scholar who studies the finest specimens of Hindū poetry in the quiet seclusion of his own library.

CHAPTER V.

THE BRĀHMAṆAS.

THE SECOND GRAND DIVISION OF VEDIC LITERATURE—AGE OF THE BRĀHMAṆAS—BURDEN OF CEREMONIES—PENANCE FOR BAD DREAMS—SACRIFICES—EXTRACT FROM FOURTH BRĀHMAṆA—THE STORY OF ŚUNAḤŚEPA—A HUMAN SACRIFICE—TRADITION OF THE FLOOD AS FOUND IN ŚATAPATHA-BRĀHMAṆA.

THE second grand division of Vedic literature is devoted almost entirely to directions and rules for the various rites and ceremonies. The oldest of them, according to leading Sanskṛit scholars,[1] was written seven or eight centuries before Christ, or from twelve to fourteen hundred years after Abraham. Their composition is rambling and unsystematic, and full of repetition and trivial detail.

Brāhmaṇa means originally the sayings of Brāhmans or priests. It is a name applicable not only to books, but to the old prose traditions, whether contained in the Saṉhitās, the Brāhmaṇas, the Āraṇyakas, the Upanishads, or even, in some cases, the Sūtras. (See Wilson.) At the conclusion of his long and exhaustive labors, Julius Eggeling, the faithful translator of the Śatapatha-brāhmaṇa, speaks of his thankless task as follows: "The translator of the Śatapatha-brāhmaṇa

1 Prof. H. H. Wilson, Sir Monier Williams, and others.

can be under no illusion as to the reception his production is likely to meet with at the hand of the general reader. In the whole range of literature, few works are probably less calculated to excite the interest of any, outside the very limited number of specialists, than the ancient theological writings of the Hindūs, known by the name of Brāhmaṇas. For wearisome prolixity of exposition, characterized by dogmatic assertion, and a flimsy symbolism, rather than by serious reasoning, these works are perhaps not equalled anywhere."

Still they represent the period in the history of that country when the priests had succeeded in transforming the primitive worship of the powers of nature into a highly artificial system of rites, ceremonies and sacrifices. Human nature appears to be much the same in all ages of the world, and the Hindū priests did not fail to avail themselves of the religious instincts of a naturally devout race; they were always intent upon deepening their hold on the minds of the people, by surrounding their own vocation with the halo of sanctity and divine inspiration. With them it was a matter of position, of influence, and of money to urge the necessity of frequent and liberal offerings to the gods, and to invoke worldly blessings upon the devotee. The priestly bard often pleaded his own cause, as well as that of his employer. For instance, Kanva sings in the Ṛig-veda, "Let him be rich, let him be foremost, the bard of the rich, of so illustrious a maghaven, (wealthy patron of priests,) as thou, O Lord of the bay steeds."[1]

[1] Int., pp. 9-11.

Hence the people were loaded down with rites and ceremonies upon all possible occasions. The devout Brāhman must have spent nearly all his time in unmeaning rites, penances and oblations. For instance, if a man dreams of being killed by a black man with black teeth, or of being killed by a boar, or if he dreams that a monkey jumps upon him, that the wind carries him along quickly, or that having swallowed gold he spits it out; if he dreams of eating honey, of chewing stalks, of carrying a red lotus, of wearing a wreath of red flowers, or of driving a black cow, with a black calf, facing the south, he must fast, and cook a pot of milk and sacrifice it, accompanying each oblation with a verse of the Ṛig-veda, and then, after having feasted the priest (with other food prepared at his house) he must eat all of the oblation himself.

The method by which man arrived at the knowledge of the virtues of sacrifices is thus explained in the Aitareya-brāhmaṇa.

"The gods killed a man for their victim, but from him thus killed the part which was fit for a sacrifice went out and entered a horse. Hence the horse became an animal fit for being sacrificed. The gods then killed the horse, but the part that was fit for being sacrificed went out of it and entered a sheep. Thence it entered a goat. The sacrificial part remained for the longest time in the goat, then the goat became pre-eminently fit for being sacrificed. The gods went up to heaven by means of offerings. They were afraid that men and sages, after having seen their ceremonies, might inquire how they could obtain some knowledge of sacrificial rites, and follow them. They therefore debarred them, by means of the Yupa (or post to which the victim was fastened), turning its point downwards. Thereupon, the men and sages dug the post out, and turned its point upwards. Thus they became aware of the sacrifice and reached the heavenly world."[1]

Besides the daily devotional acts, there were two semi-monthly sacrifices enjoined upon every Brāhmanical householder, each of which lasted two days. This must be continued during the first thirty years of housekeeping, and according to some authorities it must be kept up through life. The ceremonies began with a preparation of the sacrificial fires. The fireplaces were thrice swept, thrice besmeared with gomaya, three lines being drawn across them from west to east, or from south to north, with a wooden sword, after which the dust was removed from the lines with the thumb and ring finger, and the lines sprinkled thrice with water, etc. Many pages are filled with minute instructions in relation to these long ceremonies, and with a description of the vegetables and clarified butter, which the Brāhman and his wife were to eat before finally taking a vow.

Many pages are devoted to the washing or the brushing of the spoons, and to the particular method of laying the sacrificial grass upon the altar, for the numerous periodical oblations and for sacrifices in general. The instructions in relation to making the offerings to Agni (fire) are also both minute and multitudinous. A very brief extract upon this subject will satisfy the reader, as it is a fair sample of the literary style of hundreds of pages:

[1] Book 2: (Haug. 1-8.)

FOURTH BRĀHMAṆA.

1. "They (the sticks for the sacrificial fire) should be green, for that is their living element—by that they are vigorous, by that possessed of strength, for this reason they should be green.

2. "The middle sticks he lays down first on the west side of the fire, with the text 'May the Gandharva Visvasu lay thee around for the security of the all. Thou art a fence to the sacrificer. Thou art Agni, invoked and worthy of invocation.'

3. "He then lays down the southern one, with the text 'Thou art Indra's arm for the security of the all. Thou art a fence to the sacrificer, thou Agni, invoked and worthy of invocation.'

4. "He then lays down the northern one with the text 'May the Mitra Varuṇa lay thee around in the north with firm law for the security of the all. Thou art a fence to the sacrificer, thou Agni, invoked and worthy of invocation.'"

Thereupon he puts on the fire a kindling stick; he first touches with it the middle inclosing stick; thereby he first kindles those (three Agnis). After that he puts it on the fire—thereby he kindles the visible fire.

This, however, is only the beginning of interminable pages of description, as to the meaning of each stick, each motion, and each mumbled invocation on the part of the sacrificer. While the Brāhmaṇas are almost exclusively devoted to the formulas of domestic sacrifice, and the almost endless succession of petty details, they also contain some legends on other subjects.

One of these represents the gods and demons in a mighty warfare, in which the evil demons formed the earth into an iron citadel, changed the air into a silver fortress, and the sky into a fort of gold. Whereupon the gods said, "We will build other worlds in opposition to these." Then they constructed sacrificial palaces, where they made a triple burnt oblation. By the first sacrifice they drove the demons out of their earthly fortresses, by the second they expelled them from the air, and by the third they routed them from the sky. Thus were the evil spirits chased by the gods in triumph from the world.[1]

THE STORY OF ŚUNAḤŚEPA.

The Aitareya-brāhmaṇa, written about 600 B. C., contains also the story of Sunaḥśepa, in which the doctrine of human sacrifice is introduced, and a father is represented as selling his son to be offered to Varuṇa.

As the story goes, King Hariśćandra had no son. He therefore went to the god Varuṇa and promised that deity that if he would grant him a son he would sacrifice the child to him. A son was then born to him and was named Rohita. At last the royal father told his son that he was devoted to sacrifice and must prepare for it. But the boy refused to comply with his father's demands, and taking his bow he left his home and took up his abode in the forest, whereupon Varuṇa afflicted the king with dropsy for failing to fulfill his pledge.

After a time Rohita found in the forest a half-

[1] Aitareya-brah., Haug's Ed., 1-23.

starved hermit who had three sons. The young prince purchased one of the boys for a hundred cows and took him to his father. The god Varuṇa accepted the substitute, and the sacrificial post was made ready; but no one was found who was willing to bind the victim. The father of Śunaḥśepa then came forward and said:

"'Give me a hundred cows and I will bind him.'
They gave them to him and he bound the boy.
But now no person would consent to kill him.
Then said the father, 'Give me yet again
Another hundred cows and I will slay him.'
Once more they gave him a hundred and the father
Whetted the knife to sacrifice his son.
Then said the boy, 'Let me implore the gods;
Haply they will deliver me from death.'
So Śunaḥśepa prayed to all the gods
With verses from the Veda, and they heard him.
Thus was the boy released from sacrifice,
And Hariśćandra was restored to health."[1]

THE FLOOD.

In common with other nations and peoples, the ancient Hindūs possessed their tradition of a universal deluge. Concerning this great historic event the same voice comes to us from the archives of Babylon, from the clay tablets of old Assyria, from the hieroglyphs of Egypt, from the annals of Greece,[2] from the parchments of China, and from the pages of the

[1] Haug's Ed., 7-18, Williams' trans.

[2] According to the Greek tradition of a general deluge, every living being was destroyed except those who escaped in a boat, and these repeopled the earth after the flood subsided, as in the traditions of many other

Śatapatha-brāhmaṇa. This Indo-Āryan tradition of the deluge, which has existed for so many generations in India, represents the ark as being saved by Vishṇu in his character as a fish, which is his first incarnation. It reads as follows:

"There lived in ancient time a holy man
Called Manu, who by penances and prayer
Had won the favor of the Lord of heaven.
One day they brought him water for ablution;
Then as he washed his hands a little fish
Appeared, and spoke in human accents thus:
'Take care of me and I will be thy saviour.'
'From what wilt thou preserve me?' Manu asked.
The fish replied, 'A flood will sweep away
All creatures. I will rescue thee from that.'
'But how shall I preserve thee?' Manu said.
The fish rejoined, 'So long as we are small,
We are in constant danger of destruction,
For fish eat fish. So keep me in a jar;
When I outgrow the jar, then dig a trench
And place me there; when I outgrow the trench,
Then take me to the ocean; I shall then
Be out of reach of danger.' Having thus
Instructed Manu, straightway rapidly
The fish grew larger. Then he spoke again,
'In such and such a year the flood will come;
Therefore construct a ship and pay me homage;
When the flood rises enter thou the ship

nations. The principal personage thus saved, according to Greek tradition, was Deukalion, the ruler of Thessaly and the son of Prometheus. His father had told him to build a ship and furnish it with provisions, and when the flood came he and his wife Pyrrha were the only people who escaped.—*Sci. of Rel.*, p. 63.

And I will rescue thee.' So Manu did
As he was ordered, and preserved the fish.
Then carried it in safety to the ocean.
And in the very year the fish enjoined
He built a ship, and paid the fish respect,
And there took refuge when the flood arose.
Soon near him swam the fish, and to its horn
Manu made fast the cable of his vessel.
Thus drawn along the waters, Manu passed
Beyond the northern mountain; then the fish
Addressing Manu said, 'I have preserved thee.
Quickly attach the ship to yonder tree,
But lest the waters sink from under thee,
As fast as they subside, so fast shalt thou
Descend the mountain gently after them.'
Thus he descended from the northern mountain.
The flood had swept away all living creatures;
Manu was left alone. Wishing for offspring,
He earnestly performed a sacrifice.
In a year's time a female was produced;
She came to Manu, then he said to her,
'Who art thou?' She replied, 'I am thy daughter.'
He said, 'How, lovely lady, can that be?'
'I came forth,' she rejoined, 'from thine oblations
Cast upon the waters; thou wilt find in me
A blessing; use me in the sacrifice.'
With her he worshiped, and with toilsome zeal
Performed religious rites, hoping for offspring.
Thus were created men called sons of Manu.
Whatever benediction he implored
With her, was thus vouchsafed in full abundance."[1]

[1] Williams' trans., Ind. Wis., p. 32.

This legend in the Śatapatha-brāhmaṇa is afterwards repeated in the Mahā-bhārata. The Brāhmaṇas have more allusions to a future life, and contain stronger statements on that subject than can be found in the earlier vein of Hindū literature, but the doctrine of the transmigration of souls appears not to be fully developed until we reached the Code of Manu and the Upanishads.

CHAPTER VI.

THE CODE OF MANU.

THE DATE OF THE CODE—THE TRIBE OR SCHOOL OF MĀNAVAS—THE CODE A MEANS OF PERPETUATING THE RULES OF CASTE—DIVINE ORIGIN CLAIMED FOR THE LAWS OF MANU—CASTE—DIVINE RIGHTS OF BRĀHMANS—THE KSHATRIYA—THE VAIŚYA—THE ŚŪDRA—MARRIAGE A PURIFYING RITE—RULES FOR CHOOSING A WIFE—MARRIAGE—WOMAN'S RIGHTS—PENANCES—CRIMINAL CODE—FUNERAL CEREMONIES.

INTIMATELY connected with the ceremonies of the Vedas, we find the Code of Manu, which in its present form dates back to about the fifth century before Christ. Some parts of it were doubtless current at a considerably earlier date, as the gods mentioned are principally Vedic. Originally, it merely represented certain rules and precepts, probably by different authors, which were observed by a particular tribe or school of Brāhmans called Mānavas. This tribe appears to have been adherents of the Black Yajur-veda, and their Mantras and Brāhmaṇa are still extant. Ultimately, however, the code was accepted by the Hindū people generally, and received a reverence which was second only to that which was accorded to the Vedas. It became also the chief authority in Hindū jurisprudence.

The Laws of Manu plainly reveal the strenuous rules by which the Brāhmans sought to perpetuate an organized system of caste which should definitely define and maintain their own superiority. They were drawn largely from earlier authorities, but the real compiler and promulgator of them is unknown. In common with other Hindū works, the code claims a divine origin.

A sage named Manu is represented as saying: "The god Brahmā having formed this system of laws himself, taught it fully to me in the beginning. I then taught it to Marīći and the nine other sages, my offspring. Of these (my sons) Bhṛigu is deputed by me to declare the code to you (Ṛishis), for he has learned from me to recite the whole of it."[1]

CASTE.

The Hindū theory of caste is that the gods created one class of men superior to another—that there is as much difference between the various classes of men as between the different kinds of birds and animals. The creation of this great distinction is thus accounted for in one of the latest hymns of the Ṛig-veda:[2]

"The embodied spirit has a thousand heads,
A thousand eyes, a thousand feet around
On every side enveloping the earth,
Yet filling space no larger than a span.
He is himself this very universe.
He is, whatever is, has been and shall be.
He is the Lord of Immortality.

[1] Ind. Wis., pp. 212–215.
[2] As the whole of this celebrated hymn has been given in the first chapter a brief quotation here will suffice.

"How did they cut him up? What was his mouth?
What were his arms? and what his thighs and feet?
The Brāhman was his mouth—the kingly soldier
Was made his arms, the husbandman his thighs,
The servile Śūdra[1] issued from his feet."[2]

Hence, the divine order of caste seems to be:

1. The Brāhman, who is supposed to issue from the mouth of Brahmā.

2. Kshatriya, or "kingly soldier," who issues from the arms.

3. The husbandman, or Vaiśya caste, who comes from the thighs.

4. The servile Śūdra, who issues from his feet.

It is therefore claimed that the divine right of kings is emphasized and exaggerated in the divine right of priests; that a Brāhman is such by virtue of his birth; and that he was created with special reference to his position as the head of all mankind.

It is said that "Since the Brāhman sprang from the most excellent part (the mouth of Brahmā), since he has the priority arising from primogeniture, and since he possesses the Veda, he is by right the Lord of this whole creation," and again, "Even when Brāhmans employ themselves in all sorts of inferior occupations, they must under all circumstances be honored, for they are to be regarded as supreme divinities." "From his high birth alone, a Brāhman is regarded as a divinity, even by the gods. His teaching must be accepted by the rest of the world as an infallible authority."

[1] Slave or lowest caste. [2] See Man. 10-90, Williams' trans.

He is also declared to possess power which is in perfect harmony with his divine position and character. In Book 9, pp. 313–314, it is said, "Let not a king, although fallen into the greatest distress, provoke Brāhmans to anger (by taking revenue from them), for they, if once enraged, could instantly (by pronouncing curses and mystical texts) destroy him with all his army and retinue."[1]

THE KSHATRIYA,

or military and kingly caste, ranked next to the Brāhmans in position and influence. They introduced into India the scepticisms of philosophical speculation, but with the natural adhesiveness peculiar to monopolies, Brāhmanism and rationalism soon made a compromise to the effect that however inconsistent with each other, neither should denounce the other as a false guide, and thereafter they co-operated with each other in retaining their ascendency over the lower classes.

THE VAIŚYA,

or agricultural class, forms the third rank, and they, as well as the Brāhmans and Kshatriyas, claim to be "twice born."

THE ŚŪDRA,

or servile class, is only once born, and forms the lowest rank. But they are just as particular as their superiors to retain their proper position and caste. They would not intermarry with a higher order, and if they did their children would not be even Śūdras. All the rules of caste are sacred as ordinances of their religion;

[1] Ind. Wis., pp. 240, 241.

hence, the man who dresses hair would not clean clothes, neither could a table waiter be induced to carry an umbrella.[1]

MARRIAGE OF A BRĀHMAN.

The most elaborate and tedious details are given for the endless ceremonies connected with all the minutiæ of a Brāhman's life. Sometimes a great sacrifice lasts for weeks or months, or even years. The ceremonies and purifications connected with his student life are as long as his course of study, which comprises a knowledge of the three Vedas. He must go through twelve "purificatory rites," and it is a noticeable fact that the last of these is marriage, which is, in the language of Williams, "a religious duty, incumbent upon all completing the purification and regeneration of the twice born."

He also receives explicit directions in relation to

THE CHOICE OF A WIFE,

in the following words:

"Let him not marry a girl with reddish hair, nor one with a superfluity of limbs (as, for instance, one with six fingers), nor one who is sickly, nor one with either too little or too much hair; nor one who talks too much; nor one who is red-eyed; nor one named after a constellation, a tree, or a river; nor one with a barbarous name, or the name of a mountain, a bird, a snake, a slave, or any frightful object. But let him marry a woman without defective or deformed limbs, having an agreeable name, whose gait is like that of a

[1] Ind. Wis., XXV.

flamingo or elephant, whose teeth and hair are moderate in quantity, and whose whole body is soft."[1]

The marriage rites in Manu's Code are evidently taken from older works. The following is quoted by Prof. Williams as the

MARRIAGE CEREMONY.

"West of the sacred fire a stone is placed, and northeast a water jar. The bridegroom offers an oblation standing, looking toward the west, and taking hold of the bride's hands, while she sits and looks toward the east. If he wishes only for sons, he clasps her thumbs, and says, 'I clasp thy hands for the sake of good fortune;' the fingers alone if he wishes for daughters; the hairy side of the hand, along with the thumbs, if he wishes for both sons and daughters. Then, whilst he leads her toward the right three times around the fire and around the water jar, he says in a low tone, 'I am he, thou art she; thou art she, I am he. I am the heaven, thou art the earth. Come, let us marry; let us possess offspring. United in affection, illustrious, well disposed toward each other, let us live a hundred years.' Every time he leads her around, he makes her ascend the mill-stone, and says, 'Ascend thou this stone—be thou firm as a stone.' Then the bride's brother, after spreading melted butter on the joined palms of her hands, scatters parched grains of rice on them twice and after pouring the oblation of butter on the fire, some Vedic texts are recited. Then the bridegroom loosens the two braided tresses of hair—one on each side of the top of the

[1] Book 3, 8-10.

bride's head—repeating the Vedic text, 'I loose thee from the fetters of Varuṇa, with which the very auspicious Savitṛi has bound thee.' He now causes her to step seven steps towards the northeast quarter, saying to her, 'Take thou one step for the acquirement of sap-like energy; take thou two steps for strength; take thou three steps for the increase of wealth; take thou four steps for well being; take thou five steps for offspring; take thou six steps for the season; take thou seven steps as a friend. Be faithfully devoted to me. May we obtain many sons; may they attain to a good old age.' Then bringing both their heads into close juxtaposition, some one sprinkles them with water from the jar. He should remain for that night in the house of an old Brāhman woman whose husband and children are alive. When the bride sees the polar star and Arundhatī and the seven Ṛishis, let her break silence and say, 'May my husband live, and may I obtain children.' When he (the bridegroom) has completed the marriage ceremonial, he should give the bride's dress to one who knows the Sūryā-sūkta, and food to the Brāhmans. Then he should make them pronounce a blessing upon him."

The marriage ceremony once completed, the bridegroom at once enters upon the endless round of ceremonies which are enjoined upon the householder—the sacred fire, the daily ablutions, etc., etc. Five chapters are devoted to domestic ceremonies connected with the birth and treatment of children, and still others to the investiture with the sacred thread, which the Brāhman child receives in his eighth year, the Kshatriya, in his eleventh, and the Vaiśya in his twelfth.

As this rite is supposed to confer the second or spiritual birth, the Śūdra child does not receive it at all, only the three upper classes being "twice born."[1]

WOMAN'S RIGHTS.

So far as the woman's position in the household is concerned, it is one of complete subordination to the will of the "lord of the manor." Still, great respect is paid to the mother by her children, and it is claimed that the seclusion of Hindū wives was largely the result of the introduction of Moslem customs, when the Mohammedans invaded India. The following extracts will give an intelligible idea of the Hindū law upon this point:

"Day and night must women be made to feel their dependence on their husbands. But if they are fond of worldly amusements, let them be allowed to follow their own inclinations."[2]

"Let not a husband eat with his wife, nor look at her eating."[3]

"Women have no business to repeat texts of the Veda—thus is the law established."

"Domestic rites are to be performed in common with the wife—so it is ordained in the Veda."[4]

"As far as a wife obeys her husband, so far is she exalted in heaven. A husband must be continually revered as a god by a virtuous wife."[5]

With the lapse of time civilization appears to be having some effect upon the unmitigated despotism of

[1] Book 1, 7.
[2] Book 9, 2.
[3] Book 4, 4-8.
[4] Book 9, 18-96.
[5] Book 5, 154-160.

the Hindū householder towards his wife. The Mahābhārata, some parts of which it is claimed were written during the Christian era, contains the following tribute to the faithful wife:

> "A wife is half the man, his truest friend.
> A loving wife is a perpetual spring
> Of virtue, pleasure, wealth. A faithful wife
> Is his best aid in seeking heavenly bliss.
> A sweetly speaking wife is a companion
> In solitude; a father in advice;
> A mother in all seasons of distress;
> A rest in passing through life's wilderness."[1]

That such sentiments live upon the pages of their own sacred literature must be a great source of strength to the missionaries who are trying to educate and elevate the womanhood of India. Still, it must be confessed, that it is only in countries which are illumined by the teachings of Christianity that woman takes her true position at her husband's side, and works with him for the elevation of the human race.

PENANCES.

Lying is pronounced sometimes justifiable: "In certain cases a man stating a fact falsely from a pious motive, even though he knows the truth, is not excluded from heaven—such a statement they call divine speech." Yet severe penances are required for trivial sins of omission, or for the performance of any act causing loss of caste.

If a Brāhman receives a present from a wicked per-

[1] Maha. I, 3028, William's trans.

son, he must repeat the Sāvitrī[1] "three thousand times, with a collected mind," and drink milk for one month in a cow house. If he has eaten improper food, he is absolved by repeating for three days certain texts in the Ṛig-veda. If a twice-born man, through infatuation, should drink intoxicating liquor, he might drink of the same liquor boiling hot, and if his body is completely scalded by the process he is absolved from guilt.

"A Brāhman performing the penance called hot and severe, must swallow hot water, hot milk, hot clarified butter, and hot air, each for three days successively, after bathing, and keeping his organs of sense all restrained."[2]

Many others are prescribed, some of them being of the most loathsome nature, and entirely unfit for publication; for instance, the penance called Sāntapana.[3]

CRIMINAL CODE.

The civil and religious code is strangely combined in the laws of Manu. Sometimes the criminal seems to be under the jurisdiction of a purely civil law, and again he is threatened with the most terrible punishments in various forms, through which his soul must pass after leaving the body.

As future punishment will be treated in its proper place, under the doctrinal teachings of the Upanishads, we distinguish here between the civil punishment bestowed upon the criminal, and that with which he is threatened

1 A sacred text which is said to have been milked out of the Vedas.
2 Book II, 214. 3 Book II, 212.

in the world to come. Sir Wm. Jones says that "The cruel mutilations practiced by the native powers are shocking to humanity," and Sir Monier Williams declares that "The three most conspicuous features of Manu's penal laws were severity, inconsistency, and a belief in the supposed justice of *lex talionis*." This learned Orientalist made a careful study of this particular form of legislation, and to him we are indebted for much valuable information. In the light of the following extracts, we cannot wonder that he considered the "punishment unjustifiably disproportionate to the offences committed, and sometimes barbarously cruel."

"With whatever member of the body a low-born man may injure a superior, that very member of his body must be mutilated."[1]

"A once-born man insulting twice-born men with abusive language must have his tongue cut out."

"Should he mention their name and caste with insulting expressions, a red-hot iron spike, ten fingers long, is to be thrust into his mouth."

"Thieves are to have their hands cut off, and then to be impaled on a sharp stick."[2]

"A goldsmith detected in committing frauds is to have his body cut to pieces with razors."[3]

We can hardly imagine any form of humanity sufficiently low and cruel to inflict these horrible punishments, even upon the vilest of criminals, neither could the legal student believe that such enactments had ever been made, if they were not actually present in the record.

[1] Book VIII, 279. [2] Book IX, 276. [3] Book IX, 292.

FUNERAL CEREMONIES.

The rules for disposing of the dead were evidently derived from the Gṛihya-sûtras, an authority on domestic rites, which was extant in India before the laws of Manu were compiled. The most explicit directions are given as to the washing of the body, the trimming of the nails, hair, and beard. It is enjoined also that a piece of ground must be dug southeast or southwest of the place where the man lived and died. It should be in length as long as the man with his arms raised, a fathom wide, and a span in depth.

The burning and burying ground should be open on all sides, rich in shrubs, particularly of thorny and milky plants, and elevated in such a manner that water would run down on every side. If the deceased happened to die in the midst of a sacrifice (which is very liable to be the case among a people the greater part of whose time is occupied with religious ceremonies), his relations take his three sacred fires and his sacrificial implements and carry them to the place of cremation. Behind follow the old men, without their wives, carrying the corpse. Their number should not be even. In some places, however, the corpse is carried on a wheel cart, drawn by an ox or some other animal. Either a cow or a black kid, or a kid of any one color, is led behind by a rope tied to its left leg. This animal is to be slain and afterwards strewn over the corpse and burnt with it.

After the procession has reached the ground, he who has to perform the sacrifice steps forth, walks three times around the place towards the left, sprinkles it with water from the branch of a tree, and repeats a verse from the Veda.

The fires are placed on the borders of a pit, according to the following formula: The Āhavanīya fire is placed to the southeast, the Gārhapatya to the northwest and the Dakshiṇa to the southwest. The dead body must be placed with its feet toward the Gārhapatya fire and the head towards the Āhavanīya. If the Āhavanīya fire reaches the dead man first, his spirit is borne to heaven; if the Gārhapatya reaches him first, then his spirit is taken to the middle region; if the Dakshiṇa, then it remains in the world of mortals. When all three of these fires reach him at the same time, it is the most auspicious omen of all. The wooden pile is properly laid in the midst of these fires, sacrificial grass is then strewn upon the pile, and the skin of a black antelope, with the fur on the outside, is placed over it. The wife is made to lie down to the north of her husband, and if he be a Kshatriya, a bone is also placed there. If the wife is not to be immolated, she is then led away, and the animal is brought. The fat of the animal is cut out, and put like a cover over the face of the dead, while the following verse from the Ṛig-veda is recited:

"Put on this armor (taken) from the cows to protect thee against Agni, and cover thyself with fat, that he, the wild one, who delights in flames, the hero, may not embrace thee, wishing to consume thee."[1]

The kidneys, also, are taken out and put into the

[1] R-v. 8, 16-17.

hands of the dead, while the following quotation is repeated: "Escape on the right path the two dogs, the four-eyed, tawny breed of Saramā, then approach the wise fathers, who, happy with Yama, enjoy happiness."[1]

The heart of the animal is laid on the heart of the corpse, and after considerable ceremony the antelope skin is covered over the whole and various oblations are offered, each accompanied with a text from the Veda. After this the fire is lighted, and they walk away without looking back, at the same time reciting a verse from the Veda.

This is the *briefest possible* sketch of an almost interminable ceremony, after which all parties concerned must go through with the long ceremonies of purification. The ashes and bones are gathered and buried, with as much ceremony as attended the burning, and again all parties must go through the process of purification. The medical advice is equally complicated, and the patient is compelled to perform for himself the most exhaustive rites; if he recovers, there are a multitude of sacrifices and oblations demanded of him. Thus the whole life of the patient Hindū, from the cradle to the grave, is burdened with ceaseless rites and offerings to the various gods of the pantheon.

The extracts here given will serve to give an intelligible idea of the voluminous law books of Manu, about twenty of which are still in existence. This collection of laws is one of the most sacred portions of Sanskṛit literature. It presents an early picture of the moral and intellectual condition of the people, fully illustrating the severity with which the priestly class enforced

[1] R.-v, 10, 10-14.

the rules of caste, and their own superiority even over kings and princes.

It is a compilation of rules which had been handed down orally, perhaps for many generations, and were at last gathered and arranged in a systematic collection. They soon reached a position where they were held to be infallible, and Manu says, "By Śruti is meant the Veda, and by Smṛiti the books of the law; *the contents of these must never be questioned by reason.*" "Nevertheless," says Williams, "in almost every place where the Mantras of the Ṛig-veda are alluded to by Manu, errors disfigure the text and commentary."

CHAPTER VII.

THE UPANISHADS.

THE THIRD GRAND DIVISION OF VEDIC LITERATURE — THE UPANISHADS — THE DOCTRINAL PORTION OF THE VEDA — DERIVATION — RAMMOHUN ROY — NUMBER OF THE UPANISHADS — PLACE IN VEDIC CHRONOLOGY — ŚRUTI OR REVEALED KNOWLEDGE — ĆHĀNDOGYA UPANISHAD — IMPORTANCE OF OM — EXTRACTS FROM THE ĆHĀNDOGYA — THE KENA UPANISHAD — EXTRACT FROM THE KENA — THE KATHA UPANISHAD — THE AITAREYA UPANISHAD — EXTRACT FROM THE AITAREYA — THE KAUSHĪTAKI-BRĀHMAṆA UPANISHAD — DISCOURSE UPON FUTURE LIFE — THE VĀJASANEYI-SAmHITĀ UPANISHAD — EXTRACT FROM THE VĀJASANEYI — THE ĪŚA — THE COMPLETION OF REVELATION.

WE now come to the third grand division of the Vedas, called the Upanishads or mystical doctrine.

As has been stated, the earliest hymns of the Vedas are mostly in praise of the various gods of the earth, sky, or air, and include invocations to their deities for food, rich herds, large families, and long life, for which blessings the gods are to be rewarded with sacrifices and oblations of clarified butter, or of the soma juice, offered in their sacred groves.[1] The speculative, or theological portion of the Vedas is explained in separate books, called Upanishads. These are therefore the doctrinal portions of the Vedas.

This word, derived from the root *sad* (to sit), preceded by the two prepositions *ni* (down) and *upa* (near), expresses the idea of a number of pupils sitting down near their teacher to listen to his instructions. It also implies something which underlies the surface, and the doctrine contained in these treatises does, in fact, underlie the whole system of Hindū teaching.

These books are of later origin than the Ṛigveda,[2] but they were called by Rammohun Roy, "the kernel of the Vedas." This distinguished native scholar translated several of the books at his own expense.

The number of Upanishads has been variously estimated, but a list of about one hundred and fifty has been obtained by Europeans, many of them bearing distinctive titles, which are almost unprononnceable by any one except the natives.

[1] The worship of Baal pertained to the planting of groves, and to offerings to the sun and moon, and all the host of heaven; this was the form of idolatry for which the children of Israel were repeatedly punished. "The children gather wood, and the fathers kindle the fire, and the women knead their dough to make cakes to the Queen of Heaven, and to pour out drink offerings unto other gods."—Jer. vii: 18. The great difference between the Sabeanism of the Chaldeans and that of the Hindus is that the Chaldeans made the stars prominent in their worship, while the Hindus adored principally the sun and moon.

[2] Prof. Wilson, Dr. Mill, and other Orientalists at last succeeded in convincing the most learned natives that the Upanishads belonged to a later age than the early hymns of the Veda. This is only one of many instances in which European scholars have been able to give information to the Hindus concerning their own sacred books.

AGE OF THE UPANISHADS.

According to the chronology usually received by Sanskṛit scholars, the most ancient of these books must have slightly preceded the rise of Buddhism (600 B. C.). Sir Monier Williams, however, assigns 500 B. C. as the utmost limit of their antiquity. But, according to Max Müller, the germs of the doctrines taught in the Upanishads may be found in the early period of Vedic literature, which has been provisionally fixed at from 800 to 1000 B. C.

There are many whose exact chronology it is almost impossible to determine, although it is easy to see that they belong to very different periods of Hindū thought, and some of them must be quite modern, as mention is even made of an Allah Upanishad.

Several Upanishads occur in the later Brāhmaṇas, but the recognized place for the most ancient of these works is in connection with the Āraṇyakas[1] (or forest books), which generally form an appendix to the Brāhmaṇas, but are also sometimes included under the general name of Brāhmaṇa.

The Upanishads belong to what the Hindūs call the Śruti, or revealed literature, in opposition to Smṛiti, or traditional literature, which is supposed to be founded upon the former, and therefore can claim only a secondary importance and authority. The first in the list is

THE ĆHĀNDOGYA UPANISHAD.[2]

This work belongs to the Sāma-veda, and is one of

1 These works, as well as the Upanishads, are so obscure that it is said to be necessary to read them in the loneliness of the forest.

2 Prof. Max Müller, the translator, gives "*Kh*andogya" as the orthography of this Upanishad and this is of course absolutely correct, but, if

the most important contributions to the orthodox philosophy of India, viz., the Vedānta. This important Upanishad purports to give a full account of the syllable Om. The opening sentence is "Let a man meditate on the syllable Om—called the udgîtha, for the udgîtha (a portion of the Sāma-veda) is sung beginning with Om."

This sacred syllable has been the source of no little trouble and perplexity on the part of European scholars, as it had to be pronounced at the beginning of each Veda, and at every recitation of Vedic hymns. As connected with the Sāma-veda, Om is called udgîtha. Müller says that the syllable originally meant "that" or "yes," but it is also considered the symbol of all speech and of all life. It is also the name for all physical and mental powers; also the principle of life, or living spirit, which is identified with the spirit in the sun. Therefore, he who meditates upon Om, meditates on the spirit in man as identical with the spirit in nature, or in the sun, and thus he is supposed to be led to a recognition of the self in man as identical with the highest self, or Brahman.

Meditation on that syllable is supposed to mean the long-continued repetition of it, until the mind is drawn away from all other subjects and concentrated upon a higher object of thought, which is symbolized by the sacred syllable. The exposition of Om, or of udgîtha, as given by this Upanishad, is as follows: "The full

this method of transliteration is followed, the first two letters must always be italicized or else the K will be pronounced like the English K, whereas it should be pronounced like ch in church. Many scholars therefore prefer to write the name "Chandogya," as it is more liable to be correctly pronounced by the English reader.

account, however, of Om is this: The essence of all beings is the earth; the essence of the earth is water; the essence of water, the plants; the essence of plants, man; the essence of man, speech; the essence of speech, the Ṛig-veda; the essence of the Ṛig-veda, the Sāma-veda; the essence of the Sāma-veda, the udgîtha, (which is Om). That udgîtha (Om) is the best of all essences, the highest, deserving the highest place, the eighth. . . . By that syllable does the threefold knowledge (the sacrifice, more particularly the Sāma-sacrifice, as founded on the three Vedas) proceed. When the Adhvaryu priest gives an order, he says Om. When the Hotṛi priest recites, he says Om. When the Udgātṛi priest sings, he says Om—all for the glory of that syllable.

"The threefold knowledge (the sacrifice) proceeds by the greatness of that syllable (the vital breaths), and by its essence (the oblations). Now, therefore, it would seem to follow that both he who knows this (the true meaning of the syllable Om) and he who does not, perform the same sacrifice; but this is not so, for knowledge and ignorance are different. The sacrifice which a man performs with knowledge, faith, and the Upanishad, is more powerful. This is the full account of the syllable Om."[1]

There were three classes of priests engaged in the soma sacrifices, and each one was obliged to begin his part of the ceremonial with Om, therefore the whole sacrifice was said to be dependent on that syllable,

[1] 1st Prap.—1st Khan.

The quotations from the Upanishads, unless otherwise indicated, are from Müller's translations.

and for the glory of that syllable as an emblem of the Highest Self, the knowledge of whom is the indirect result of all sacrifices. The great importance of this syllable is expressed by the vital breaths of the priest, the sacrificer and his wife.

The essence of the syllable is supposed to be many things: for instance, the rice and corn and other articles used in the oblation. The sacrifice which is dependent upon the syllable Om is supposed to ascend to the sun, and as the sun sends rain, and rain produces food, and food produces life, breath and food are due to the syllable Om. This syllable seems to have been used on all occasions, both in sacrifice and in fables, sometimes apparently without meaning, as in the 12th Khanda of the 1st Prapā*th*aka.

1. "Now follows the udgîtha of the dogs. Vaka Dālbhya . . . went out to repeat the Veda in a quiet place.

2. "A white dog appeared before him, and other dogs gathered around him (the white dog), and said to him, 'Sir, sing and get us food, we are hungry.'

3. "The white dog said to them, 'Come to me to-morrow morning.' Vaka Dālbhya watched.

4. "The dogs came on, holding together, each dog keeping the tail of the preceding dog in his mouth, as the priests do (hold each other's garments) when they are going to sing praises with the Vahish-pavamāna hymns. After they had settled down, they began to say Hin.

5. "Om let us eat. Om let us drink. Om may the divine Varuṇa-pra*g*âpati Savitṛi bring us food. Lord of food, bring hither food, bring it Om."

Here it is represented as being used by dogs in order to obtain their food, but the *kh*anda closes as abruptly as it began and gives no information as to whether they received the food or not. The allusion to the priests in the fourth verse applies to the ceremony where the priests have to walk in procession, each holding the gown of his predecessor. Varuṇa (the sky) and Pra*g*âpati (year), alluded to in verse 5, are explained as different appellations of Savitṛi (the sun), meaning rain-giver and man-protector. The syllable Om is elsewhere explained as representing all the deities of the earth, the air, and the sky.

THE KENA UPANISHAD.

The Kena or Talavakâra was one of the Upanishads published in English by Rammohun Roy. It was also published in Germany, and has been more or less investigated by many scholars. The prominence given to this important Upanishad both by native and European scholars, would seem to justify the quotation of the 1st *kh*anda:

1. "The pupil asks: 'At whose wish does the mind sent forth proceed on its errand? At whose command does the first breath go forth? At whose wish do we utter this speech? What god directs the eye or the ear?'

2. "The teacher replies: 'It is the ear of the ear—the mind of the mind—the speech of the speech—the breath of the breath—and the eye of the eye. When freed (from the senses) the wise on departing from this world become immortal.

3. "The eye does not go thither, nor speech, nor mind. We do not know, we do not understand, how any one can teach it.

4. "It is different from the known; it is also above the unknown. Thus have we heard from those of old, who taught us this.

5. "That which is not expressed by speech, and by which speech is expressed, that alone, known as Brahman, not that which people here adore.

6. "That which does not think by mind, and by which they say mind is thought, that alone, known as Brahman, not that which people here adore.

7. "That which does not see by the eye, and by which one sees (the work of) the eyes, that alone, known as Brahman, not that which people here adore.

8. "That which does not hear by the ear, and by which the ear is heard, that alone, known as Brahman, not that which people here adore.

9. "That which does not breathe by breath, and by which breath is drawn, that alone, known as Brahman, not that which people here adore."

This peculiar metaphysical work closes with the declaration that "The feet upon which the Upanishad stands are penance — restraint — sacrifice. The Vedas are all its limbs. The True is its abode.

"He who knows this Upanishad, and has shaken off all evil, stands in the endless unconquerable world of heaven — yea, in the world of heaven."

THE KAṬHA UPANISHAD.

This is one of the oldest and most important of these books, and is quite familiar to European students of Sanskṛit. It formed part of the Persian translation, was rendered into English by Rammohun Roy, and has been quoted by many scholars as one of the most perfect specimens of the mystic philosophy and poetry of the ancient Hindūs.

This document opens with the story of Naćiketas. The father of this unfortunate youth had given all of his property to the priests and devoted his son to death.

Naćiketas is represented as going to the abode of Yama, the King of Death, by whom he is kindly received. He is requested to choose three boons. For the first boon, the boy chose that he might be restored to life and see his reconciled father once more; for the second that he might know the fire by which heaven is gained; for the third he requested the King of Death to teach him whether or not the soul existed after death. Yama entreated him to choose any other boon than this, but the youth persisting in his demand to be enlightened upon this subject, Yama finally explained the matter to him in the following language:

"The good, the pleasant — these are separate ends —
The one or the other all mankind pursues;
But those who seek the good alone are blest;
Who choose the pleasant miss man's highest aim.
The sage the truth discerns — not so the fool.
But thou, my son, with wisdom hath abandoned
The fatal road of wealth that leads to death.
Two other roads there are, all wide apart,
Ending in widely different goals — the one
Called ignorance, the other knowledge — this,

O Naćiketas, thou dost well to choose.
The foolish follow ignorance, but think
They tread the road of wisdom, circling round
With erring steps—like blind men led by blind
The careless youth, by lust of gain deceived,
Knows but one world, one life; to him the Now
Alone exists, the Future is a dream.
The highest aim of knowledge is the soul.
This is a miracle beyond the ken
Of common mortals, thought of though it be,
And variously explained by skilful teachers.
Who gains this knowledge is a marvel, too.
He lives above the cares—the griefs and joys
Of time and sense—seeking to penetrate
The fathomless unborn, and eternal essence.
The slayer thinks he slays, the slain
Believes himself destroyed; the thoughts of both
Are false, the soul survives, nor kills, nor dies;
'Tis subtler than the subtlest, greater than
The greatest—infinitely small, yet vast,
Asleep, yet restless, moving everywhere
Among the bodies—ever bodiless.
Think not to grasp it by the reasoning mind,
The wicked ne'er can know it. Soul alone
Knows soul; to none but soul is soul revèaled."[1]

Thus is the immortality of the soul distinctly taught in this Upanishad; but the soul is represented as being asleep, yet moving restlessly everywhere. It is also stated that the "wicked ne'er can know it," thereby broadly hinting that only the good are immortal; it

[1] Williams' trans., Ind. Wis., p. 43.

is perhaps as lucid an explanation of a future life as we could expect to receive from Yama, the King of Death.

THE AITAREYA UPANISHAD.

This Upanishad which was translated for the "Bibliotheca Indica" by Dr. Röer, appears to be almost hopelessly mixed with the Āraṇyakas or forest books, and the first chapter is simply a continuation of the Aitareya-brāhmaṇa.

Sāyaṇa speaks of the Aitareya-āraṇyaka as a part of the Brāhmaṇa, and Śankara, who is a still earlier authority, conveys the idea that both the Upanishad and the Āraṇyaka may be classed as Brāhmaṇa.

In this Upanishad we find much repetition of matter which, even at first, was useless and absurd. For instance, in relation to men and deities, it is said: "By repeating the first verse three times they (men) become twenty-five. The trunk is the twenty-fifth, and Pra*g*âpati (the year) is the twenty-fifth. There are ten fingers on his hands, ten toes on his feet; two legs, two arms and the trunk, the twenty-fifth. Now this day consists of twenty-five, and the stoma hymn of that day consists of twenty-five. It becomes the same through the same. Therefore, the two, the day and the hymn, are twenty-five. This is the twenty-fifth with regard to the body. Next, with regard to the deities: The eye, the ear, the mind, the speech and breath — these five deities (powers) — have entered into that person (purusha), and that person entered into the five deities. He is wholly pervaded there with his limbs to the very hairs and nails. Therefore, all beings, to the very insects, are born as pervaded (by the deities or senses)."[1]

THE KAUSHĪTAKI-BRĀHMAṆA UPANISHAD.

This Upanishad discourses upon the future life and teaches that all who leave this world (or this body) go to the moon. Those who reach the light half of the moon meet with a glad reception, for "the moon delights in their spirits," while those who reach the dark half are not joyously received, but are sent on to be born again. The moon is represented as the door to the heavenly world. If a man objects to her, she sets him free; but if the man does not object, she sends him down as rain upon the earth. His next birth is favorable or otherwise, in direct proportion to his virtue and wisdom; he may be born as a worm or an insect; as a fish or a bird; as a lion, or a boar, or a serpent. He may assume the shape of a tiger or a man. He may happen to be in favorable or unfavorable localities, and he is as likely to be found in hell as anywhere else. If, upon returning to the earth in any of these forms, any one asks him from whence he came, he is to reply: "From the wise moon, who orders the seasons—when it is born consisting of fifteen parts—from the moon who is the home of our ancestors. . . Therefore, O ye seasons, grant that I may attain immortality (knowledge of Brahman), by this my true saying, by this my toil. I am like a season, and the child of the seasons. 'Who art thou?' the sage asks

[1] 1st Aran., 3 Adhy., 8 Khan.

[2] This work was translated for the "Bibliotheca Indica" by Prof. Cowell of Cambridge.

again. 'I am thou,' he replies. Then he sets him free to proceed onward."[1]

THE VĀJASANEYI SAmHITĀ UPANISHAD.

The peculiar character of this book appears to be the recognition of the necessity of good works as a preparation for the reception of the highest knowledge. The doctrine that the moment a man is enlightened he becomes free, as taught in the other Upanishads, led (according to Müller) to a rejection of all discipline and a condemnation of all sacrifices, which could hardly have been tolerated in the last chapter of the Yajur-veda Sa*m*hitā.

In this Upanishad Brahman is called *Īs*, or lord; it treats of the demoniacal and sunless worlds, to which all go who have lost their identity. It is said that "All who worship what is not true cause enter into blind darkness. Those who delight in true cause enter, as it were, into greater darkness."

"One thing they say is obtained from (knowledge of) the cause, another, they say, from (knowledge of) what is not the cause. . . He who knows at the same time both the cause and the destruction (the perishable body) overcomes death by destruction (the perishable body), and obtains immortality through (knowledge of) the true cause. . . Breath to air and to the immortal. Then this my body ends in ashes, Om! Mind, remember! Remember thy deeds! Mind, remember! Remember thy deeds!"

[1] 1st Adhy., 2.

THE ĪŚA.

This is a very short Upanishad which has been translated by Max Müller, and also by Sir Wm. Jones and Dr. Röer, but we here give the poetical rendering by Sir Monier Williams of about half the work.

"Whate'er exists within this universe
Is all to be regarded as enveloped
By the great Lord, as if wrapped in a vesture.
Renounce, O man, the world, and covet not
Another's wealth, so shalt thou save thy soul.
Perform religious works, so mayst thou wish
To live a hundred years; in this way only
Mayst thou engage in worldly acts untainted.
To worlds immersed in darkness, tenanted
By evil spirits shall they go at death
Who in this life are killers of their souls.
There is one only Being who exists
Unmoved, yet moving swifter than the mind;
Who far outstrips the senses, though as gods
They strive to reach him; who himself at rest
Transcends the fleetest flight of other beings;
Who like the air, supports all vital action.
He moves, yet moves not; he is far, yet near;
He is within this universe, and yet
Outside this universe; whoe'er beholds
All living creatures as in him, and him—
The universal spirit—as in all,
Henceforth regards no creature with contempt.
The man who understands that every creature
Exists in God alone, and thus perceives
The unity of being, has no grief

And no illusion. He, the all-pervading,
Is brilliant, without body, sinewless,
Invulnerable, pure, and undefiled
By taint of sin; he also is all-wise,
The Ruler of the mind, above all beings,
The Self-existent. He created all things
Just as they are from all eternity."[1]

There are many other Upanishads, but an examination of these extracts will give an idea of their general literary character, and the tenor of their teachings, as a whole.

These treatises were considered the completion of revelation; they were held to be a very important portion of the Veda, or knowledge, and in the estimation of their best thinkers, like Rammohun Roy, they were by far the most important portion, being the grandest and noblest utterances of the Veda—the point to which all previous revelation tended.

The three grand divisions of Vedic literature which have been discussed under the heads of Mantra, Brāhmaṇa and Upanishad, all come under the head of Śruti—that which is directly heard or revealed. The voice of divine knowledge heard by the Ṛishis, or sages, and by them either orally transmitted or written down exactly as heard.

We shall now consider the teaching of these oracles upon the most important doctrinal points of the Hindū faith. Too much care and discrimination cannot be used in the examination of this subject, in view of the fact that they are considered the most vital portion of the Veda.

[1] Ind. Wis., p. 38.

CHAPTER VIII.

THE MONOTHEISM OF THE UPANISHADS.

PANTHEISM — CONFESSION OF FAITH — DEATH OF THEIR SUPREME GOD — DESCRIPTIONS OF BRAHMA — THE FEET OF BRAHMAN — VISHṆU AS THE SUPREME GOD — THE ŚVETĀŚVATARA UPANISHAD — PANTHEISM THE CREED OF VEDIC LITERATURE.

IT has been claimed by some that the Upanishads are devoted to the worship of the one God — the Supreme — who bears the name of the Highest Self — Brahman. But here again, as in other portions of the Vedas, the monotheism, upon closer examination, seems to be simple pantheism. In other words, there is only one Being in the universe, and that is the universe itself. This being is also thought of as the one Universal Soul, with which all existing material substances are identified, and into which the souls must be ultimately merged.

"This," says Williams, "is the pantheistic doctrine, everywhere traceable in some of the more ancient Upanishads. It is often wrapped up in mystic language and fantastic allegory, but in the Ćhāndogya Upanishad is found the following simple

CONFESSION OF FAITH.

"'All this universe indeed is Brahma; from him does

it proceed; into him it is dissolved; in him it breathes, so let every one adore him calmly.'"[1]

It is also taught that "This whole is Brahma, from Brahma to a clod of earth. Brahma is both the efficient and the material cause of the world. He is the potter by whom the vase is formed; he is the clay from which it is fabricated. Everything proceeds from him, without waste or diminution of the source, as light radiates from the sun. Everything merges into him again, as bubbles bursting mingle with the air—as rivers fall into the ocean. Everything proceeds from and returns to him, as the web of the spider is emitted from and retracted into itself."[2]

DEATH OF THEIR SUPREME GOD.

Brahmā, as the Supreme God, is represented as dying, and in strict accordance with the pantheistic creed so generally taught, the whole universe expires with him, to be reorganized again when the Supreme God comes again from the death state

The Devas, or deities, are also frequently mentioned, and many of the descriptions of God are so absurd that the student of Vedic literature wonders what kind of a conception the writer could have had of an Infinite Creator. He is sometimes represented as being the guardian of the world—having swallowed the others. It is also claimed that he is the self of the Devas (or gods), the creator of all. He is represented as having golden tusks; he is called "the eater," and is said to be "not without intelligence." "His greatness is said

[1] Chan. Upa., 8-14, Williams' trans. [2] Wilson, Vol. II, p. 95.

to be great indeed, because without being eaten, he eats even what is not food."[1] It is claimed that though mortals see him not, he sees and knows them. He is the god who, as Vāyu, swallows all the gods, but produces them again, and who swallows during sleep all senses, but produces them again at the time of waking.

THE FEET OF BRAHMAN.

Satyakāma, a religious student, is said to have received the following expositions of the feet of Brahman[2] from a bull, from fire (Agni), from a flamingo, and from a diver bird, respectively. "The bull of the herd said to him ' . . . I will declare to you one foot of Brahman . . . The eastern region is one quarter, the western region is one quarter, the southern region is one quarter, the northern region is one quarter. This is the foot of Brahman and called Prakāsavat (endowed with splendor). He who knows this and meditates on the foot of Brahman consisting of four quarters, by the name of Prakāsavat, becomes endowed with splendor in this world. He conquers the resplendent worlds, whoever knows this and meditates on the foot of Brahman consisting of four quarters by the name of Prakāsavat.'

"After these words of the bull, Satyakāma on the morrow drove the cows toward the house of the teacher, and when they came towards the evening he lighted a fire, penned the cows, and sat down behind the fire, looking toward the east. Then Agni (the fire) said

1 Chan. Upa., 4-3.

2 In the Code of Manu the name of Brahman is applied to the supreme Being, while Brahma is called the creator of the universe—Brahman (the Highest Self) being the neuter form.

to him, ' . . . I will declare unto you one foot of Brahman . . . The earth is one quarter, the sky is one quarter, the heaven is one quarter, the ocean is one quarter. This is the foot of Brahman, consisting of four quarters, and called Anantavat (endless). He who knows this and meditates on the foot of Brahman by the name of Anantavat, becomes endless in this world. He conquers endless worlds, whoever knows this and meditates on the foot of Brahman consisting of four quarters, by the name of Anantavat.'

"After these words of Agni, Satyakāma on the morrow drove the cows onward, and when they came towards the evening, he lighted a fire, penned the cows . . . and sat down behind the fire, looking toward the east. Then a Hamsa (flamingo, meant for the sun), flew near and said to him; . . . . I will declare unto you one foot of Brahman . . . Fire is one quarter, the sun is one quarter, the moon is one quarter, lightning is one quarter. This is the foot of Brahman consisting of four quarters, called Gyotishmat (full of light). He who knows this and meditates on the foot of Brahman consisting of four quarters, by the name of Gyotishmat, becomes full of light in this world. He conquers worlds which are full of light, whoever knows this and meditates on the foot of Brahman consisting of four quarters, by the name of Gyotishmat.'

"After these words of the Hamsa, Satyakāma on the morrow drove the cows onward, and when they came towards evening he lighted a fire, penned the cows, and sat down behind the fire, looking toward the east.

Then a diver (bird) flew near and said to him, ' . . . . . I will declare unto you one foot of Brahman . . . Breath is one quarter, the eye is one quarter, the ear is one quarter, the wind is one quarter. This is the foot of Brahman, consisting of four quarters and called Āyatanavat (having a home). He who knows this and meditates on the foot of Brahman, consisting of four quarters, by the name of Āyatanavat, becomes possessed of a home in this world. He conquers the worlds which offer a home, whoever knows this and meditates on the foot of Brahman, consisting of four quarters, by the name of Āyatanavat.'"[1]

VISHṆU AS THE SUPREME GOD.

Vishṇu, especially in the Purāṇas, is often addressed as the Supreme God, who is described under all the different forms of this deity. Only a few years since, one of the finest literary men in India commenced a paper with an earnest invocation to the "Heavenly Boar." In this form it said that his feet were the Vedas, his tusks the sacrificial stakes; his teeth were the offerings; his mouth was the pyre; his tongue was the fire; his hair was the sacrificial grass; the sacred texts were his head; his eyes were day and night; his ears were the two bundles of Kusa grass; his earrings were the two ends of those two bundles of Kusa grass; his nose the clarified butter; his snout was the ladle of oblations. . . . The Lord, the Creator, the great Yogin[2]—plunging into the one ocean from love of the world—raised up by the edge of his tusks the earth

1 Chan. Upa., 4th Prap., 5-8 Khan.
2 In the character of "lord of abstract meditation" Śiva is called Yogin.

bounded by the sea, together with its mountains, forests, and groves, which was immersed in the water of the one ocean, and created the universe anew.

THE ŚVETĀŚVATARA UPANISHAD.

One of the most modern Upanishads (the Śvetāśvatara)[1] represents the Supreme God as having a thousand heads, and also describes the hydra-headed deity as having a thousand eyes and a thousand feet—one eye and one foot for each head. The quotation is as follows:

"The perfect spirit with a thousand heads,
A thousand eyes, a thousand feet, the ruler
Of all that is, that was, that is to be,
Diffused through endless space, yet of the measure
Of a man's thumb, abiding in the heart,
Known only by the heart. Whoever knows him
Gains everlasting peace and deathlessness."[2]

Although the Supreme Being is here represented as having a superfluity of heads and feet, he is described in another Upanishad as being entirely without body or mind, as in the following extract:

"That heavenly Person is *without body, without breath* and *without mind*—pure, higher than the high Imperishable. From him, (when entering on creation), is born breath, mind, and all organs of sense; ether, air, light, water, and the earth, the support of all.

[1] The word signifies "white mule," and as mules have been known and prized in India from the earliest time, the name is not considered inappropriate for either a Upanishad or a person.

[2] Williams' trans.

Fire (the sky) is his head; his eyes, the sun and moon; the quarters, his ears; his speech, the Vedas disclosed; the wind, his breath; his heart, the universe; from his feet came the earth. . . . . Brahman the highest immortal. He who knows this, O friend, scatters the knot of ignorance here on earth."[1]

PANTHEISM THE CREED OF VEDIC LITERATURE.

It appears, therefore, that the monotheism of the Upanishads represents the Supreme Being in the most repellent forms, and also that the great underlying principle of Upanishad theology is one of the cardinal doctrines of Hindū teaching, viz., pure pantheism.

"As golden bracelets are in substance one
With gold, so are all visible appearances,
And each distinct existence one with Brahma."

This pantheistic creed is traceable even in the Ṛig-veda, and it gathers force all the way down the stream of Hindū literature. The Upanishads, both ancient and modern, teach the same doctrine. It is re-echoed by both of the great epic poems, and finally presented in the strongest colors, amidst the endless mythologies and theogonies of the Purāṇas. Thus the Vedic creed upon this subject is simplified into a belief in the unity of all existing beings. But while this doctrine is everywhere traceable in Hindū literature, we find side by side with it in all their later works a pantheon containing three hundred and thirty millions of deities, many of them engaged in the most terrible conflicts with one another.

[1] Mundaka Upa., 1st Khan.

CHAPTER IX.

COSMOGONY.

ABSURD THEORIES—EXTRACT FROM ĆHĀNDOGYA UPANISHAD—COSMOGONY OF MANU—A DAY OF BRAHMĀ—SLEEP OF BRAHMĀ AND ITS RESULTS—RE-CREATION—LENGTH OF BRAHMĀ'S LIFE—THE SERPENT ŚESHA—THE NĀGAS OR SERPENT DEMONS—DEATH OF BRAHMĀ—REPEATED CREATIONS—THE WILL OF BRAHMĀ—INDESTRUCTIBILITY OF MATTER—EVOLUTION AND PANTHEISM—COSMOGRAPHY OF THE MAHĀ-BHĀRATA AND THE PURĀṆAS—THE LENGTH OF A KALPA—TEACHING OF THE RĀMĀYAṆA—CREATION BY VISHṆU—COMPARISON BETWEEN COSMOGONY OF THE VEDAS AND OTHER ANCIENT WRITINGS—TESTIMONY OF BARON VON HUMBOLDT—MOSAIC COSMOGONY.

THE various cosmogonies of the Hindūs are so absurd in their theories, and so contradictory in themselves, that the historian shrinks from the repetition of them. But justice has no choice; her decisions are inevitable, and the only fair verdict that can be rendered must come from an examination of the books themselves. Hence, we give

AN EXTRACT FROM THE ĆHĀNDOGYA UPANISHAD,

in relation to the theory of the sun's origin:

1. "Āditya (the sun) is Brahman; this is the doctrine, and this is the fuller account of it: In the beginning this was non-existent. It became existent—it grew. It turned into an egg; the egg lay for the time of a year; the egg broke open. The two halves were one of silver, the other of gold.

2. "The silver one became this earth; the golden one, the sky; the thick membrane (of the white), the mountains; the thin membrane (of the yolk), the mist with the clouds; the small veins, the rivers; the fluid, the sea.

3. "And what was born from it? That was Āditya, the sun. When he was born shouts of hurrah arose, and all beings arose, and all things which they desired. Therefore, whenever the sun rises and sets, shouts of hurrah arise, and all beings arise, and all things which they desire."[1]

COSMOGONY OF MANU.

This mundane egg is a little differently presented by Manu.

The collected wisdom found in his laws represents the universe as first existing in darkness, as if immersed in sleep. Then the Self-existent, having willed to produce various beings from his own substance, first with a thought created the waters and placed upon them a productive seed, or egg. Then he himself was born in that egg, in the form of Brahma. Next, he caused the egg to divide itself, and out of its two divisions formed the heaven above and the earth beneath. Afterwards, having divided his own substance,

[1] 14th Prap., 1 Khan.

he became half male and half female, and that female produced Virāj, from whom was created Manu, the secondary progenitor of all things.[1]

In the Vishṇu-purāṇa we learn that there is a great multitude of these cosmic eggs, and it is said that the boundless cause of all things—the Supreme Prakṛiti—is "the cause of all mundane eggs, of which there are thousands, and tens of thousands, and millions, and tens of millions."[2]

The elements of the primary forms thus developed from these cosmic eggs are supposed to remain unchanged during a single

DAY OF BRAHMĀ,

which consists of two billion, one hundred and sixty millions of years. At the end of this time Brahmā is represented as sleeping. The contents of this world and also of the other spheres of the universe are consumed by fire during his sleep. The fire is then extinguished by such heavy and long-continued rains that a universal cataclysm is produced, and a shoreless ocean engulfs all life, except the sages and the gods, who have managed to escape the fire and the deluge.

RE-CREATION.

Brahmā finds, however, that the elements still exist, and by skilful combinations of these he soon creates anew the earth and its inhabitants. For some unexplained reason, it is found necessary for Brahmā to repeat this creation every day during the hundred

[1] For a further elucidation of this cosmic egg see Chap. XXII of this volume.

[2] Vish. Pur., Vol. II, p. 232, Wilson's trans.

years of his life, the sum total of his existence being 311,400,000,000,000 years, a number quite beyond the ordinary comprehension. During these intervals of creation he is supported on the thousand heads of

THE SERPENT ŚESHA.

For this reason the Nāgas, or serpent demons are held sacred in India. A particular day is devoted to them, and a festival is kept in their honor about the end of July. The lower regions are supposed to be peopled with serpents, all of them having jewels in their heads. The never-failing imagination of the Hindū has furnished names for all the chiefs of the serpent tribe, and these are supposed to rule over the snakes on the earth as well as those in the lower regions.

DEATH OF BRAHMĀ.

At the close of the enormous periods presented as the sum of the hundred years of Brahmā's life, Brahmā himself expires, and with him the other gods, when every form of the world has been resolved back to primary matter, or primary spirit, according to the different theories of various philosophies.

REPEATED CREATIONS.

But the Hindū mystic is not long left without a world. Similar causes again produce similar results and the whole programme of creation is repeated. Thus the whole universe fluctuates between existence and non-existence throughout the ages of eternity.

In the Ćhāndogya Upanishad it is said that "In

the beginning there was the mere state of being—only one without a second. . . It willed, 'I shall multiply and be born.' It created water. The water willed, 'I shall multiply and be born.' It created aliment. Therefore, whenever rain falls much aliment is produced. That deity willed, 'Entering these three divinities I shall develop name and form.'"[1]

THE WILL OF BRAHMĀ.

An explanation of the mode in which the will of Brahmā operates, seems never to have been attempted. He wills creation to be, and it is; still, various schools of India seem to unite in according to matter the property of eternal existence, and also claim that it is indestructible—the most of the Hindū sages having advocated the doctrine of *ex nihilo nihil.* All of these schools agree in advocating the infinity and eternal succession of creation, and the periodical dissolution and reorganization of the world.

EVOLUTION AND PANTHEISM.

At times these books teach instead of a creation, a system of evolution in its clearest type. First, there was simple matter, then being sprang out of non-being, and finally Brahma became the universe. Says Prof. Duncker, Brahma, according to the Vedānta, "is the one eternal self-existent essence, unutterable and unchangeable. It develops into the world and is thus creative and created. As milk curdles, as water becomes snow and ice, Brahma congeals with matter."[2]

[1] Chan. Upa., 6-2, Williams' trans. [2] Hist. of Antiq., Vol. IV, p. 300.

COSMOGRAPHY OF THE MAHĀ-BHĀRATA AND THE PURĀṆAS.

The cosmography which is taught in the Mahā-bhārata, and afterwards adopted by the Purāṇas, divides the earth into seven concentric circles or rings, each of which is surrounded by a circumambient ocean or belt, which separates it from the next annular continent. The first ocean is a sea of salt water; the second is composed of the juice of the sugar cane; the third, of wine; the fourth, of clarified butter; the fifth, of curdled milk; the sixth, of sweet milk; and the seventh, of fresh water. In the center of this vast annular system a mountain called Meru rises to the height of sixty-four thousand miles.[1]

These seven circumambient worlds are supposed to rest on the thousand heads of the serpent Śesha, which support the Supreme Being in the intervals between the creative acts, and which also support the worlds which are created at the commencement of each Kalpa, or two billion, one hundred and sixty millions of years.

It is claimed in the Rāmāyaṇa that the earth is supported on the heads and backs of sixteen immense elephants; eight of these are males and eight are females. In order to be explicit, the names of the elephants are given[2] and it is said that when one of them shakes his body the motion produces earthquakes. Hence, it is fair to suppose that if they all happened to shake their bodies at the same time, a universal earthquake would be the result.

[1] Vish. Pur., Wilson's trans., p. 166. [2] Ind. Wis., p. 430.

CREATION BY VISHṆU.

There are almost as many creations in Hindū literature as there are gods in the pantheon, the most of them being represented as creators; for as the Hindūs have the past eternity filled with successive creative acts, there is time enough for each deity to assume the part of Brahmā in the work of creation. The Vishṇu-purāṇa gives an eloquent description of the process of reconstruction by Vishṇu. This deity, who is repeatedly addressed as the Supreme Being, is described as a huge boar, a thousand yojanas (forty-five hundred miles) in height, and ten yojanas (forty-five miles) in breadth. He had the color of a dark cloud; his roar was like thunder; his bulk vast as a mountain; his tusks white, sharp, and fearful. Fire flashed from his eyes like lightning, and he was radiant as the sun. His shoulders were round, fat, and large, and he strode along like a powerful lion.

This "auspicious supporter of the world," whose eyes were like the lotus after receiving hymns of praises, emitted a low murmuring sound, like the chanting of the Sāma-veda, and uplifted the earth from the lower regions by means of his ample tusks. As he raised his enormous head from the water the drops which fell therefrom purified the great sages, Sanandana, and others residing in the sphere of the saints. Through the indentations made with his hoofs, the water rushed into the lower worlds with a thundering noise, while the Munis sought for shelter among his sacred bristles as he rose up supporting the earth and dripping with moisture. Then the great sages were inspired with delight, and bowing lowly they praised the stern-eyed upholder of the earth.

EULOGY OF THE GREAT BOAR.

The Yogis then eulogized the great boar as follows: "Triumph lord of lords, supreme, sovereign of the earth, wielder of the mace, the shell, the discus and the sword, cause of production, destruction, and existence. Thou lord art the person of the sacrifice, for thy feet are the Vedas; thy tusks are the stake to which the victim is bound; in thy teeth are the offerings; thy mouth is the altar; thy tongue is the fire; and the hairs of thy body the sacrificial grass.

"Thine eyes, oh omnipotent, are the day and night; thy head is the seat of all—the place of Brahma. Thy mane is all the hymns of the Vedas; thy nostrils are all the oblations. Oh thou, whose snout is the ladle of oblations—whose deep voice is the chanting of the Sama veda—whose body is the hall of sacrifice—whose joints are the different ceremonies and whose ears have the properties of both voluntary and obligatory rites. Do thou who art eternal—who art in size a mountain, be propitious.

"We acknowledge thee who hast traversed the earth, oh universal form, to be the beginning, the continuance, and the destruction of all things.

"Have pity upon us, oh lord of conscious and unconscious beings!

"The orb of the earth is seen seated on the tip of thy tusks, as if thou hadst been sporting amidst a lake where the lotus floats, and hadst borne away the leaves covered with soil.

"The space between heaven and earth is occupied by thy body, oh thou of unequaled glory, resplendent with the power of pervading the universe for the benefit of all. . . . Thou art the aim of all, there is none other than thee, sovereign of the world! This is thy might by which all things, fixed and movable are pervaded.

"This form which is now beheld is thy form, as one essentially with wisdom. Those who have not practised devotion conceive erroneously the nature of the world. The ignorant who do not perceive that this universe is of the nature of wisdom and judge of it as an object of perception only, are lost in the ocean of spiritual ignorance.[1]

"The supreme, being thus eulogized, upholding the earth, raised it quickly and placed it on the summit of the ocean where it floats like a mighty vessel and from its expansive surface does not sink beneath the waters.

"Then, having leveled the earth, the great eternal deity divided it into portions by mountains. He who never wills in vain, created by his irresistible power those mountains again upon the earth, which had been consumed at the destruction of the world.

"Having thus divided the earth into seven great portions or continents as it was before, he constructed in like manner the four (lower) spheres, earth, sky and heaven, and the sphere of the sages.

"Thus Hari, the four-faced god, invested with the quality of activity, and taking the form of Brahma, accomplished the creation."

The cosmogonies of India and Egypt, of Assyria and

[1] Vishnu-purana, Wilson's trans., pp. 31-32.

Persia, of Greece and Rome, and of the isles of the seas, have been canvassed in vain for satisfactory expositions of physical law.

The sublime sentence "In the beginning God created the heavens and the earth" stands forever without a rival in literature. It is the closed gateway between the illimitable past and the long aisles of earthly time. In the dim vista beyond it lies a silence as profound as the primeval darkness that rested on the face of the deep. In a few brief sentences is given a graphic description of the great cycles of time, during which the stars were lighted and the earth was born. "And the earth was without form and void." How long? The question is rolled backward through the halls of time, but its echoes bring no answer. Chronology has tried in vain to measure these cycles, and geology has opened her rock-bound pages, but her clear-cut inscriptions tell not of "the beginning." God wrought alone in those grand periods, but tide and torrent, restless surge and burning mountain, were His agents. At last, through the unvarying laws of nature's God, a finished globe, with sunlit vales and snow-crowned mountains, with silvery streams and peaceful hills rolled in its orbit, while the morning stars sang together and all the sons of God shouted for joy.

CHAPTER X.

THE ORIGIN OF MAN.

DESCENT OF MAN FROM A SINGLE PAIR—THE EARTHLY AND HEAVENLY PART OF MAN—RECONSTRUCTION OF MEN AT THE END OF EACH KALPA—CREATION OF ANIMALS—DIFFERENT CHARACTERS AND RACES OF MEN—RUDRA—DEVOLUTION—EXTRACT.

THE philosophical systems of India seem to take little notice of man except in the abstract. It is easy, however, to detect through all the embellishments of Hindū literature, the tradition of the descent of mankind from a single pair.

Brahma is repeatedly fabled to have divided himself into two creatures—one male and the other female—and from the union of these two one man and one woman were born, from whom came not mankind alone, but all other living creatures as well. This general outline is found in the Vedas themselves, but it has been changed, remodeled, and repeated in a variety of shapes.

The origin of the human species is sometimes strangely mixed up with the creation of the world. For instance, in the Upanishads we find the following expositions:

"Adoration to the highest self, Hari, Om.

"1. Verily in the beginning all this was self—one only there was; nothing else blinking (living) whatsoever.

"2. He thought, 'Shall I send forth worlds?' He sent forth these worlds:

"3. Ambhas (water), marîki (light), and mara (mortal).

"4. That Ambhas (water) is above the heaven; and it is heaven, the support. The marîkis (the lights), are the sky. The Mara (mortal) is the earth, and the waters under the earth are the Ap (world).

"5. He thought, 'There are these worlds; shall I send forth guardians of the worlds?' He then formed the Purusha (the person) taking him forth from the water.

"6. He brooded on him, and when that person had thus been brooded on, a mouth burst forth like an egg. From the mouth proceeded speech; from speech, Agni (fire).

"Nostrils burst forth; from the nostrils proceeded scent; from scent, air.

"Eyes burst forth; from the eyes proceeded sight; from sight, Āditya (sun).

"Ears burst forth; from the ears proceeded hearing; from hearing the Dis (quarters of the world).

"Skin burst forth; from the skin proceeded hairs; from the hairs, shrubs and trees. The heart burst forth; from the heart proceeded mind, etc. . . . He thought, 'There are the worlds and the guardians of the worlds. Let me send forth food for them.' He brooded over water. From the water thus brooded on, matter was born . . . that verily was food.

When this food had been sent forth it wished to flee, crying and turning away. He (the subject) tried to grasp it by speech. If he had grasped it by speech, man would be satisfied by naming food. He tried to grasp it by scent. If he had grasped it by scent, man would have been satisfied by smelling food. He tried to grasp it by the eye . . . If he had grasped it with the eye, man would have been satisfied by seeing food. He tried to grasp it with the ear . . . If he had grasped it with the ear, man would have been satisfied by hearing food. He tried to grasp it by the skin . . . If he had grasped it by the skin, man would be satisfied by touching food. He tried to grasp it by the mind . . . If he had grasped it by the mind, man would have been satisfied by thinking of food. He tried to grasp it by the down breathing breath, which helps to swallow food by breathing through the mouth . . . He got it." Hence man is satisfied only by the eating of food.[1]

These endless vagaries are pursued through a wilderness of literature, apparently without thought or purpose. Vāyu, the getter, is then represented as saying: "How can all this be without me?" and then he thought "By what way shall I get there?" Then opening the suture of the skull he got in by that door and found there were three dwelling places for him, viz.: the eye, the throat, and the heart.

"When born (that is, when the Highest Self had entered the body), he looked through all things in order to see whether anything wished to proclaim here

[1] Aitareya Aran., II, 4, 2-3.

another (Self). He saw this person only (himself) as the widely spread Brahman." This verse is understood to mean that the Self looked carefully around in order to learn what there was which might proclaim another self; and when he saw there was nothing which did not come from himself, he recognized the fact that the person which he had created was the developed Brahman, the Atman — in other words, himself. Again, we are taught that "Every man is indeed like an egg; there are two halves of him. This half is the earth; that half, heaven. And there between them is the ether (the space of the mouth) like the ether between heaven and earth. In this ether there (in the mouth) the breath is fixed, as in that other ether the air is fixed. And as there are those luminaries (in heaven) there are these luminaries in man. As there is that sun in heaven, there is this eye in the head. As there is that lightning in the sky, there is this heart in the body."[1] The half of man which represents the earth is that part from the feet to the lower jaw, and the part which represents heaven is the intellectual part found between the upper jaw and the skull.

RECONSTRUCTION OF MEN AT THE END OF EACH KALPA.

Created beings, although destroyed in their individual forms, are never exempted from the consequences of their acts; for whenever Brahmā creates the world anew they are at the mercy of his will, either as gods, men, animals, or inanimate things. Brahmā being desirous at one of these periods of creating gods, de-

[1] Aitareya, 2, 4-1.

mons, progenitors and men, collected his mind into itself. Whilst thus concentrated, the quality of darkness pervaded his body, and the demons were born first, issuing from his thigh. Brahmā then abandoned the form he had used, and the form thus abandoned became night. Then from his mouth proceeded gods, and the form which he then abandoned became day, for goodness predominated in it. He next adopted another form, and the progenitors (the pitnis) were born from his side, and the body which he then abandoned became the evening twilight. Brahmā then assumed another body pervaded by foulness, and from this men were born, and the body thus abandoned became the morning twilight

Thus gods, men, demons and progenitors were reconstructed from previous forms, and the bodies which Brahmā abandoned became day, night, dawn and evening. Afterward the hairs of Brahmā which were shriveled up, fell from his head and became serpents. The creator of the world, being incensed by the loss of his hair, created fierce beings who were denominated goblins; they were malignant fiends and eaters of flesh. The divine Brahmā then created birds from his own vitality, sheep from his breast, goats from his mouth, cows from his sides, horses, elephants, and other animals from his feet, whilst from the hairs of his body grew herbs, roots, and plants.

THE DIFFERENT CHARACTERS AND RACES OF MEN

are accounted for in the Vishṇu-purāṇa by the following legend of Rudra: The mind-engendered progeny of Brahmā were inspired with holy wisdom, and being estranged from the world, they were not desirous of progeny. When Brahmā perceived this "he was filled with wrath capable of consuming the three worlds; the flame of his anger invested like a garland heaven, earth, and hell. Then from his forehead, darkened with angry frowns, sprang Rudra, radiant as the noontide sun, fierce and of vast bulk, and of a figure which was half male and half female. 'Separate yourself,' commanded Brahmā. Obedient to the command, Rudra immediately disjoined his two natures and became twofold. His male being he again divided into eleven persons, of whom some were agreeable and some were hideous; some were fierce and some were mild of disposition. He also multiplied his female nature manifold, some of them being of fair complexion and others very dark, or even black."[1]

DEVOLUTION.

The Upanishads also teach that the lower animals are descended from man, and seem to claim that degeneracy is easier than improvement. The doctrine that the lower animals are the direct descendants of man is taught in the fourth Brāhmaṇa and also in the Upanishads, from which we quote as follows:

"In the beginning there was Self alone in the shape of a person (purusha), and looking around he saw nothing but his Self. He wished for a second. He then made this his Self to fall in two, and thence arose husband and wife." . . .

Then men were born, and afterward the brute cre-

1 Vish-Pur., Wilson's trans., p. 50.

ation, whose origin from degenerate man is expressed in the most explicit terms. "She became a cow . . . hence cows were born. They then became one-hoofed animals . . . and one-hoofed animals were born . . . They became goats, and goats were born . . . They became sheep . . . and sheep were born . . . and thus he created everything that exists in pairs, even down to the ants." In this quotation the universal doctrine of pantheism is presented in the following words: "He knew I, indeed, am this creation, for I created all this. Hence he became the creation, and he who knows this lives in his creation."[1]

In intimate connection with this doctrine of devolution, we find Prof. Wilson quoting the statement of the Commentator Madhwa, who asserts that in the compilation of his own work he consulted eight other commentaries, one of which was written by a monkey, and Prof. Wilson's comment upon the statement is that "While the Hindū disputant may believe in the reality of such a compilation, yet we may receive its citation as a proof that Madhwa was not very scrupulous in the verification of his authorities."[2]

There is a story in Hindū literature of a great drama in fourteen acts, composed by the monkey chief Hanuman, but it is claimed that this was not preserved, because Vālmīka feared that it would cast his poem (Rāmāyaṇa) into the shade. Therefore the generous ape who wrote it threw it into the sea.

We read, too, in the Rāmāyaṇa of the ourang-outang

[1] Upanishads, Part 2, pp. 85, 86 [2] Wilson, Vol. VI, p. 49 of Int.

who lived on the banks of Lake Pampa. He is Sugrīva, the king of the monkeys, with whom Rāma makes an alliance. Several of the monkey generals are mentioned, and a wonderful feat in bridge building by the privates of this strange army is recorded.

If the Hindūs believed that the monkeys wrote commentaries in the days of Madhwa and dramatic poems in the time of Vālmīka, that they commanded armies and built bridges, as recorded in the Rāmāyaṇa, we cannot wonder that they feel that the theory of evolution is working the other way—that degeneracy and not development is the law of nature, so far at least as the quadrumanous family is concerned; and yet we find a certain class of the natives of India advocating the claims of the Sānkhya philosophy.

CHAPTER XI.

METEMPSYCHOSIS.

TRANSMIGRATION NOT TAUGHT IN THE ṚIG-VEDA — THE TRIPLE SYSTEM OF TRANSMIGRATION — THE DOCTRINE OF THE ĆHĀNDOGYA — GREATEST DANGER DURING TRANSMIGRATION — DISTINCTION BETWEEN ASCENDING AND DESCENDING SOULS — HINDŪ EXPLANATION OF INEQUALITIES OF FORTUNE — SINS AGAINST CASTE RECEIVE THE GREATEST PUNISHMENT — NO CRIME BECOMES A SIN IF THE WORDS OF THE ṚIG-VEDA BE REMEMBERED.

THE Ṛig-veda, not being a doctrinal work, does not teach the theory of metempsychosis in any decided way. But there are freqnent allusions to the immortality of the soul, and one of the hymns in the last Maṇḍala is addressed to the spirits of departed ancestors, who have attained to a state of heavenly bliss and are supposed to occupy three stages of blessedness, the highest inhabiting the upper sky, the middle the intermediate air, and the lowest the regions of the atmosphere near the earth.

THE TRIPLE SYSTEM OF TRANSMIGRATION.

A most elaborate theory, however, of the transmigration of the souls of men through plants, animals, and gods, was inculcated in the Code of Manu, which, dates back to about 500 years B. C. According to

Manu (12 : 3), every act and every thought produces either good or evil fruit, and the various transmigrations of men are the result of their conduct upon earth. A threefold alternative is presented to the soul: it may pass through deities, through men, or through beasts and plants. It will go through deities if goodness predominates in its nature; through men if it is ruled by passion; through beasts and plants if it dwells still lower in the moral scale. Each of these three degrees of transmigration has three sub-degrees. The highest and first is Brahmā himself, and the lowest is either a vegetable or a mineral. But souls in these latter forms may ascend through various insects, fish, reptiles, snakes, tortoises, etc.[1] "Let the man who has renounced the world reflect on the transmigration of men caused by their acts; on their downfall into hell and their torments in the abode of Yama; on their formation again in the womb and the glidings of the soul through ten millions of other wombs."[2]

A passage in the Śatapatha-brāhmaṇa is quoted by Weber and Dr. Muir, asserting that in a future state animals and plants will revenge upon men the injuries and death received here. The absence of all memory of wrong done, and indeed of all consciousness of a former existence, does not appear to the Hindū as any objection to this creed which has been handed down to him through so many generations, although mythology claims to record cases where men were gifted with the power of remembering former existences.

The Upanishads which contain the doctrinal teachings of the Vedas have not by any means neglected the

[1] Manu, 1: 2-40. [2] 6: 61-63.

doctrine of metempsychosis, which forms so important a part of the Hindū faith. This doctrine is found and most enthusiastically taught in the very first of the series.

DOCTRINE OF THE ĆHĀNDOGYA UPANISHAD.

This book, belonging to the Yajur-veda, has supplied the most important materials for what is called the Vedānta, which is the end, the purpose, and the highest object of the Veda.

This Upanishad teaches that after various changes, the bodies of those who have performed good works are turned to water; so that when a man is dead and his body burned, the water from the body rises upward with the smoke and carries him to the moon, where he enjoys the fruit of his good works as long as they last. When, like the oil in the lamp, they are consumed, he is obliged to return to a new round of existences.

"When born he (man) lives whatever the length of his life may be. When he has departed his friends carry him as appointed to the fire, from whence he came and from whence he sprang."[1]

1. "Those who know this, and those who in the forest follow faith and austerities go to light; from light to day, from day to the light half of the moon; from the light half of the moon to the six months when the sun goes to the north; from the six months when the sun goes to the north, to the year; from the year to the sun; from the sun to the moon; from the moon to the lightning. There is a person not human.

[1] 5th Prap., 9th Khan.

2. "He leads them to Brahman; this is the path of the Devas.

3. "But they who living in a village practice sacrifices, works of public utility, and alms, they go to the smoke; from smoke to night; from night to the dark half of the moon; from the dark half of the moon to the six months when the sun goes to the south; but they do not reach the year.

4. "From the months they go to the world of the fathers; from the world of the fathers to the ether; from the ether to the moon. That is Soma, the king. Here they are loved (eaten) by the Devas; yes, the Devas love (eat) them.

5. "Having dwelt there till their good works are consumed, they return again the way they came to the ether; from the ether to the air. Then the sacrificer having become air, he becomes smoke. Having become smoke, he becomes mist.

6. "Having become mist, he becomes a cloud; having become a cloud, he rains down. Then he is born as rice and corn, herbs, and trees, and beans. From thence the escape is beset with most difficulties, for whoever the persons may be who eat the food and beget offspring, he henceforth becomes like unto them.

7. "Those whose conduct has been good will quickly attain to some good birth. But those whose conduct has been evil will quickly attain to an evil birth—the birth of a dog, or a hog.

8. "On neither of these two ways those small creatures (flies and worms) are continually returning, of whom it may be said, they live and die. Theirs is a

third place. Therefore, that world never becomes full. Hence, let a man take care to himself."[1]

TIME OF GREATEST DANGER DURING TRANSMIGRATION.

In these stages of transmigration, the greatest danger is incurred after the man has been changed into rain. For if the rain should fall into the sea it might be swallowed up by the fishes; if it should fall upon a desert it might be swallowed by serpents or other reptiles; so that it would require an almost endless round of existences to reach any comfortable degree either of intelligence or dignity. But even if the rain is fortunate enough to be absorbed by the rice, the corn, and the beans, these products might be eaten by a man who has foresworn marriage, in which case the victim of unfortunate circumstances would lose the opportunity of a new and more desirable birth. There are also perils arising from the uncertain character of the man who eats the rice and corn, who thus becomes a new seed, and still another danger that even if he is good himself, he may marry a wicked wife, and make her the mother of this wandering soul. All these dangers must be safely passed before a new birth as a Brāhman, Kshatriya, or Vaiśya can be secured.

DISTINCTION BETWEEN ASCENDING AND DESCENDING SOULS.

Another peculiar distinction is made by Śankara in his commentary. There are some, he says, who assume the form of rice and corn, etc., not in their descent from a higher world, as described in the Upani-

[1] 5th Prap., 14th Khan.

shad, but as a definite punishment for certain evil deeds which they have committed. They remain in that state until the consequences of their evil deeds are past, when they assume a new body, like caterpillars. These guilty ones retain a consciousness of these states and of the acts which caused them to assume the particular body which they wear.

This is not the case with those who, in their descent from the moon, pass through the same vegetable forms; for while in their ascent to the moon they are conscious, they lose this consciousness in coming down. Otherwise, a man who by his good works deserved rewards in the moon would suffer while corn is being ground the very tortures of hell, and the object of good works, as taught by the Veda, would be defeated. As a man who is made unconscious by a severe blow, so it is with souls in their descent, until they are born again as men and thus get a new start toward the highest Brahman.[1]

HINDŪ EXPLANATION OF INEQUALITIES OF FORTUNE.

The popular theory is that every being must pass through eighty-four lakhs of births, a lakh being one hundred thousand, making a grand total of eight milllion, four hundred thousand births for every human being. By this doctrine the Hindūs easily explain all inequalities of fortune and all diversities of character. The fortunate are supposed to be enjoying the benefits of their good deeds in a former life, while the unfortunate man, however virtuous he may be, is being punished for former misdeeds. Even intellect-

[1] Upanishads, Pt. I, pp. 81-83.

ual strength or ability in any given direction is supposed to have been acquired by careful training in some previous form of existence, and to have been cultivated through millions of previous bodies. Disease is looked upon as a legitimate punishment, not for disobedience to nature's laws, but for some sin committed in a previous state — a murder, or the omission of some penance, or some act of disrespect toward the priesthood.

SINS AGAINST CASTE OR THE PRIESTHOOD RECEIVE THE GREATEST PUNISHMENT.

It is noticeable, however, that the ecclesiastical sins and offenses against caste are more severely punished than the crimes against morality. For instance, if a man steals grain, he will be born a mouse; if he steals brass, he will be born a gander; but if a Brāhman neglects his own appointed caste, he will be born a vomit-eating demon. If a Kshatriya violates the rules of his caste, he will be born a demon, feeding on excrement and dead bodies. If a Vaiśya is guilty of the same offense, he will become a demon, feeding on putrid carrion.

NO CRIME BECOMES A SIN TO A BRĀHMAN IF THE WORDS OF THE ṚIG-VEDA BE REMEMBERED.

But there is no crime so heinous that it cannot be forgiven, provided only the criminal is a priest and retains his caste remembering the sacred text. Hence, it is said in the Code of Manu, "A Brāhman by retaining the Ṛig-veda in his memory incurs no guilt though he should destroy the inhabitants of the three worlds, *and even eat food from the foulest hands.*"[1]

[1] Book II, 26.

CHAPTER XII.

REWARDS AND PUNISHMENTS.

IMMORTALITY OF THE SOUL — HEAVEN ONLY A STEPPING-STONE TO HAPPINESS — EXPERIENCE OF THE FAITHFUL HINDŪ — THE HEAVEN OF INDRA — THE HEAVEN OF VISHṆU — FUTURE PUNISHMENT — TWENTY-ONE HELLS — VICTIMS SEE THE INHABITANTS OF HEAVEN — TRANSMIGRATION OF SINNERS.

THE survival of the soul after the death of the body is everywhere implied; but Manu's doctrine is that if a man has been wicked the soul is clothed in a body composed of coarse and impure elements, which goes with it into hell; whereas, if he has been virtuous, the soul is invested with a luminous and ethereal body, composed of the purer elements of air and fire, and this body goes with the righteous soul into heaven.

A place of reward and punishment is indeed very necessary for the proper compensation of man's conduct, but neither the reward of heaven nor the punishment of hell, according to the Hindū theology, is full, effectual, or final.

HEAVEN ONLY A STEPPING-STONE TO HAPPINESS.

The heavens of the Hindū system are only steps on the road to complete happiness, and the hells, though places of terrible torture, are merely temporary purgations.

The soul must leave both heaven and hell, and return to corporeal existence, migrating into higher, intermediate and lower forms, according to its degrees of guilt or virtue, and passing in its progress towards emancipation from separate existence, through the four stages of bliss, called saloka (living in the same heaven with God); samipya (nearness to God); sarupya (assimilation to the likeness of God), and sayujya, when a complete union with the Supreme is attained.

EXPERIENCE OF THE FAITHFUL HINDŪ.

The faithful Hindū after death soon reaches the path of the gods and comes to the world of fire and air—to the world of Indra and Brahma. Here is the beautiful river of eternal youth, whose banks are crowned with majestic trees, and by whose side stands the city and the palace of "the unconquerable." Here is the magnificent hall of Brahman, with the imperial throne and luxurious couch of splendor. Here also are the crystal streams which lead to the knowledge of Brahman. When the devotee approaches, Brahman orders his servants to run and meet him, and to render him the same homage which they yield to their lord. Then five hundred celestial nymphs approach him. One hundred of them bring him beautiful garlands of flowers; one hundred bear precious ointments; one hundred come laden with choice perfumes; one hundred are burdened with rich and luxurious garments for his apparel, and one hundred bring the choicest fruits for his enjoyment, and adorn him like Brahman himself.

In the beautiful waves of the ageless river he shakes off his good and evil deeds, and receives the crown of eternal youth. The good deeds here disposed of are bequeathed to his beloved relatives, who are to receive the benefits arising from them, while his unfortunate relatives, who are not beloved, receive the full value of his transgressions.

He approaches the beautiful tree Ilya, and the odor of Brahman reaches him. He approaches the great city, and finds there the flavor of Brahman. He then approaches the magnificent palace, and the splendor of Brahman greets him. He approaches the spacious hall, and the glory of Brahman meets his eyes. He finally comes to the great throne and the royal couch, where he finds Brahman himself, who catechises him very carefully and, his answers being satisfactory, bestows the whole Brahman world upon him.[1]

HEAVEN OF INDRA.

The beautiful heaven of Indra is supposed to be situated upon the very summit of Mount Meru, which is the centre of the earth and many thousand miles in height. Here the heavenly gardens are found planted with luxuriant trees, which are burdened with delicious fruits. The fragrant groves are haunted with fairy nymphs, whose faces and forms are visions of loveliness. Low, sweet strains of music are borne upon the air. The city of Indra is eight hundred miles in circumference and forty miles high. Its pillars are of diamonds and its palaces are of pure gold. The air is laden with the rich perfume of the rose-colored flowers of the

[1] Kaushitaki Upanishad, 1-3.

Camalata, the beauty of which has brought it the name of Love's Creeper; by this delicate flower all wishes are granted to the inmates of Indra's heaven.

THE HEAVEN OF VISHṆU.

The home of Vishṇu is built entirely of gold and is much larger than Indra's, being eighty thousand miles in circumference. The crystal waters of the Ganges fall from the higher heavens upon the head of Śiva, and from there into the hair of the seven sages, from which they descend to the earth and form a river. On a throne of white lotus blossoms sits Vishṇu, and his wife Lakshmī beside him. She is radiant with the splendor of precious stones, and the sweet perfume of her body extends eight hundred miles.

FUTURE PUNISHMENT.

Realizing that this is a subject which attracts universal interest, the Hindū philosophers have elaborated it very extensively. They have provided ample accommodations for sinners of all classes and degrees, in twenty-one hells of various descriptions, each of which is provided with an unpronounceable name in addition to other horrors.

The names and number of these places of punishment vary with different authors, the Vishṇu-purāṇa and also the Bhāgavata giving a list of twenty-eight instead of twenty-one. The names of these places of punishment as translated are: 1st, darkness; 2d, complete darkness; 3d, place of howling; 4th, place of much howling; 5th, thread of time or death; 6th, great hell; 7th, restoring to life; 8th, waveless; 9th, burning; 10th, parching; 11th, pressing together; 12th, ravens; 13th, bud; 14th, stinking clay; 15th, iron spiked; 16th, frying-pan; 17th, rough or uneven roads; 18th, thorny salmali tree; 19th, flame river, which has a fearful odor and is full of blood (it is a torrent of hot water carrying bones, hair, and other refuse in its course); 20th, the sword-leaved forest; 21st, iron fetters.

This enumeration is from the institutes of Vishṇū. The Purāṇa has also the following details: "Men when they die are bound with cords by the servants of King Tartarus, and beaten with sticks, and have then to encounter the fierce aspect of Yama, and the horrors of their terrible route. In the different hells there are various intolerable tortures, with burning sand, fire, machines, and weapons. Some are severed with saws, some roasted in forges, some are chopped with axes, some buried in the ground, some are mounted on stakes, some cast to wild beasts to be devoured, some are gnawed by vultures, some torn by tigers, some are boiled in oil, some rolled in caustic slime, some are precipitated from great heights, some are tossed upwards by engines. The number of punishments inflicted in hell, is infinite."[1] There is also a description of the Kṛishṇa, a black hell, a red-hot iron hell which appears to have been prepared expressly for traitors and horse dealers, a swine hell which is provided for wine drinkers and for those who associate with them, and the "hell of pincers" for those who violate vows or break the rules of their order. "These hells," say the Purāṇa, and indeed "hundreds and thousands of

[1] Vis. Pur., Wilson's trans., p. 640.

others are the places in which sinners pay the penalty of their crimes. As numerous as the offences which men commit are the hells in which they are punished."[1]

VICTIMS SEE THE INHABITANTS OF HEAVEN.

The inhabitants of heaven are beheld by the sufferers in hell as they move with their heads inverted, whilst the gods, as they cast their eyes downward, behold the sufferings of those in hell. This arrangement has a twofold purpose. It serves to enhance the sufferings of the wicked and to temper the enjoyment of the righteous, who are thereby reminded that even the happiness of heaven is but temporary in its duration; for when they have received their due proportion of reward, they, too, must be born again as stones or plants, or must gradually migrate through the inferior conditions until they again become human. After this their future is in their own hands, and their future births are in direct proportion to their merit.

The time to be spent in hell is a kalpa (two billions and one hundred and sixty millions of years). The criminal then reaches the stage of metempsychosis, when he is relieved from the acute sufferings and has an opportunity to ascend to a higher mode of existence through the bodies of worms, reptiles, or demons. For instance, a gold stealer must pass a thousand times into the bodies of spiders, snakes and noxious demons; a spirit drinker becomes a worm, insect, or moth.

[1] Vish. Pur., Wilson's trans., p. 209.

In these various changes there is sometimes a curious consistency. For instance, a man who has stolen perfumery becomes a musk-rat; one who has stolen grain becomes a rat; one who has stolen water becomes a water-fowl; one who has stolen honey becomes a gad-fly; one who has stolen meat becomes a vulture; one who has stolen oil becomes a cockroach; one who has stolen linen becomes a frog, etc., etc., etc.

When the evil-doers have undergone all these transmigrations and passed through various animal bodies, they are born as human beings, with the following marks indicating their crime: A criminal of the highest degree has leprosy; a killer of Brāhmans, pulmonary consumption; a drinker of spirits, black teeth; a malignant informer, an offensive breath; a stealer of food, dyspepsia; the breaker of a convention, a bald head. After these changes and a multitude of others follows a list of penances comprising many pages.[1]

Having briefly presented the character and teaching of the Upanishads with correlative testimony from other works, we shall now consider a much more fascinating department of Sanskṛit literature. Following the Upanishads chronologically come the Epics of the Hindūs, a very important division of their literature. The Rāmāyaṇa and the Mahā-bhārata are the two great poems of India and, although by no means historical from a European point of view, they comprise nearly all of history that we have from Hindū sources.

1 Institutes of Vish., pp. 140-149.

CHAPTER XIII.

THE RĀMĀYAṆA.

ONE OF THE SACRED EPICS OF INDIA—THE LAND OF THE HINDŪ—THE RĀMĀYAṆA AND THE ILIAD—HELEN AND SĪTĀ—HECTOR CHAINED TO THE CHARIOT WHEEL—FUNERAL HONORS PAID TO RĀVAṆA—AGE OF THE RĀMĀYAṆA—THE SANCTITY OF THE POEM—AUTHOR OF THE WORK—BASIS OF THE POEM—LENGTH OF THE RĀMĀYAṆA.

THE land of the Hindū is the natural birthplace of poetry and song. The great Himālayas, with raiment of cloud and robe of sunlight, seem to commune with the stars that crown with radiance their snowy brows; in their wild crags are the silvery fountains of the rivers which flash and sparkle through forest and vale. The Ganges, the "bride of the heavens," receives in her crystal tide the sins of her people and bears them away between her flowery banks. The wild swans float amid the lotus blossoms upon her bosom, and the gazelles come down to slake their thirst at her sacred brink.

The tropical forest is darkened with the shade of lofty trees and perfumed with the odor of a thousand blossoms. The long, deep grass and feathery ferns are kissed here and there by the stray sunbeams that find their way between the glossy leaves of dense thickets, and the dreamy song of the kokila is borne on the air.

The wide plains are illumined with the dazzling flowers of the cactus and the snowy wreath of jessamine blossoms, while here and there the sweet lime-tree and feathery acacia wave their delicate boughs in the sunlight, and the orange groves unfold their pearly cups of rich perfume.

Delicate butterflies float slowly away on the fragrant air, and golden bees nestle amid the rose petals and revel in life and beauty.

Down by the gleaming shores of the ever sounding sea, the white-crested waves come marching in; with song and psalm and chanted praise they come, and the children of the wildwood hear in their waves the song of the sea-nymphs, and see in coral groves the home of the ocean queen. So they bring oblations to the fair goddess of the sea, who is robed in azure and pearl, with garlands of scarlet flowers in her heavy hair and her snowy hands gleaming amidst the darkling waves.

Above the mountain crest and beyond the silvery sea is the changeful sky of crimson and gold—of amethyst and azure—which is to them the "Mantle of Indra." Whether this radiant mantle is tinted with the rosy light of morning, or gilded with the golden glory of noon, or flashing with diamonds in the halls of night, it receives the earnest adoration of the worshipers. They bring their oblations to the morning light, their songs of praise to the god of day, and their reverent thanksgiving to the silvery soma that illumines the night. The imagination of the Hindū has long been cultivated by the beautiful scenes around him, and the results are manifested, not only in the songs of the Vedas, but also in the great Hindū Epics.

The two colossal poems of Sanskṛit literature, the Rāmāyaṇa and the Mahā-bhārata, have been called "The Iliad and the Odyssey of the Hindūs."

THE RĀMĀYAṆA AND THE ILIAD.

The Rāmāyaṇa has been beautifully termed "The Iliad of the East," and in some respects this great Indian production does resemble the Grecian classic.

The subject of both Epics is a war undertaken to recover the wife of one of the warriors, who was carried off by the hero on the other side. In this respect Rāma, the hero of the Rāmāyaṇa, corresponds to Menelaus, while in others he more nearly represents Achilles. Ayodhyā may be compared to Sparta and Laṇkā to Troy. But it would be unjust to compare Sītā, the chaste and beautiful wife of Rāma, with the treacherous Helen. The Indian princess, pleading eloquently to be allowed to follow her husband into exile, is a loyal, loving woman, while the beautiful Helen is a faithless, fickle wife, utterly unworthy of the life-blood of an honest man.

The descriptions of Ayodhyā and of Laṅkā imply greater luxury and a higher degree of refinement than those of Sparta and Troy. But so far as art and harmony are concerned the Asiatic poems cannot compete with those of Greece. The Rāmāyaṇa and Mahābhārata are burdened with description and simile, with wearisome repetition and amplification, while the Iliad and Odyssey have the polish and the rounded proportions of Grecian sculpture.

The Indian Epics sometimes lay aside all delicacy and give the most revolting particulars of ancient legends, but the Rāmāyaṇa shows far more humanity to a fallen foe than does the Iliad.

The duty of returning good for evil, which had been so clearly taught in a previous age,[1] is well illustrated in the character of Rāma, who ordered elaborate funeral honors to be paid to his conquered foe.

In striking contrast with this scene is the barbarous picture so vividly described in the Iliad when the dying Hector pleaded with his foe :

"By thy own soul, by those who gave thee breath,
By all the sacred prevalence of prayer,
Ah, leave me not for Grecian dogs to tear!
The common rites of sepulture bestow,
To soothe a father's and a mother's woe.
Let their large gift procure an urn, at least,
And Hector's ashes in his country rest."

But the furious Greek, who is almost glorified by Homer, degrades his own manhood and taunts the dying man with insult :

"No, wretch accursed, relentless he replies,
(Flames as he spoke shot flashing from his eyes),
Not those who gave me breath should bid me spare,
Nor all the sacred prevalence of prayer;
Could I myself the bloody banquet join.
No—to the dogs that carcass I resign.
Should Troy, to bribe me, bring forth all her store,
And giving thousands, offer thousands more,

[1] Ex. xxiii: 4, 5; 2d Sam. xvi: 12; Prov. xxv: 21, 22.

Should Dardon Priam and his weeping dame,
Drain their whole realm to buy one funeral flame,
Their Hector on the pile they should not see,
Nor rob the vultures of one limb of thee."

The funeral pyre of Rāvaṇa was adorned with wreaths of flowers and costly jewels at the command of the victor, while the body of the gallant Hector was chained to the chariot wheel of Achilles and dragged around the walls of Troy, in full view of his aged father and broken-hearted mother.

"Purple the ground and streak the sable sand,
Defamed, dishonored in his native land.

. . . .

And the whole city wears one face of woe,
No less than if the rage of hostile fires,
From the foundations curling to her spires,
O'er the proud citadel at length should rise,
And the last blaze send Ilion to the skies."

AGE OF THE RĀMĀYAṆA.

Quite a difference of opinion prevails among scholars in relation to the age of this work. Dowson and Sir Monier Williams claim its earliest origin to be about 500 B. C., and Williams speaks of "the beginning of the third century B. C." as the time of the first orderly completion of the work in its brāhmanized form. He also assigns a portion of it to the early centuries of our own era.

Prof. Weber claims that it belongs to the begin-

[1] Ind. Wis., pp. 319, 320.

ning of the Christian era "after the operation of Greek influence upon India had already set in."[1]

The noted Indian scholar, Kāshinath Trimbak Telang, in a note on the Rāmāyaṇa says, "The received chronology refuses to allow to the bulk of classical literature an antiquity of more than eighteen centuries, if so much."[2]

But while there is a variety of opinion on the subject, it seems to be well established that the work belongs' to an age subsequent to the Iliad, and this fact in connection with the striking similarities of the two poems certainly gives some weight to the opinion of Prof. Weber that the Indian poets really borrowed ideas from Homer.

THE SACREDNESS OF THE POEM.

The Rāmāyaṇa is held to be one of the most sacred of all the Hindū productions.[3] Like other works of the same class, it boldly lays claim to supernatural powers, declaring that "Whoever reads or hears the Rāmāyaṇa will be freed from all sin . . . Those who read or hear it for the sake of riches will certainly acquire wealth. . . . The Rāmāyaṇa heals diseases, removes all fear of enemies, compensates for the loss of wealth or fame, prevents loss of life, and secures all that is desired. The mere utterance of the name of Rāma is equal in religious merit to the giving of a hundred ornamented cows to a Brāhman, or

[1] Sans. Lit., p. 194. [2] Ind. Ant., Vol. iii, p. 267.

[3] The Hindus, who are the devoted followers of Rama, acknowledge two bibles in two different versions of the great Epic, the one by Valmiki and the other by Tulasi-dasa.

the performance of an Aśva-medha.[1] A follower of Rāma enjoys happiness in this world, and in the next is absorbed into Rāma in the heaven of Vishṇu." Rāma is still faithfully worshiped in India, and devotees will sit for days and nights together upon the sacred banks of the Ganges or beneath the stately pipal trees repeating in low monotonous tones, "Rām, Rām, Rāma." The mere utterance of the words without any conception of the ideas accompanying them will secure a birth into a higher life either to men, birds, or animals.

AUTHOR OF THE WORK.

The plot and unity of the poem show it to have been originally the work of one man; but his name is lost to the historian, and there are three different versions now in existence. The one best known and most popular among Europeans is ascribed to Vālmīki; another to Tulasī-dāsa, who was born A. D. 1544, and is said to have written in A. D. 1575, two copies of whose work, claimed to be in his own handwriting, are still preserved in India; while the third is ascribed to Vyāsa (the editor or arranger). These authors took a crude legend which had for generations been repeated from father to son, and remodeled and finished it, each in his own peculiar style. Wilkins and some other Oriental scholars claim that the passages in the Hindū Epics which speak of Rāma as an incarnation of Vishṇu are among the interpolations of a much later date than the original.

[1] The great horse sacrifice, which required a year of preparation. A hundred of these offerings entitled the sacrificer to the throne of Indra.

BASIS OF THE RĀMĀYAṆA.

Prof. Williams and J. Talboys Wheeler think that it may have some foundation in fact; that at some early period soon after the settlement of the Āryan races in the plains of the Ganges, a body of invaders headed by a bold leader may have attempted to force their way into the peninsula of India, in which case the heroic exploits of the chief would naturally become the theme of song and the hero himself would be deified. Prof. Weber claims that the work is purely allegorical, being based upon the single historical fact of the spread of Āryan civilization toward the south and the feuds connected therewith. Be this as it may, we have in the Rāmāyaṇa a mass of literature which, although radiant with Oriental coloring, is a wilderness of myths and extravagant fables.

LENGTH OF THE POEM.

This interminable Indian Epic consists of twenty-four thousand slokas, or verses, but even this statement does not give us an intelligible idea of the formidable volumes through which it leisurely wanders. Its literary value would be greatly increased by condensation. Few busy people of modern times would find time to read it in its present form, even if it possessed the marvelous properties which are ascribed to it. We therefore give briefly in the following chapters the principal story of the poem, which is here presented in a simple style of narration.

CHAPTER XIV.

THE STORY OF THE RĀMĀYAṆA.

AYODHYĀ — DAŚARATHA AND THE AŚVA-MEDHA — THE CONCLAVE OF THE GODS — PLEA MADE TO BRAHMĀ — REFERRED TO VISHṆU — HIS HOME IN THE SEA OF MILK — REQUEST GRANTED — THE BIRTH OF RĀMA — THE BOW OF ŚIVA — MARRIAGE OF RĀMA — RĀMA APPOINTED YUVA-RĀJA — KAIKEYĪ — KAUŚALYĀ — SĪTĀ — THE FAREWELLS — THE DEATH OF THE RAJA — BHARATA.

THE opening scene of this fascinating Indian romance is laid in the ancient city of Ayodhyā, which in modern times is called Oude. Beautifully situated upon the banks of the river Sarayū, Ayodhyā was in olden times one of the most magnificent cities of Hindūstān. But the great scythe of time has swept her glories away, leaving only a pitiful scene of ruin. Even the name of her river has been changed, which now sweeps along its course under the name of Gogra. She was the capital of the great raj of Kośala, which extended from the Gogra to the banks of the Ganges. But little is now known of this fertile kingdom. The rajas who governed it claimed to be descendants of the sun, and hence they were called the solar kings.

History claims that the ancient Ayodhyā was a city of considerable importance, but the vivid imagination of the Hindū poet has made it a dream of fairyland. In the Rāmāyaṇa it is represented as being built entirely of large and well-arranged houses, while the streets were continually cooled with streams of running water. Its temples were richly decorated with gold and gems, and its stately palaces lifted their great domes toward the heavens, like the crowns of the distant mountain tops.

Its parks were filled with tropical flowers and shaded here and there with massive trees. Birds of bright plumage darted like flames through the heavy foliage. Crystal fountains sparkled in the air, and on the quiet pools below them the white lotus blossoms, fair daughters of the moon, raised their fragrant cups in rich profusion. On the banks of the great river the stately plantain trees drooped with golden fruit, and the magnolias loaded the air with the rich odor of their creamy blossoms.

The whole city shone in splendor and waved its gorgeous banners on the fragrant breeze, and strains of richest music mingled with the twanging of bowstrings and the low chanting of Vedic hymns.

The city was encompassed with great walls, which were set with jewels, and her towers and the porticoes above her gates were filled with archers. Every part of the city was guarded by heroes, who were as strong as the eight gods that rule the universe, and vigilant as the many-headed serpents who watch at the entrance of the regions below.

There was no poverty within her gates, but every merchant owned storehouses, which were filled with jewels. There were no misers, nor thieves, nor liars inside her beautiful walls, and no one lived less than a thousand years. Men loved their own wives only, none of whom was without a marriage crown, or rich laces and jewels. Their clothing never became soiled; their gold was never tarnished. All the women were beautiful, witty, and wise, for there was no disease or unhappiness in the favored city.

"In bygone ages built and planned
By sainted Manu's princely hand,
Imperial seat! her walls extend
Twelve measured leagues from end to end;
Three in width, from side to side
With square and palace beautified.
Her gates at even distance stand,
Her ample roads are wisely planned.
Right glorious is her royal street,
Where streams allay her dust and heat.
On level ground in even row
Her houses rise in goodly show.
Terrace and palace, arch and gate
The queenly city decorate.
High are her ramparts, strong and vast,
By ways at even distance passed,
With circling moat both deep and wide,
And store of weapons fortified."[1]

In the midst of the wonderful city was the magnificent palace of the raja, encompassed by walls so high that the birds could not fly above them, while over the massive gateways, strains of music floated by day

1 The poetical extracts in this story, unless otherwise indicated, are from Griffiths' translation.

and by night. In the midst of the palace was the throne, which was set with precious stones. The palace itself was guarded by thousands of warriors, who were as fierce as flames of fire and as watchful as the lions which guard their mountain dens.

DAŚARATHA AND THE AŚVA-MEDHA.

In the midst of all this magnificence there lived a childless king, Daśaratha. Although descended from the sun, his line threatened to become extinct, for there was no heir to his royal throne, his beautiful city, and his fertile kingdom. He was a perfect charioteer, a royal sage, and famous throughout the three worlds for his virtues and his magnificence. His kingdom was inspected by his spies as the sun inspected it by its rays, but the great Daśaratha found in it all no disloyalty or disobedience. The raja resolved to perform the great Aśva-medha[1] sacrifice in order to propitiate the gods and obtain a son. So the long ceremony was begun and the rajas from all the surrounding kingdoms came to attend the sacrifice. Thousands of priests were feasted by themselves, the most delicious viands were served to them in dishes of gold and silver, and their attendants were the warriors of the kingdom. Eighteen sacrificial pits were pre-

[1] The horse for this sacrifice was turned out to wander at his will for a year, followed by a faithful priest or perhaps a large body of attendants. If no one touched him during the year of preparation, he was considered fit for the sacrifice, but if he had been caught another had to be turned loose and the ceremonies postponed. If the first horse proved fit for the offering, when the year was completed and the long preliminary arrangements were finished, the sacrifice was performed with almost endless ceremonies, which were purposely made very difficult and tedious. No one could perform them except Brahmans, who received enormous gifts in return for their services.

pared in the form of the bird Garuḍa, and the pits which represented the wings of the bird were lined with bricks of gold. The king gave to the priests a million cows, one hundred million pieces of gold and four hundred million pieces of silver, besides generous presents to the whole multitude. Then the horse and the birds and the animals were duly sacrificed, and the presiding priests proclaimed to Daśaratha the welcome news:

> "Four sons, O monarch, shall be thine,
> Upholders of the royal line."

THE CONCLAVE OF THE GODS.

The gods assembled at the sacrifice in obedience to the summons of the priests, who slowly chanted:

> "For you has Daśaratha slain
> The votive steed, a son to gain.
> Stern penance rites the king has tried,
> And in firm faith on you relied."

Having partaken of the food furnished them by the offering, and being pleased with the sacrifice, they went in a body to Brahmā to intercede with him on behalf of the raja, and to present a petition of their own.

The whole body of deities, with the glorious Indra at their head, presented themselves at the heaven of Brahmā, and there beneath the golden dome and before the throne of white lotus blossoms they pleaded with their sovereign to grant the petition of Daśaratha and also to rid the world of the hideous ten-headed demon, Rāvaṇa, who had long persecuted the gods and the priests, destroying the sacrifices and violating every law of virtue and every principle of right.

The celestial band stood before Brahmā in all their beauty and brightness, surrounded on every side by a host of joyous storm gods, and with joined hands chanted their petition:

"O, Brahmā, mighty by thy grace,
Rāvan, who rules the giant race,
Torments us with his senseless pride,
And penance-loving saints beside.
For thou, well pleased in days of old,
Gavest the boon that makes him bold,
That gods nor demons ere should kill
His charméd life, for so thy will.
We honoring that high behest,
Bear all his rage, though sore distrest.
That lord of giants, fierce and fell,
Scourges the earth and heaven and hell.
Mad with thy boon, his impious rage
Smites saint and bard and god and sage.
The sun himself withholds his glow;
The wind, in fear, forgets to blow;
The fire restrains his wonted heat
Where stands the dreaded Rāvan's feet;
And necklaced with the wandering wave,
The sea before him fears to rave.
Kuvera's self in sad defeat
Is driven from his blissful seat.
We see, we feel the giant's might,
And woe comes o'er us and affright.

To thee, O lord, thy suppliants pray
To find some cure this plague to stay."

Rāvaṇa had secured from Brahmā the promise that he should not be slain by gods or demons or genii. This assurance had been gained by a long penance on the part of Rāvaṇa, during which he had stood upon his head in the midst of five fires for ten thousand years. In addition to this wonderful boon he had thereby gained a gratuity of nine additional heads, with a full complement of eyes, ears, noses, and other features, besides eighteen additional arms and hands. Brahmā having bestowed these gifts upon Rāvaṇa, found himself in a dilemma. He therefore replies:

"One only way I find
To slay this fiend of evil mind.
He prayed me once his life to guard
From demon, god, and heavenly bard,
And spirits of the earth and air.
And I, consenting, heard his prayer.
But the proud giant in his scorn
Recked not of man of woman born.
None else may take his life away,
And only man the fiend can slay."

Brahmā then conducted them to the home of Vishṇu, on an island in the sea of milk, which is the sixth circumambient ocean of the world. When they arrived at the gorgeous court of Vishṇu, the god was not to be seen. They began, however, to sing his praises, and soon the glorious lord of the world appeared, arrayed in garments of golden texture and riding upon his eagle steed (Garuḍa). In his four hands were the symbols of his power—the shell, the mace, the ćakra, and the lotus, while his beautiful wife, Lakshmī, sat upon his lap. Then the assembled gods fell upon their knees before him and implored him to deliver them from the fatal power of Rāvaṇa. The great Vishṇu was gracious to his noble petitioners, and answered: "Be no longer alarmed; your foe shall fall before my feet. Rāvaṇa in his pride of power did not ask Brahmā to preserve him from men or from monkeys, for he deemed them beneath his notice. But I will take advantage of this omission, and cause his destruction by the very means which he despises. I will myself be born as the son of Daśaratha, you shall assist me by assuming the form of monkeys, and together we will overthrow this terrible enemy of gods and men." Then the gods rejoiced and sang the praises of Vishṇu as they went away to do his bidding, and were borne to their homes across the creamy billows of the sea of milk.

RĀMA.

Soon after the conclave of the gods had received from Vishṇu a favorable answer to their petition, the principal wives of Daśaratha bore him four sons. Kauśalyā was the mother of Rāma, and Kaikeyī the mother of Bharata, while Sumitrā became the mother of two sons, Lakshmaṇa, who was always the firm friend of Rāma, and Śatru-ghna, who was equally attached to Bharata.

It is claimed that when Rāma was born he wore a

crown set with jewels. In his ears were rings in the form of crocodiles. He had four arms, and in each hand he held one of the symbols of Vishṇu. A string of rubies was around his neck, and a million suns and moons would hide their faces at the sight of his countenance. After explaining to his mother his reason for assuming a human form, he concealed his four arms, and in the form of a human babe began to cry. When it was announced in the streets of Ayodhyā that four heirs were born to the raja, the great city was filled with rejoicing. The happy father distributed generous gifts among the people, and received in return their congratulations and praises. From every gate of the city the joyful notes of music rang out upon the clear air, and the houses were decorated with the blossom-laden branches of the mango tree. Rāma, the beautiful boy,[1] grew rapidly toward manhood, and even in his childhood became an expert archer. In early youth he was the best shot in the kingdom, and his strength was such that everything he touched yielded to the power of his hands.

THE BOW OF ŚIVA.

The raja Janaka, who ruled over a neighboring province, was the possessor of the wonderful bow of Śiva. This was said to be the veritable bow with which Śiva had destroyed the gods, when he overturned the altars and tore up the groves of Daksha, because

[1] Each nation has an undoubted right to its own ideal, but the personal appearance which is ascribed to Rama hardly accords with modern ideas of beauty. He is represented as being of "a beautiful color like green grass, with fine glossy hair and a large head. His nose was like that of the green parrot, his legs resembled plantain trees, and his feet were red as the rising sun."

Daksha, having prepared a great sacrifice, invited all the gods to the festival except Śiva and his wife. But no man could handle the great bow or the heavy arrows of the vindictive god. Janaka therefore issued a proclamation that he who could bend the bow of Śiva should receive in marriage his beautiful daughter, Sītā.[1] The loveliness of this young girl had attracted rajas from all parts of the country to enter the contest for her hand, but they had gone home in dismay when they saw the mammoth bow. The fame of Sītā's beauty had also reached the city of Ayodhyā, and Rāma determined to test his strength and win, if possible, the lovely princess. One beautiful morning he started with Lakshmaṇa, who was ever his devoted companion, to the city of Mithilā, where the raja Janaka lived.

When they arrived and the raja saw them, he inquired of his attendants, "Who are those two young men who are as majestic as elephants, as heroic as tigers, and as beautiful as the two Aśvins?"[2] And they answered, "They are the sons of Maharaja Daśaratha, and they come hither to inquire about the great bow." Then the raja exhibited to his royal guests the great bow with which Śiva destroyed the gods at the sacrifice of Daksha, and which had ever since been preserved in the royal house of Mithilā, and worshiped by devotees.

[1] It is claimed that Sita was born of the earth and not of woman. Janaka said that one day while he was ploughing, the ploughshare struck a silver vessel, and taking it out of the ground he opened it and found a beautiful babe therein, whom he adopted as his own daughter.

[2] Two deities, ever young and beautiful, who riding in a golden car announced the coming of Ushas (the dawn). They are also called divine physicians.

When the bow was brought into the royal presence it lay in a great car, which moved upon eight wheels and was drawn by five thousand strong men. Then said raja Janaka to the young princes, "I have promised to give my beautiful daughter Sītā to the raja who shall succeed in bending the bow, and all the rajas of the earth have come hither; but no one has been strong enough even to lift it from its resting-place." No sooner had he uttered these words then Rāma stepped forth in his magnificent strength and took the bow from the car with his right hand, while the multitude around him were hushed with amazement and expectation. Then, taking the other hand he bent the bow nearly double, so that it broke with a crash, like one of the thunder-bolts of Indra. The people were stunned as if a mountain had fallen into the sea, and many of them were thrown to the ground. Raja Janaka turned to his attendants and said, "This deed of Rāma's is without a parallel, and he shall receive my daughter Sītā in marriage. Let messengers be mounted upon swift horses, and let them carry this joyful news to the raja Daśaratha, and bring him to this city."

MARRIAGE OF RĀMA.

When the messengers arrived at the palace of Daśaratha the king was rejoiced to learn of the prowess of his son, and also that the two royal lines were to be joined by the marriage of Rāma with the lovely princess Sītā.

Early the next morning the raja set out with a magnificent train of attendants upon the four days' journey to the city of Mithilā. In his splendid retinue a large corps of royal archers rode upon swift horses, and the priests of the royal household were mounted upon elephants with rich trappings and decorations. All the treasures of the king were also carried in a long line of chests, which were drawn by elephants. The raja and his household were mounted upon white elephants and attended by dancing girls and musicians. The great procession moved gaily out of the city, amidst the rejoicing of the people, and wound its way slowly along to the city of Mithilā. It was joyfully received, the raja Janaka and his court coming out to meet his royal guest, whom he saluted, saying to Daśaratha, "Happy am I this day and delivered from all distress, for by this alliance with your royal line my family will be honored and purified."

On the morrow when the two kings with their priests and other attendants were assembled, the great sage Vaśishṭha recited to raja Janaka the names of all the ancestors of Daśaratha, and Janaka repeated to his guest the long list of his own progenitors. Thus the two royal lines were compared and the marriage was decided upon. Then Daśaratha retired from the scene and performed the great ceremony of Śrāddha, or offering, to the ghosts of his ancestors, giving a great number of cows to the officiating priests. Each cow had horns of pure gold.

When the ceremonial night had passed away, Daśaratha, attended by his four sons, all richly adorned with jewels, went again to the raja of Mithilā. When they reached the chamber of the gods where the ceremony was to be performed, they found it draped on every side with the richest flowers of the tropics.

There were great vases filled with the branches of magnolias, whose white blossoms loaded the air with their fragrance. The pearly flowers of the orange tree surrounded its golden fruit, contrasting with the rich green of its foliage. The floor was carpeted with the sacred kusa grass, and the sacred fire was lighted upon the altar, where the homa, consecrated with mantras, was placed upon the flame. While Rāma stood upon the eastern side of the altar, Janaka led his peerless daughter to the other side. Costly jewels studded the folds of her white robe and glittered in the braids of her dark hair. Then raja Janaka placed her hand in that of Rāma and said to him, "This is my daughter Sītā, endowed with every virtue. Take her hand in yours, O son of Daśaratha, and she will ever attend you like a shadow. Maintain her for life, and be not offended if she commits a fault." The bride was consecrated with holy water, the trumpets sounded, and Rāma led her three times around the sacred fire upon the altar and performed all the ceremonies according to the Hindū law. Then a shower of blossoms fell upon them from the heavens, and celestial music was heard in the sky, as the Gandharvas, or celestial musicians, played a sweet and solemn wedding hymn.

After Rāma and his bride were taken to an inner room, her veil was removed, and he looked for the first time upon her lovely face. Her large dark eyes were veiled with heavy lashes and cast down in the presence of her lord, while her crimson blushes lighted up with new beauty her soft golden complexion. As Rāma took his trembling bride in his arms and gazed upon her girlish form, a great love was born in his heart for the woman upon whom he now looked for the first time. Her ruby lips were pressed with a warm and eager kiss, which was at once a lover's tribute and a husband's offering. And she, the timid girl, felt the brave heart of her husband beating against her own, and nestled in his bosom, like a trembling bird that has found a refuge from the storm.

The next morning after the marriage of Rāma, the raja Daśaratha and his family took leave of Janaka, who caressed his daughter Sītā and loaded her elephant with valuable presents. The splendid troops of archers and the great retinue of horses and elephants with their rich trappings were made ready, and amidst the strains of joyous music the procession set out for the capital city of Daśaratha. Couriers had announced their approach, and upon their arrival they found Ayodhyā adorned with banners and decorated with flowers. The air was filled with the clangor of trumpets, and thousands of people thronged the gates to welcome their king, the heir apparent, and his beautiful bride. After a great feast to the musicians and the warriors, the dancers and the singers, the priests and the kinsmen, they were dismissed with rich presents, and the royal party entered their own apartments within the beautiful palace.

RĀMA APPOINTED YUVA-RĀJA.

It was the custom for the heir to the throne to receive the appointment of Yuva-rāja, that he might assist in the management of the affairs of state, even during the life of the raja. This arrangement introduced the young prince to his life work, and at the same time lightened the burdens of the reigning king, while it effectually prevented any dispute as to the proper successor when the death of the raja occurred. Therefore, the ministers and counselors went to the palace and entreated Daśaratha to appoint Rāma as the Yuva-rāja, for all the people loved the young heir and were anxious to see him share in the honors of the government. The ministers said to Daśaratha, "O Maha-raja, listen to the voice of your people. You are the raja of rajas. You are the greatest among men. At a great sacrifice of your happiness you have governed us for nine thousand years, and under your rule every one has been happy and no one has dreamed of misfortune. Now it is the wish of all that Rāma should also be placed upon the throne."

So Daśaratha called together all of his ministers and counselors, and the chieftains and officers of the army, and all the people of the city to hear his proclamation. Then from the throne of the Council Hall the raja addressed them as follows: "To-day I am the happiest of men, and I cannot reward you sufficiently for the joy which your proposal has given me. I have long been desirous of placing Rāma upon the throne, but have waited to know your wishes. Therefore, let there be no further delay. I have constantly preserved my subjects to the utmost of my power, but this frame of mine has grown old under the shadow of the royal canopy. I am worn out with the weight of my duties, and desire rest. My excellent son I wish to appoint Yuva-rāja. To him I commit the government of the raj. This delightful month, Ćaitra, in which the forests are adorned with flowers, is sacred and auspicious; prepare all things for the installation of Rāma as Yuva-rāja." Then all the chieftains and the people rejoiced and great shouts went up from the assembled multitude. But the raja turned to Vaśishṭha and said, "O chief of sages, it is proper for you to say what ceremonies shall be performed at the installation of Rāma." And Vaśishṭha said to the servants of the king, "Prepare the gold and the jewels and the purifying bath of the gods, the incense, the garlands of white flowers, the parched grain, the honey, the clarified butter, the insignia of royalty, and all things necessary for the installation of the Yuva-rāja, and place them in the house set apart for the sacred fire. Provide, also, abundance of food, with curds and milk for one hundred thousand priests, and fill the golden pots with water from the sacred rivers. Let the Brāhmans be invited to attend and the throne be prepared and the banners be elevated, and let the musicians and beautiful dancing girls gaily adorned, fill the inner court of the royal palace, and let garlands of flowers be placed in all the temples and beneath the sacred trees."

Then Daśaratha said to his chosen counselor Sumantra, "Bring hither the accomplished Rāma." So Rāma was brought to the great council hall of the palace, and descending from his royal chariot went into the presence of his father and bowed himself at his feet. But the raja clasped both the hands of his son and drew him toward him, and commanded a lofty throne set with jewels to be placed before the heir apparent. Then addressing his son he said,

"All men owe three great debts: the first to the gods, the second to the Ṛishis, and the third to their ancestors. The first I have paid with sacrifices and ceremonies; the second, by learning the Vedas, and your birth has freed me from the third. I have now one wish remaining, which you must not refuse. You are my eldest son, born of my first wife, and all my chieftains, counselors, and subjects are anxious to see you upon the throne. I wish you, therefore, to comply with their request. Do not hesitate because I am alive, for it has always been the rule of my race for the raja to take his son to the throne when he grows old. To-morrow is auspicious; therefore, to-morrow I will install you as Yuva-rāja." And Rāma bowed his head to the king and went away to the apartments of his devoted mother to inform her of his good fortune, before he began the ceremonies which were to purify him for the morrow.

KAIKEYĪ.

The youngest and most beautiful wife of Daśaratha was Kaikeyī, the mother of Bharata. Her heart had been burning with jealous rage ever since the joy and feasting over Rāma's marriage began. The magnificent presents and the beautiful wife of the heir apparent had filled her with envy, and now the great preparations to install him as Yuva-rāja made her resolve to defeat him if possible. She therefore retired to her own apartments to work out her wicked scheme. She remembered that some years before, when the raja was wounded in battle, she had nursed him tenderly, and in his gratitude he had promised her any two boons that she might ask. A promise of this kind is peculiarly sacred in the East, and as she had never yet claimed its fulfilment, she felt that she now held the key to the situation.

When the preparatory ceremonies were over, the king hastened to the apartments of his beloved Kaikeyī, to give her the joyful tidings and receive her congratulations upon the accession of his son. He hurried along the hall, which was decorated with peacocks and made vocal with the songs of birds, where beautiful vines and flowers twined around the marble pillars, filling the air with their fragrance. With a joyful heart he entered a magnificent room, which was as bright as the southern sky beneath a mantle of fleecy cloud. But he saw only the magnificent appointments of the room; the beautiful creature who had hitherto met him with her smiles was not there. Then his heart sank within him, for he longed to see her. But the doorkeeper said, "Oh, raja of rajas, the rani is in a great rage, and she has fled to the chamber of displeasure."

Puzzled and grieved, the king hurried to the chamber of displeasure, and beheld his beautiful rani lying upon the floor, in sordid garments He caressed her and tried to arouse her, like one who awakens a sleeping serpent that will surely cause his death. "Why, my beloved, are you in the chamber of displeasure? Why are you without ornaments, and why do you weep? Surely I have never offended you by night or by day. Say if you are ill, that I may send for the most eminent physicians, or if any one has offended you, that I may punish him according to your pleasure. I will do whatever you command; I will slay the innocent or release the guilty, for I am a raja of rajas. I will give you whatever you request, even if it be my own life." And he clasped the evil creature in his arms, even as men will sometimes take a serpent to their bosoms.

Seeing that he was still infatuated with her, Kaikeyī told him of the boons he had promised and that the time had come when he must grant them, if, indeed, he really loved her.

> "Now pledge thy word if thou incline
> To listen to this prayer of mine.
> If thou refuse thy promise sworn
> I die despised before the morn."

Then the foolish raja smiled upon her and said, "Know, beautiful one, that no one is more beloved than you except my son Rāma, and by Rāma, who is dearer than my life, I swear that I will perform your request, whatsoever it may be. May I lose all the merit of every good deed that I have done upon earth if I fail to perform your request."

Then the evil creature demanded of him, "Grant me the boon, even as thou hast sworn. Let all the gods, with Indra at their head, and all the regents of the universe bear witness to the promise of the illustrious, the upright, the faithful Maha-raja." Then putting her arms around him, she entreated him to remember the two favors which he had promised when she had saved his life by her care, and which she now claimed. "The first favor is that my son Bharata be installed this day instead of Rāma, and the second is that Rāma may be banished to the forest of

Daṇḍaka,[1] to lead the life of a hermit, and to clothe himself in deerskins and in the bark of trees for fourteen years."

When the raja heard these fatal words, he fell upon the floor in his anguish, like a majestic plantain tree that has been prostrated by the wind.

Then Kaikeyī said to herself, "After he has installed Bharata I shall not be sorry for his death, but now I must bring him to his senses, for if he dies Rāma will surely receive the kingdom." So she called her attendants to apply restoratives, and at last he became again sensible of his pain and exclaimed, "Am I tormented with demons or have I lost my reason?" When he fully remembered all that she had said, he quivered in pain like an antelope in the grasp of a tigress, but he felt as powerless in her vile presence as a bird in the face of a serpent that has charmed it. At last he recovered himself enough to exclaim, "Oh, cruel wretch! what has Rāma done to you? He has always yielded to you the same reverence that he pays to his own mother; why, then, are you bent upon his ruin? You, the daughter of a raja, have crept into my house like a venomous serpent in order to destroy me. Oh, Kaikeyī! have pity upon an old man, who humbly supplicates you. Save my life by relinquishing your evil purpose. Take jewels instead—take a thousand cities, or anything else that will satisfy you," and he fell at her feet while he pleaded. But the cold-hearted woman replied, "I am in possession of my senses. People call you truthful, and it is said that you always adhere to your promise. The time has

[1] This forest is described as a terrible wilderness infested with wild animals and inhabited by savages or demons.

come for you to grant me the two favors that you swore should be mine." She was met with a torrent of indignant reproach, to which she angrily replied by accusing him of falsehood.

He remembered his oath, and bitterly exclaimed: "Oh, Kaikeyī! in what evil hour have I entered your room? I have been entrapped by my love for you as a mouse is entrapped by a bait. The race that has descended from the sun has hitherto been without stain; and I am the first to pollute it. Never before was it heard that a father sent his eldest son into exile in order to gratify a capricious woman. Be the consequence what it may, I shall place Rāma upon the throne as soon as it is morning. But I fear lest Rāma should hear of my promise. Then he would voluntarily go into exile rather than send his father to a liar's hell.[1] Oh, Kaikeyī! relinquish this cruel wish! What will the rajas say when I tell them that, tortured by you, I have given the kingdom to Bharata and sent Rāma into the jungle? The whole world will abhor me for the sake of the female who sends my beloved son into the forest. Oh, Kaikeyī! I fall at your feet; be gracious to me." But the evil creature replied, "I have three times repeated my requests, and your promises must be fulfilled or I will take poison in your presence." Then answered the raja, "I reject you forever, and your son Bharata I reject with you, although

[1] J. Talboys Wheeler remarks that the "great stress which is here laid upon the performance of a promise is somewhat remarkable, from the fact that it scarcely tallies with the charges which have been so frequently brought forward against the truthfulness of Hindus." Neither is it quite consistent with the teaching of their sacred Code of Manu, that lying is sometimes justifiable. (See Manu VIII, 103, 104.) A similar precept occurs in another ancient code, but an expiation is there prescribed.

he is my son as well as yours." While the king still lingered in this chamber of torture darkness came down upon him and he passed a terrible night of agony, a helpless raja within his palace walls.

REVELATION TO RĀMA.

The morning dawned clear and beautiful. Bright banners and garlands of flowers saluted the rising sun, and all was made ready for the great installation of the heir to the kingdom. The golden throne was set up and covered with the white canopy, which was the symbol of royalty. The sacred tiger's skin, the bow and the cimeter, and the sacrificial fire, with the elephants and the chariots and horses were at hand. The golden pots were filled with water from the sacred Ganges, and surrounded with the fruits and gorgeous flowers of the favored clime. There, too, were the priests, and the eight beautiful damsels to rub tumeric on the body of the raja; there was the great white bull, girded with a golden rope, and the shaggy lion, and a multitude of musicians, and thousands of people, besides the beautiful dancing girls.

At the rising of the sun the magnificent procession filled the street leading to the palace, and there the patient people waited for the coming of the raja and the excellent Rāma. Vaśishṭha requested Sumantra to go and hasten the Maha-raja, "so that Rāma may receive the raj as the moon enters the mansion of Pushya." Sumantra joyfully entered the palace, and approaching the curtain of the door he remained outside of the apartment and saluted the raja thus: "As the ocean when illumined by the rising sun gives pleasure to the beholders, so a great raja by his benign presence diffuses happiness around him. As the charioteer of Indra aroused the mighty god before he went forth, so do I arouse you. As the moon awakens the earth, permit me this day to awaken you. The god of day rises propitious from his couch; may he and all the gods command that success attend you. Oh, Maha-raja, all is ready for the installation of Rāma. As an army without a commander, as the night without the moon, so is a country when the Maha-raja does not appear." These joyous words fell upon the ear of a monarch who was speechless with anguish: but the heartless Kaikeyī responded, "Go you, Sumantra, and bring Rāma hither, for the raja has something of great importance to tell him."

Then Sumantra went out of the palace and hastened to the home of Rāma, which was as resplendent as the palace of Indra. In the lovely grounds the deer were feeding in fearless serenity, and the gay peacocks displayed their gorgeous feathers in the morning sunlight. Sumantra passed the brilliant militia guard at the door, and going toward the inner apartments, he ordered the attendant to inform Rāma immediately that Sumantra waited for an audience.

When Rāma heard that his father's chosen counselor had come, he directed that the guest should be conducted at once to his presence. When the great counselor entered the room he beheld Rāma sitting on a golden couch, tastefully draped with the richest fabrics of the Indian looms. The air of the room was fragrant with the odor of sandalwood and rich masses of tropical flowers. The beautiful Sītā stood by her lord fanning him with peacock's feathers, while her young face was lighted with love and happiness. Then Sumantra delivered his message, and Rāma turned to Sītā with the words, "Oh, divine one! I will go at once to the Maha-raja, and you may remain here and amuse yourself with your maids." The dark-eyed wife followed her lord to the door saying, "May the gods of all the four quarters of the universe protect you. May Indra who wields the thunderbolt, Yama the judge of the dead, Varuṇa, god of the waters, and Kuvera, the lord of wealth, guard you from harm." Then Rāma went gaily out with Sumantra, and they ascended Rāma's bright chariot, lined with tiger skins, adorned with gold and gems, and drawn by magnificent horses. Lakshmaṇa, his younger brother, attended the crown prince, standing behind him in the chariot.

His appearance on the street was greeted with shouts and cheers and the great multitude pressed around his chariot, while thousands of horses and trained elephants followed and the brightly uniformed militia guarded the line of his approach. Thus amidst the strains of music and the triumphal acclamations of the multitude he was escorted to his father's palace, where he was met with garlands of flowers, the palace itself appearing as resplendent as the milk-white cars of the gods. Having passed through the five outer courts he ordered his people to halt, while with his brother only he entered his father's presence.

The whole multitude waited without in joyous anticipation, while a terrible scene was enacted within the palace walls. Rāma beheld his wretched father sitting by the side of Kaikeyī on a magnificent couch, with his whole face and form withered and blasted by the terrible hand of sorrow. Rāma knelt at his feet, but the eyes of the raja were overflowing with tears. Sobbing with anguish, he could only exclaim, "Oh, Rāma! Rāma!" The young heir shrank from the presence of Kaikeyī as if he had been touched by a loathsome serpent, for his father was convulsed with grief, like an ocean which is swept by a tempest.

But Kaikeyī displayed neither grief nor shame. She coolly said, "Rāma, the Maha-raja is not angry, neither is he in distress; but he has something on his mind which he forbears to tell you, though it is necessary that you should know it. The Maha-raja has made me two solemn promises and confirmed them with an oath; but he now repents of it like one of low caste. In former times when I saved his life he offered me two boons and swore to perform them. I have now requested that my son Bharata may be installed as coadjutor with the Maha-raja, and that you may be sent into exile in the wilderness of Daṇḍaka for fourteen years. If, therefore, you desire that your father shall act according to his oath, you will go out of the city this day and return not for fourteen years."

She coolly uttered this merciless speech, well knowing that it was a dagger which pierced the hearts of both father and son. The Maha-raja was overcome with grief, but Rāma bravely replied: "Be it so. I will depart into the forest that the Maha-raja may fulfil the promise he has made. Let messengers be sent upon swift horses to bring Bharata here from the city of Giriv-raja, and I will hasten to the forest of Daṇḍaka and abide there fourteen years." And Kaikeyī replied, "So let it be. Let not your father's shame affect you, but depart immediately, for your father will neither eat nor bathe until you are out of the city." Although goaded thus by her merciless tongue, he quietly answered, "I obey the will of the Maha-raja, for there is no act of virtue greater than that of obeying the command of a father and fulfilling his engagements. But I go first to take leave of my loving mother, Kauśalyā, and to comfort my beautiful Sītā." And bowing himself again at the feet of his wretched father, he left the apartment, followed by Lakshmaṇa, who had witnessed the whole interview.

KAUŚALYĀ.

When Rāma entered the elegant rooms of his devoted mother, he saw that she was propitiating the gods in his behalf. She was even then fanning the sacrificial fire, while around her lay the curds, the rice, the sweetmeats, the white garlands, the sacrificial wood, and the jars of holy water. She joyfully arose and embraced her son, saying, "May you attain the age, the renown, and the virtue which are worthy of your race, oh, Rāma, for even this day you are to be installed in the office of coadjutor of the raj, according to your father's promise." Then Rāma saluted her, and said, "Oh, mother! Are you unacquainted with the heavy calamity now pending? It is Bharata who is to be installed, and as for me, I am to go for fourteen years into the forest of Daṇḍaka and live upon roots and fruits."

When Kauśalyā heard these terrible words she fell

in the agony of her grief to the floor. But her son raised her up and tenderly comforted her. At last she exclaimed: "Oh, Rāma! Oh, my son! If you had never been born I should have been saved this bitter sorrow. A barren woman has only the grief of being childless; she knows not what it is to lose a son. Oh, Rāma! I am the chief rani, the first and the rightful wife; I am the mother of the heir to the throne, and yet even whilst you are here I have been supplanted and am insulted by the very servants of my rival, and now even my own servants will see Kaikeyī's son installed in the raj! You, too, will be doomed to hunger and fatigue and all the horrors of exile. Surely there is no room in the mansions of Yama, or death would have seized upon me this day, like a lion springing upon a trembling doe. The Maharaja is the victim of a bad woman; he has brought contempt upon himself by becoming the slave of his mistress. Oh, Rāma! Before this thing is made public you ought to assume the reins of government. You can now do so without the aid of the old raja, who has sunk into his second childhood and is the slave of Kaikeyī." "You are right, mother," exclaimed Lakshmaṇa. "You have spoken what I had in my own mind. I long to see Rāma upon the throne, and should anyone oppose him, I swear to you that he shall soon behold the mansions of Yama." But Rāma answered, "I can not transgress the commands of my father. I therefore entreat your permission, oh, my mother, to depart into the forest. No one is degraded by obedience to his father, and having promised to obey him, I can not make my promise void."

SĪTĀ.

Still another terrible trial awaited the loyal heart of Rāma. Taking tender leave of his mother he went to his own home, where his loving wife awaited his coming. Seeing that he was sorrowful, Sītā inquired, "Why is it, Rāma, that you are not yet installed? Has the moon not yet entered the palace of Pushya?" He then repeated to her the sad story he had already told his mother and added, "By the command of my venerable father I go this day into the forest. It will therefore become you to devote yourself to my aged mother, who is wasted with grief. Oh, beloved one! I must depart to the great forest and you must remain here, obedient to the commands of raja Bharata." But the brave wife answered, "Oh, Rāma! What words are these? A wife must share the fortunes of her husband, and if you go to the forest, I must go with you and smooth away the thorns. Wherever the husband may be, the wife must dwell in his shadow. I shall live with you in the jungle, and we shall be happy together in the fragrant woods. I am not afraid, and I long to roam through the forest with my husband; but if you leave me, oh, Rāma! I shall die." And a flood of hot tears filled her eyes at the thought of separation, although banishment from home and throne, with the man she loved, had no power to bring them forth.

Taking his brave young wife into his arms, Rāma said, "Oh, Sītā! The forest is not always pleasant; indeed, it is dangerous. You are the delicate daughter of a raja. You have never braved even the hot sun of the city streets; how then could you live in the wilderness? Your feet are as delicate as the petals of a lily; how could you walk on the cruel thorns of the wood? There are terrible serpents and crocodiles and tigers. The rank weeds conceal snakes so venomous that even their breath will kill a man. Sometimes you would have to live upon bitter roots and fruits. You would thirst when you could have no water. For garments you would have to wear the bark of trees and the skin of an antelope, and at night sleep upon grass or the bare earth. Reptiles, mosquitoes, flies, and scorpions would bite and sting you in your sleep. Fearful Rākshasas[1] (demons) infest the wilderness, and they will eat a man at a single meal. Besides, you would be without friends, and how can that be endured by a woman? You are dearer to me than my own life, and I cannot take you into the wilderness and expose you to these terrible perils. You will always be in my thoughts, but you must remain here, where I can at least know that you are safe and comfortable." But she only nestled closer in his arms, and answered:

"A wife must share her husband's fate. My duty is to follow thee
Where'er thou goest. Apart from thee I would not dwell in heaven itself!

1 These Rakshasas are elsewhere described as shapeless and cruel monsters who perpetrate terrible outrages, changing their forms at pleasure. They are represented as hiding in the thickets, casting away the ladles and sacrificial vessels of the devotees, and defiling their offerings with blood. The most revolting descriptions are given of their natural appearance, although it is claimed that they can at will assume the most fascinating features. The myth has probably grown from exaggerated descriptions of the aboriginal tribes found in the jungles of India.

Deserted by her lord, a wife is like a miserable corpse.
Close as thy shadow would I cling to thee in this life, and hereafter.
Thou art my king, my guide, my only refuge, my divinity.
It is my fixed resolve to follow thee. If thou must wander forth
Through thorny, trackless forests, I will go before thee, treading down
The prickly brambles to make smooth thy path. Walking before thee I
Shall feel no weariness. The forest thorns will seem like silken robes;
The bed of leaves, a couch of down. To me the shelter of thy presence
Is better far than stately palaces, and Paradise itself.
Protected by thy arm, gods, demons, men, shall have no power to harm me.
With thee I'll live contentedly on roots and fruits. Sweet or not sweet,
If given by thy hand, they will to me be like the food of life.
Roaming with thee in desert wastes, a thousand years will be a day.
Dwelling with thee, e'en hell itself would be to me a heaven of bliss."[1]

But Rāma yielded not to her pleadings, and seeing her tears he bowed his head in sadness. Then she drew her form up to its full height, and with her dark

[1] Williams' trans. Ind Wis., p. 366.

eyes flashing through her tears, she exclaimed, "Shame on my father for giving me to a man who has no spirit! They say that Rāma is brave and courageous, but he is too effeminate to protect even his own wife in the wilderness. Surely the Maha-raja has acted wisely in not giving the kingdom into the hands of such a coward! After having married me and pretended to love me, he is willing to desert me and leave me in desolation and loneliness for fourteen years." But her love was stronger than her indignation, and breaking down in the midst of her upbraiding, she said, "If I have done wrong, oh, my husband, forgive me! I can bear anything but separation from you. I entreat you to take me with you. Do not refuse me, oh, Rāma!" and weeping bitterly she threw herself at his feet.

Rāma could no longer withstand her pitiful pleading. Taking her in his arms, he said, "Why do you blame me, beloved, without understanding me? My heart's desire is always to remain with you. I would not care for the throne of Brahmā without you. But when I thought of your delicate frame, I felt that I could not take you into the wilderness. Still, if you are determined to go, take leave of your friends, for you shall accompany me." Sītā, overjoyed, hastened to arrange for their departure. Then Lakshmaṇa approached his brother and entreated that he might be allowed to accompany them. Rāma gladly consented; whereupon they took off all their jewels and ornaments, and even their shoes, and went after the manner of devotees to the palace to take leave of Daśaratha.

THE FAREWELLS.

A rumor had spread through the city that instead of the installation, Rāma and his wife Sītā, and his half-brother Lakshmaṇa, were to be sent as exiles into the forest of Daṇḍaka. The people loved Rāma as they loved no one else, and the terrible news fell upon Ayodhyā like a funeral pall. The gorgeous procession gradually separated, and mournful crowds with tear-stained faces took its place.

At last the two princes and the wife of Rāma were seen walking with bare feet toward the palace of the Maha-raja. The indignation of the populace could not longer be suppressed and bitter denunciations were mingled with wailings. The Maha-raja was bitterly denounced, some declaring that he must be possessed of demons or he could not do so cruel a thing. Others sneered at his weakness in being controlled by a wicked woman, and others still proposed that all the inhabitants and their families should take their wealth and follow Rāma into the wilderness, leaving a deserted city for Bharata and his heartless mother to rule over.

While the people were lamenting, the little party approached the palace, and Counselor Sumantra made known to Daśaratha that Rāma was at the door. The Maha-raja had summoned all the inmates of the palace, and in their presence was still cursing Kaikeyī when Rāma and Sītā and Lakshmaṇa entered the room. The Maha-raja arose from his seat to receive them, but overcome with grief he sank back again. Rāma and Lakshmaṇa took him up in their arms and laid him upon the royal couch, while the cries of the women, mingled with the clanging of their ornaments, filled the palace. Then Rāma with joined hands said, "I entreat you, oh, Maha-raja, to look with a propitious eye upon me who am ready to depart to the wilderness of Daṇḍaka. Permit also Lakshmaṇa and Sītā to accompany me to the forest."

Then the Maha-raja answered, "Oh, Rāma! I have been infatuated with this wicked woman — set aside my command — become this day the raja of Kośala." But Rāma replied, "My lord, the Maha-raja has yet a thousand years to live upon the earth, and I will abide in the forest fourteen years, but when I have completed the vow I will again embrace the feet of my father."

"Go, then, beloved son," returned the Maha-raja, "but go in a safe and good road, and go not away to-day. Spend this night with your mother and me, and to-morrow do as you think best. Oh, Rāma! I have been deceived by a vile woman, who has covered her evil designs as a fire is covered with ashes."

But Rāma persisted in going immediately as he had promised. All the women of the palace wept bitterly except the remorseless Kaikeyī. The chief counselor also mingled his tears with theirs, but his indignation overcame his grief, and turning with fierce denunciations upon Kaikeyī, he accused her of murdering the raja and his family, and uttered the threat which the people were making — that they would with one accord desert the raj and leave her and her son in a desolate city.

Then the Maha-raja gave the following command to

Sumantra: "Order the troops to make ready at once to accompany Rāma. Let beautiful dancing girls and musicians and rich merchants adorn the train of my son. Let the warlike engines follow Rāma, and the citizens also. Let all my storehouses of grain and treasure accompany my children that they may dwell happily in the wilderness." But Rāma supplicated the Maha-raja to countermand the order, declaring he had no use for soldiers or followers. So with many loving words to the Maha-raja and tender caresses to Kauśalyā, the exiled trio left the palace. But the raja declared that Rāma should not go away on foot; if he must go, he should at least travel in a style befitting the great prince that he was. The royal chariot was ordered, and Rāma and Sītā and Lakshmaṇa were seated therein, while the chief counselor himself took the reins, and guided the willing steeds as they moved proudly away.

The whole city was now in a state of excitement, and the afflicted people ran after the chariot or hastily mounted horses to accompany it. Every carriage that happened to be ready was pressed into service, and a great crowd of people followed them. Even the Maha-raja and Kauśalyā came after them and cried to Sumantra to rein in the horses that they might once more look into the face of Rāma. But the young prince commanded his charioteer to drive on and said, "When the Maha-raja asks you why you did not obey him, tell him that you did not hear his order. My deep distress has driven me to this falsehood."

And so the great chariot went out of the city, followed by a vast concourse of mourning people; while those who were left behind were overcome with grief. The black pall of sorrow rested upon the great city.

DEATH OF THE RAJA.

The Maha-raja entered the palace with a breaking heart, and said to his attendants, "Carry me at once to the apartments of Kauśalyā, the mother of Rāma, for only with her can I find rest for my tortured heart." They carried him in and laid him upon a gorgeous couch, from which he never arose. As the city watchman called the hour of midnight, he said, "Oh, excellent Kauśalyā, take my hand while I confess to you the great sin of my youth—the sin for which the gods are now sending this terrible woe upon me." And holding the hand of his faithful wife he confessed that he had years before accidentally caused the death of an only child, and that the father in cursing the author of his suffering, had declared that sorrow for a child should one day bring the wanton prince to his grave. Said the heart-broken king:

"One day when rains refreshed the earth and caused
my heart to swell with joy,
When after scorching with his rays the parched
ground, the summer sun
Had passed toward the south; when cooling breezes
chased away the heat,
And grateful clouds arose; when frogs and pea-fowl
sported, and the deer
Seemed drunk with glee, and all the winged creation,
dripping as if drowned,
Plumed their dank feathers on the tops of wind-rocked
trees, and falling showers

Covered the mountains till they looked like watery heaps, and torrents poured
Down their sides, filled with loose stones, and red as dawn with mineral earth,
Winding like serpents in their course; then at that charming season, I,
Longing to breathe the air, went forth, with bow and arrow in my hand,
To seek for game, if haply by the riverside a buffalo,
Or elephant, or other animal, might cross at eve, my path,
Coming to drink. Then in the dusk I heard the sound of gurgling water;
Quickly I took my bow and, aiming toward the sound, shot off the dart.
A cry of mortal agony came from the spot,—a human voice
Was heard, and a poor hermit's son fell pierced and bleeding in the stream.
'Ah, wherefore then,' he cried, 'am I, a harmless hermit's son, struck down?
Hither to this lone brook I came at eve to fill my water jar.
By whom have I been smitten? whom have I offended? Oh, I grieve
Not for myself or my own fate, but for my parents, old and blind,
Who perish in my death. Ah! what will be the end of that loved pair,
Long guided and supported by my hand? This barbed dart hath pierced

Both me and them.' Hearing that piteous voice, I, Daśaratha,
Who meant no harm to any human creature, young or old, became
Palsied with fear; my bow and arrows dropped from my senseless hands,
And I approached the place in horror; there with dismay I saw,
Stretched on the bank, an innocent hermit-boy, writhing in pain and smeared
With dust and blood, his knotted hair disheveled, and a broken jar
Lying beside him. I stood petrified and speechless. He on me
Fixed full his eyes, and then, as if to burn my inmost soul, he said:
'How have I wronged thee, monarch? that thy cruel hand has smitten me—
Me, a poor hermit's son, born in the forest. Father, mother, child
Hast thou transfixed with this one arrow; they, my parents, sit at home
Expecting my return, and long will cherish hope,—a prey to thirst
And agonizing fears. Go to my father—tell him of my fate,
Lest his dread curse consume thee, as the flame devours the withered wood.
But first in pity draw thou forth the shaft that pierces to my heart,
And checks the gushing life-blood, as the bank obstructs the bounding stream.'

He ceased, and as he rolled his eyes in agony, and quivering writhed
Upon the ground, I slowly drew the arrow from the poor boy's side.
Then with a piteous look, his features set in terror, he expired.
Distracted at the grievous crime, wrought by my hand unwittingly,
Sadly I thought within myself how best I might repair the wrong,
Then took the way he had directed me toward the hermitage.
There I beheld his parents, old and blind; like two clipped, wingless birds
Sitting forlorn, without their guide, awaiting his arrival anxiously,
And to beguile their weariness, conversing of him tenderly.
Quickly they caught the sound of footsteps, and I heard the old man say
With chiding voice, 'Why hast thou lingered, child? Quick, give us both to drink
A little water. Long forgetful of us, in the cooling stream
Hast thou disported; come in—for thy mother yearneth for her son:
If she or I in aught have caused thee pain, or spoken hasty words,
Think on thy hermit's duty of forgiveness; bear them not in mind.
Thou art the refuge of us refugeless—the eyes of thy blind sire.

Why art thou silent? Speak! Bound up in thee are both thy parents' lives.'
He ceased, and I stood paralyzed—till by an effort resolutely
Collecting all my powers of utterance, with faltering voice I said,
'Pious and noble hermit, I am not thy son; I am the king;
Wandering with bow and arrow by a stream, seeking for game, I pierced,
Unknowingly, thy child. The rest I need not tell. Be gracious unto me.'
Hearing my pitiless words, announcing his bereavement, he remained
Senseless awhile; then drawing a deep sigh, his face all bathed in tears,
He spake to me as I approached him suppliantly, and slowly said,
'Had'st thou not come thyself to tell the awful tale, its load of guilt
Had crushed thy head into ten thousand fragments. This ill-fated deed
Was wrought by thee unwittingly, O, king, else had thou not been spared,
And all the race of Rāghavas had perished. Lead us to the place:
All bloody though he be, and lifeless, we must look upon our son
For the last time and clasp him in our arms.' Then weeping bitterly,
The pair led by my hand came to the spot and fell upon their son.

Thrilled by the touch, the father cried, 'My child, hast thou no greeting for us?
No word of recognition? Wherefore liest thou here upon the ground?
Art thou offended? or am I no longer loved by thee, my son?
See here thy mother. Thou wert ever dutiful towards us both.
Why wilt thou not embrace me? Speak one tender word. Whom shall I hear
Reading again the sacred-Śāstra in the early morning hours?
Who now will bring me roots and fruits to feed me like a cherished guest?
How, weak and blind, can I support thy aged mother pining for her son?
Stay! Go not yet to Death's abode—stay with thy parents yet one day.
To-morrow we will both go with thee on the dreary way. Forlorn
And sad, deserted by our child, without protector in the wood,
Soon shall we both depart toward the mansions of the King of Death.'
Thus bitterly lamenting, he performed the funeral rites; then turning
Towards me thus addressed me, standing reverently near—'I had
But this one child, and thou hast made me childless. Now strike down
The father. I shall feel no pain in death. But thy requital be

That sorrow for a child shall one day bring thee also to the grave.'"[1]

When he had finished the sad recital, the king fell back exhausted, but rallied under the influence of restoratives applied by the physicians around his bed, and taking her hand again he drew his stricken wife more closely to him, saying in pitiful, heart-broken tones, "Come nearer, my wife, let me feel your loving arms. I cannot see you—my sight has gone after Rāma." There was darkness in the city, but the darkness of grief lay like a pall upon the palace where the faithful watchers stood around the dying king. Soon the throbbing pulse was still, the tortured heart had ceased to beat, and the fainting wife was carried away by her attendants.

BHARATA.

The prince, who had been summoned, came with joy to attend, as he supposed, the installation of Rāma, the rightful heir to the throne. He went first, however, to his mother Kaikeyī, who told him in exulting tones all that had taken place. But instead of receiving his gratitude and congratulations, she was overwhelmed with his reproaches and denunciations for her wickedness.[2] "Have you come into this family," he demanded, "to destroy it as darkness destroys the universe? My father, the Maha-raja, who suspected no evil, has embraced burning coals, and met with his death through you! Oh, you are bent upon evil! This family has been forever robbed of happiness through your infatua-

[1] Williams' trans. Ind. Wis., pp. 350-352.

[2] It is stated in the original that the guiltless Bharata was pained by his mother's conduct as by a tumor that had been opened with a knife.

tion. The eldest among the sons of a raja is always appointed to the raj. This is the rule amongst all rajas, and especially those of our race. But I will bring back Rāma from the wilderness of Daṇḍaka. I will bring the young heir from the forest and install him upon his rightful throne."

Bharata's half-brother, Śatru-ghna, heard his words and applauded the position he had taken, and leaving Kaikeyī overwhelmed with shame and confusion the two brothers went together to the apartments of Kauśalyā with the glad news that her beloved son was to be brought back from exile and seated upon the throne which was his rightful inheritance.

On the fourteenth day after the funeral obsequies of the Maha-raja, the official time for mourning having passed by, the great council convened in the court hall of the royal palace, and the counselors formally offered the throne to Bharata. But he replied, "Oh, excellent men! in our family the raj has ever been considered the inheritance of the eldest son, and it is right that my eldest brother, Rāma, should become your raja, and that I should reside fourteen years in the forest. Therefore, prepare a large army and I will lead them into the forest and restore the rightful heir. We will go forth with a splendid retinue of troops with horses and elephants, bearing all the sacred utensils necessary for his installation, and he shall return to his throne and kingdom."

These generous words were received with shouts and cheers, even from the high officials, and as the news spread through the city, the people took up the glad refrain, and their mourning was turned to joy. Happy songs and laughter again sounded in the streets which had for days been oppressed with a pall of sadness. Strains of joyous music again floated upon the air, gorgeous banners were once more flung to the breeze, and the very trees and flowers seemed to share in the general rejoicing.

CHAPTER XV.

THE STORY OF THE RĀMĀYAṆA, CONTINUED.

LEAVING THE ATTENDANTS — THE GANGES — ĆITRAKŪṬA — LIFE IN EXILE — BHARATA'S ARRIVAL — THE INTERVIEW — A WARNING AND DEPARTURE — ATRI AND ANASŪYĀ — THE NEW HOME — ŚŪRPA-ṆAKHĀ — RĀVAṆA — THE ABDUCTION — THE SEARCH — SUGRĪVA, THE MONKEY KING — EXPEDITION OF THE MONKEY GENERAL — HANUMAN — LANKĀ — THE PALACE OF RĀVAṆA — THE AŚOKA GROVE — INTERVIEW BETWEEN HANUMAN AND SĪTĀ — HANUMAN DESTROYS THE MANGO GROVE — THE BURNING OF LANKĀ — HANUMAN REJOINS THE MONKEY ARMY.

THE people continued to follow the chariot of Rāma even after the Maha-raja had been carried back to the palace. Determined to share in his fortunes and hardships, the great procession continued almost unbroken until they reached the banks of the beautiful river Tamasa, where it was determined to encamp for the night. So the horses were loosed and allowed to drink from the clear flood before being tethered for the night, while the people ate of the wild fruits, and making beds of the forest leaves lay down to sleep beneath the great trees.

In the early morning Rāma awakened Sumantra and his brother and said to them, "These devoted people have vowed to take us back, and they will never leave us while their lives remain. Let us therefore quietly mount the chariot and depart while they are still asleep." Then Sumantra harnessed the horses as quietly as possible, and Rāma with his wife and brother entered the chariot. The charioteer, in compliance with Rāma's request, drove the horses slowly backward over the route by which they came, that the people might not be able to follow their track, and then turning took a different direction into the wilderness.

When the people awoke and found that the chariot had gone, they followed its backward track until it was lost in a multitude of others; then they returned with sad hearts to the city of mourning.

CROSSING THE GANGES.

In the meantime the chariot of Rāma pursued its way to the sacred shores of the Ganges. The deep, cool waters were dashing between the green banks in a rapid current, then rolling away into the quiet pools below, where the creamy lotus blossoms raised their heads above the bright surface and loaded the air with their fragrant breath. Just above them the fair river gleamed like a stream of silver against the golden sands upon the shore, and around them were massive trees, some of which were laden with flowers, and others bending low beneath a weight of golden fruit. Here they paused to pay their tribute of devotion to the beautiful river by chanting the musical Hindū name of Gangā! Gangâ!

Then the fair goddess of the stream raised their chariot in her hands and bore it in the air above the waters to the other side. This was the river which fell to earth from the divine feet of Vishṇu.[1] Gangā was the eldest daughter of Himavat, "Lord of the Mountains," but the beautiful river flowed only through the fields of heaven.

Sagara, an early king of Ayodhyā, had sixty thousand sons, and he sent them out one day to recover a horse which had been designed for the Aśva-medha sacrifice, but had been stolen by a Rākshasa. The gigantic sons of the solar race having searched the earth unsuccessfully, proceeded to dig through into the lower regions; they found many wonderful things in the course of their excavations, and at last met a living sage, Kapila. They promptly accused him of having stolen the horse, when he responded to their accusation by reducing them all to ashes. The grandson of Sagara attempted to perform the funeral rites, but was told that the Gangā must water the ashes with her sacred stream. Bhagīratha, the great-grandson of Sagara, then performed severe penances to induce the gods to send down the celestial river. He was told that his request should be granted, but he must secure the intervention of Śiva, or the earth would be destroyed by the force of the torrent.

"As thou prayest it shall be.
Gangā, whose waves in heaven flow,
Is daughter of the Lord of Snow.
Win Śiva that his aid be lent
To hold her in her mid descent.
For earth alone will never bear
These torrents from the upper air."

[1] The fountain of the Ganges is said to be in the great toe of this god.

He therefore propitiated Śiva, who at last consented to stand beneath the descending torrent and break its fall.

"On Śiva's head descending first,
  A rest the torrents found,
Then down in all their might they burst
  And roared along the ground;
On countless glittering scales the beam
  Of rosy morning flashed,
Where fish and dolphins through the stream
  Fallen and falling dashed.
Then bards who chant celestial lays,
  And nymphs of heavenly birth,
Flocked round upon that flood to gaze
  That streamed from sky to earth.
The gods themselves from every sphere,
  Incomparably bright,
Borne in their golden cars drew near
  To see the wondrous sight.
The cloudless sky was all aflame
  With the light of a hundred suns
Where'er the shining chariots came
  That bore these holy ones.
So flashed the air with crested snakes
  And fish of every hue
As when the lightning's glory breaks
  Through fields of summer blue.
And white foam-clouds and silver spray
  Were wildly tossed on high,
Like swans that urge their homeward way
  Across the autumn sky."[1]

[1] Griffith's trans., Vol I, p. 194.

Thus flowing down the long coils of Śiva's hair, the fearful torrent reached the earth and fell into Vindu Lake,[1] whence proceed the seven sacred streams of India. Immediately after crossing the Ganges, Rāma dismissed Sumantra, sending him back to Ayodhyā with the chariot and with admonitions to be careful of the feelings of the Maha-raja, and thoughtful for the happiness of his mother, Kauśalyā. He also sent kind salutations to Bharata, as the ruler of the raj. In vain the faithful Sumantra pleaded to be allowed to spend the fourteen years of exile with them and carry them home in the chariot. He was kindly but firmly sent back to the city without them.

ĆITRA-KŪṬA.

"Lakshmaṇa," said Rāma, "my poor Sītā will now be obliged to endure the privations of forest life, and the fear of lions and tigers and other wild animals. We will protect her as far as lies in our power. You may go on before and I will follow behind her, that she may be shielded on all sides." Then taking their bows and arrows in their hands they walked bravely into the forest. They traveled slowly and carefully, with occasional rests on account of Sītā's tender feet, until they came near to the beautiful mountain of Ćitra-kūṭa.

A fair green slope which lay at its feet was covered with flowering trees, in whose fragrant blossoms the wild bees drowsily hummed as they gathered the honey from the tinted cups and stored it away in the

[1] No such lake is known, and of the seven sacred streams mentioned in the legend only two (the Ganges and the Indus) are known to geographers.

great combs hanging beneath the shelving rocks In the crevice of the cliff the crystal springs formed cascades that went dashing down the mountain-side and poured their cool waters into the river Maṇḍākinī as it swept around the base of the slope and rolled away in the distance. Beyond the flowering trees and just at the foot of the mountain stood a group of lofty pīpals, whose trunks were enwreathed with flowering vines, like garlands festooned upon the columns of some fair temple. While they looked a gazelle, which had never been startled by man, walked carelessly out of the shade and went down to the river to drink of its clear waters.

Enchanted with the scene, Rāma turned to his brother with the words, "This shall be our wildwood home; we will build a cot beneath those trees, and in the shade of the sacred mountain we will spend the years of our exile." Then turning to Sītā, he put his arm around her and said:

"Look round thee, dear; each flowery tree
Touched with the fire of morning see.
The Kinśuk,[1] now the frosts are fled,
How glorious with his wreaths of red!
The bel trees see, so loved of men,
Hanging their boughs in every glen,
O'erburdened with their fruits and flowers!
A plenteous store of food is ours.
See, Lakshman! in the lofty trees,
  Where'er they make their home,
Down hangs the work of laboring bees,
  The ponderous honey-comb!

1 The *butea frondosa*, which has gorgeous red blossoms.

In the fair wood before us spread
  The startled wild cock cries.
Hark, where the flowers are soft to tread
  The peacock's voice replies!
Where elephants are roaming free,
  And sweet birds' songs are loud,
The glorious Ćitra-kūṭa see,
  His peaks are in the cloud.
On fair, smooth ground he stands displayed,
  Begirt by many a tree.
Oh, brother, in that holy shade
  How happy we shall be!"[1]

LIFE IN EXILE.

Beneath the dense foliage of the tropical trees Lakshmaṇa built a tent with graceful branches and entwined it with the gigantic flowering vines that grew around it, forming a bower of beauty and fragrance. Free from the cares of state, the young prince gave himself up to the offering of sacrificial rites and to the company of his beautiful wife.

To Rāma and Sītā every tree and flower were glorified by the divine light of love. Hand in hand they wandered through the long aisles of woodland beauty and gathered the rich fruits and fragrant flowers of the forest.

Luxury can never taste of happiness, if it is not offered by the hand of affection; but love can be supremely happy even in the home of poverty, for privation has no power to break the chain which gilds even her own ruggedness with beauty.

[1] Book 2, Canto 56.

As each day was ushered in by the golden light of morning, which touched the sacred peak with fire, it brought a new crown of peace and happiness to the inmates of the leafy cot in the shade of the mountain.

BHARATA'S ARRIVAL.

At the close of a peaceful day the exiles stood in the balmy air making their oblation to the setting sun, as he passed through the crimson gates of evening, when they were startled by a group of wild elephants that dashed in terror through the waves of the Maṇḍākinī and rushed into the jungle beyond. In another moment a herd of frightened deer ran by the mountain, and the birds flew over their heads in wild confusion. "My brother," said Rāma, "do you hear this ominous roar, deep and terrible as thunder? It sounds like the approach of a hostile army, but it may be that the animals and birds are terrified by lions that have come into the jungle." Then Lakshmaṇa hastily ascended an eminence and looking far away into the distance beheld the approaching army of Bharata. No wonder that the denizens of the forest had fled in wild affright, for there in the light of the setting sun were nine thousand elephants richly caparisoned, sixty thousand chariots with archers, a hundred thousand horsemen, and a multitude of footmen, the whole city having followed Bharata upon his journey into the wilderness. There were the ladies of the royal household, with Kanśalyā, the royal widow, at their head. There were the priests and the royal counselors in chariots vying in splendor with the chariot of the sun. There were musicians and dancing girls, gaily appareled in brilliant colors.

Lakshmaṇa gazed for a moment in silence upon the gorgeous pageant; then he said to his brother, "Oh, chief of men! This must be the army of Bharata, the son of Kaikeyī. Jealous even of exiles in the wilderness, he is coming to destroy us both. I see his flag upon the chariot; he comes like a destroying king."

But Rāma answered, "Perhaps Bharata has come hither for affection only, or to surrender the raj to me. Why do you speak so harshly of him?"

Lakshmaṇa replied, "Possibly the Maha-raja has come to see you, and will take us home again. I see the great imperial elephant marching at the head of the army, but I cannot see the white canopy of our royal father."

When the procession came near the mountain, Bharata ordered a halt, that only himself and his brother, Śatru-ghna, with the chief counselor, Sumantra, should first approach the exiled prince.

THE INTERVIEW.

The three men approached the mountain and came toward the large and pleasant tent. Above the door of the outer room was placed an enormous bow, gleaming with gold, like the bow of Indra, and beside it rested a great quiver of arrows, as bright as the rays of the sun and as keen as the face of a serpent. Before the door of the tent Bharata saw his elder brother, dressed in the garb of a devotee, and near him Lakshmaṇa, also wearing garments of bark, while the beautiful Sītā was nestling close to her husband, her great dark eyes dilated with wonder and fear.

Then Bharata bowed himself in tears at the feet of Rāma, saying, "This is my elder brother, who once had thousands of suits of apparel, who is now wearing vestments of bark. The body of that excellent one, which was formerly perfumed with costly sandalwood, is covered with the dust of the forest. Rāma, who is worthy of all happiness, has undergone all of these privations because of me!"

But Rāma embraced his brother, saying, "Oh, beloved brother! where is our father Daśaratha that you have come to this forest? Is the Maha-raja alive, or has he departed from this life?' Bharata replied with joined hands, "Oh, excellent one! my valiant father, having sent you into exile at the instance of my mother Kaikeyī, has departed to heaven, overwhelmed with grief." At the announcement of this terrible news, which fell upon Rāma like a thunderbolt from Indra, the prince sank upon the ground, like a lofty tree that has been felled with the ax.

It was a pitiful scene of mourning at the foot of the silent mountain, when the gallant brothers mingled their tears together over the memory of their dead father. Then Rāma and his brothers walked down to the river Maṇḍākinī, and descending into the stream performed the funeral oblations for their father. As the prince sprinkled the water toward the regions of Yama, he exclaimed, "Oh, raja of rajas! may this pure water given to you by me always quench your thirst in the spirit-land." Then holding the hands of his brothers he led them again to the door of the tent.

The troops now advanced, bringing Kauśalyā and the ladies of the royal household, including the humiliated Kaikeyī. Rāma fell down at the lotus-like feet of his mother, who wiped the dust from his hair with her soft caressing hands; then twining her arms around him as he arose to his feet, she wept for joy in the arms of her manly son.

At length Bharata addressed Rāma in the presence of the troops and the attendants with the words, "My mother Kaikeyī having given the raj to me is satisfied, and now I give it to you. Oh, Rāma! with bowed head I entreat you to wipe off the guilt of my mother's anger and deliver my father from sin. But if you turn your back upon me and persist in going farther into the forest, I will surely go with you." But Rāma answered him, "Nay, Bharata, you must be the raja of men, and I will be the raja of wild beasts. The royal canopy shall shade your head from the sun, while mine shall be shaded by the trees of the wood."

In this useless pleading the night wore away. When the morning sun again illumined the peaks of Ćitrakūṭa, Bharata brought to the prince a pair of sandals embroidered with gold and besought him to put them on. Rāma did so and returned them to his brother, who bowed low before them, saying, "For fourteen years I will wear the garb of a devotee and live upon roots and fruits. I will reside without the city, awaiting your return, and I will commit the management of the raj to your sandals. If you do not return to Ayodhyā within five days after the completion of the fourteenth year, I will enter my pyre."

Bharata then embraced his two brothers, and placing the sandals upon his head, mounted his chariot, and with all of his attendants, both horse and foot, returned to Ayodhyā. But the deserted city was traversed by bats and owls; it was bereft of music and song. It was like a necklace from which the jewels have been taken, or a star which has fallen to the earth. Bharata refused to enter its walls. The grand procession swept slowly and sorrowfully in, while Bharata stayed at Nandi-grāma, just outside the city. Here he assumed the garb and matted hair of a devotee, and here he was installed, while he himself held the royal canopy over the sandals of Rāma. All the affairs of the government were transacted under the authority of the sandals, and Bharata, while ruling the raj, paid homage to them. All the presents and offerings which were brought to the sovereign were laid before the sandals, and all matters of state were first presented there and afterward adjusted by Bharata.

A WARNING AND DEPARTURE.

After the departure of Bharata and his army, the quiet life at the foot of Ćitra-kūṭa flowed on in its peaceful channel. The seasons came and went, bringing new glory with every change. The outside world rushed on, wearing its cares and bearing its burdens, but they came not to the woodland home of the exiles. Sītā had made friends with the wild gazelles, that came down to drink from the cool waves of the Maṇḍākinī, and as she approached them they raised their beautiful eyes and looked fearlessly into her own.

The birds made their nests in the trees above her head and fluttered down to the door of her leafy home to find the food which she never failed to furnish them.

But a great sage who lived in a hermitage not far away, came to them one day and bade them beware of the Rākshasas who infested the great jungle beyond them. The Rākshasas were demons who fed upon living men and changed their own forms at pleasure. Of late they had become more abundant and obtrusive, and the hermits had all decided to leave the dangerous region. The sage besought Rāma, also, to heed the warning and go.

So they bade farewell to the bright bower beneath the massive trees and went forth again into the wilderness.

ATRI AND ANASŪYĀ.

At the close of the second day of their journey they arrived at the hermitage of a holy sage named Atri, who lived in the wild forest with his excellent wife, Anasūyā, and had sanctified his life by long penance. He gave them a cordial welcome, for even the birds seemed to have heard the story of the illustrious Rāma. He introduced his wife to the exiled prince, saying: "Oh, sinless one! This, my wife, is a Brahmāṇī, renowned for her vows and the constant performance of pious deeds. By the power of her austerities rain was brought and fruits and flowers were produced during a ten years' dearth, and the holy Gangā was brought near our dwelling. If she ask of the gods any boon it will be granted her. I beseech you to let your beautiful Sītā go into her presence." Then Rāma said to his wife, "Do you hear the words of the sage? You may go now into the presence of Anasūyā." Then Sītā approached with reverent mien the aged woman and bowed at her feet. The venerable matron said to her, "Oh, honorable Sītā! You have abandoned your relatives and friends to follow your brave husband into exile. The woman who loves her lord will obtain a great reward hereafter."

Sītā replied: "It is true that a woman should love her husband, even though he be poor and wicked, but how much more must she reverence him when he is the embodiment of virtue and kindness." The aged woman then drew the fair face of Sītā toward her, and impressed a reverent kiss upon her forehead, saying, "I am greatly pleased with thee, beautiful one, and I wish to confer a blessing upon thee. Thou shalt ever wear thy youthful beauty, and thy silken raiment shall never become soiled or frayed—thou shalt always remain thy beautiful self. Time cannot tarnish thy beauty nor soil thy fair robes."

On receiving the crown of eternal youth and beauty, Sītā thought only of Rāma and the pleasure that it would bring to his heart. "I shall be more beautiful in his sight," she whispered. "Oh, pearl amongst women! Thou hast filled my heart with gladness." When Rāma and Lakshmaṇa heard that Sītā was to retain her youthful beauty through all the coming years, they rejoiced with her that she was thus favored above all others.

They were cordially tendered the modest hospitalities of the hermitage for the night, and in the morning inquired of the devotees where they could find a pleasant home in the forest. But they were told that the whole wilderness of Daṇḍaka was infested with the terrible Rākshasas, whom it was hoped Prince Rāma would be able to destroy, or stop their depredations.

THE NEW HOME.

The morning sunlight was crowning the distant mountain tops with glory and piercing with its rays the dense foliage of the tropical forest, when the homeless ones again set out to find a resting-place. The air was perfumed with the breath of the blossom-laden mango trees; the tall tamarinds lifted their feathery plumes in the distance; flowering creepers of gigantic size and gorgeous colors festooned the jungle; and water lilies rested their pearly cups upon the bosom of every pool.

They wandered through the beautiful scene with the enthusiasm of children, for the changeful face of nature never wearies her faithful lovers, and this was the flowery forest of Pańćavatī.

"Here is beauty and happiness," exclaimed Rāma. "Let us seek a place for our hermitage in some pleasant thicket, where the sacrificial wood may be obtained, and near a flowing stream whose banks are covered with flowers and kusa grass."

They found the place they sought in a beautiful spot on the shores of the bright river Godāvarī, whose gentle current sang in a musical monotone as the clear waters wandered away. Near it, gleaming like a gem in the sunshine, was a lake, which fed the stream and made the breezes fragrant with the breath of its white lilies.

Their hermitage was built of the flexible bamboos, and the rooms were tapestried with branches of broad-leaved evergreens and beautified with floral vines and bunches of golden fruit. When Lakshmaṇa had finished his task he went down to the shores of the lake to gather fruits and water-lilies. He made an oblation of the flowers to the god of dwellings and sprinkled water, according to the ordinance, to secure peace to the new habitation. There in their leafy home the exiles dwelt happily for many days; but even amidst the fruits and flowers of Pañćavatī they were still in the doleful wilderness of Daṇḍaka. Loathsome serpents were coiled in the flower-wreathed jungle and the Rākshasas roamed the woods, unseen by mortal eye.

ŚŪRPA-ṆAKHĀ.

One of the Rākshasas was a female demon, who often watched Rāma and Sītā as they sat beneath the plantain trees or gathered lilies from the clear surface of the lake. Their innocent love and happiness was gall and bitterness to her vile nature, and as evil creatures cannot witness domestic happiness without wishing to destroy it, Śūrpa-ṇakhā began to plot for their ruin. As she gazed upon the noble form and rich complexion[1] of Rāma, she became enamored of his manly beauty, which formed so strong a contrast to her own repulsive features; for while he was pure, noble, and chaste, she was so vile that she failed to win the respect even of the low creatures with whom she lived.

[1] Rama is frequently represented as having a complexion which is of a bright green "like new grass," although as an incarnation of Vishnu his color should be dark blue.

"She, grim of eye and foul of face,
Loved his sweet glance and forehead's grace—
She, whose foul wig uncleanly hung,
Him, whose dark locks on high brows clung."

Day after day she haunted their footsteps, becoming more and more infatuated with Rāma, and more determined to destroy their happiness and ruin this pure man by polluting him with her vile associations. She saw him chaste and true, and longed to degrade him to her own level by bringing him under her vile influence. What a grand chief he would make for a Rākshasas tribe, if she could but decoy him into their camp and use his noble life for her own base service!

She loved Rāma, if it be lawful to call that love, which was only the passion of a degraded creature seeking to pollute and destroy her victim. If, then, she could steal from Sītā the loving heart of her husband and rob them of their leafy home, both her lust and her avarice would be gratified. As she lingered one day gazing upon them, she turned green with envy and ground her teeth in her rage. But she could assume other forms at her pleasure, and she muttered, "I, too, can wear the face and form of beauty; I, too, can assume the manners of an innocent woman, and I will show her that she cannot stand between me and my wishes."

So saying, she sprang to her feet and assumed a form of beauty and grace. Then going out into the thicket she uttered a piercing shriek of distress to lure Rāma from the side of his wife. He gallantly rushed into the forest to rescue a woman in distress and beheld the beautiful creature, who appealed to his sympathies so effectually that he could not at once tear himself away from her. She approached him and with pleading eyes besought him to flee from the terrible Rākshasas of the wood, while her own loveliness and apparent helplessness appealed to him for protection. Drawing nearer and holding her beautiful face up toward his own she poured forth a passionate story of her love for him. Flattered by the approaches of the siren he addressed her with winning compliments, but at last explained that he was already bound by the marriage tie, and she would not wish to share his caresses with a rival. "There shall be no rival between me and Rāma!" she screamed; "I will destroy this odious Sītā." She ran towards the tent; but Lakshmaṇa divined her cruel purpose and with a drawn sword cut off her nose and ears, whereupon she rushed into the woods, making the echoes ring with her shrieks and vowing vengeance upon the mortals who had thus thwarted and disfigured her. She cast off her disguise and wore a personal appearance corresponding to her moral depravity; her claw-like hands returned, and demon that she was she bounded through the forest, howling with rage and pain, and rushed into the presence of her brother Khara.

Seeing his sister covered with blood and almost exhausted with fury, he exclaimed, "Who has done this? Who is there, who even in sport would vex with his finger a black serpent full of venom? Who would take the rope of death and tie it around his own neck? Yet the man who has done this has drunk of the deadly poison."

Then Śūrpa-ṇakhā told her story in her own way, and the enraged brother, calling fourteen powerful Rākshasas, commanded them to go with his sister and bring the three exiles to him as prisoners. Wild with rage and filling the air with their maledictions the Rākshasas fell upon the hermitage, but only to receive from the bow of Rāma fourteen bright arrows, which sped through the air like meteors, piercing their black hearts and carrying them to the regions of Yama.

Śūrpa-ṇakhā gave one piercing shriek and fled to Khara with the tidings that his bravest warriors were slain. He replied in a voice like thunder, "Wipe away your tears and shake off your terror, for this day I will send these mortals to the abode of Yama." Then turning to his brother Dushana, he said, "Equip fourteen thousand Rākshasas who are dreadful as a thunderbolt and valiant as tigers. Bring also my chariot, my bows, and my arrows. I myself will go to the front and drink the life-blood of Rāma."

When Rāma heard the demon troops approaching with loud beating of drums and terrible war cries, he commanded Lakshmaṇa to carry Sītā for safety to a cave in the mountains, while he prepared to meet the foe alone. The black horde came on with screams and yells and peals of hideous laughter. They poured down upon Rāma like a black, raging sea, but he received their missiles as the ocean receives her rivers, and drawing his bow in a circle sent his death-dealing arrows into their ranks until the conquered army lay in slaughtered heaps upon the plain. Khara then rushed toward Rāma in his own chariot, but Rāma seized the bow of Vishṇu and discharged a flaming arrow, which laid the demon dead at his feet.

The contest being over, Lakashmaṇa and Sītā came out of the cave. The young wife joyfully embraced her brave husband, and as he took her into his arms he appeared to his adoring brother as glorious as Indra in his heaven of the golden dome.

RĀVAṆA.

On the beautiful island of Lankā, where the wealth of art had vied with the luxuriance of nature, stood the palace of Rāvaṇa, the demon king of Ceylon. He was the enemy of gods and men. There were ten hideous heads upon his colossal form, and twenty strong arms bade defiance to his foes. His immense black body was as smooth as polished ivory, but it bore the marks of his terrible contests. The lightning bolts had scorched him and a monstrous elephant had torn him with his tusks, while on his broad chest was a great scar that had been left from a wound made with the shield of Vishṇu. His ten necks were ornamented with ten huge golden necklaces set with flashing gems, and on his twenty wrists gleamed costly bracelets of gold and jewels. Each frightful head wore a golden serpent as a crown. He was taller than the Himālayas, and reaching upward he could stop the stars in their courses. He could shake the sea with his fearful strides, and with his mighty arms rend asunder the tops of mountains. This was he who went to Bhogavatī, the city of resplendent serpents, and conquering Vāsuki, carried away the beloved wife of the glittering snake Takshaka.[1] Such was the fear he inspired, that every living thing shuddered and shrunk out of sight upon his approach. Even the winds crept silently by, and the angry sea forgot to rave and only moaned in terror when he looked upon her billows. "The courage of the Three Worlds," as he was often called, sat upon the golden throne in the great council hall of his palace, surrounded by his chieftains and counselors.

On either side of the languid demon were great masses of fragrant flowers which had been gathered and brought to him as offerings, while at his feet were piles of gold and jewels which he had extorted as tributes from his terror-stricken subjects. Over his numerous heads his attendants in misty Oriental garb waved fans whose handles were of pearl and set with diamonds. As they moved them gracefully to and fro they kept time to a dreamy musical measure, which floated through the air. But while the demon sat holding council with his chiefs, he was disturbed by a confusion among his courtiers outside the palace, and in a moment, to his angry astonishment, his sister, the terrible Śūrpa-ṇakhā, dashed into the room. Her garments were torn, her long hair was disheveled, and her mangled face was covered with blood.

The dreadful Rāvaṇa sprang to his feet, and shouted, "Speak! who has dared to molest the sister of Rāvaṇa, the victor of the gods?" "Who has dared, indeed!" burst from the lips of the vindictive female fiend. "Here I find you surrounded by luxury and fanned to

[1] Vasuki and Takshaka are leading Nagas, to whom a separate dominion over a portion of the serpent race is sometimes assigned. In company with Sesha, they rule over snakes in general and their dominion is in the lower regions.

sleep by the perfumed breath of flowers, while I come bleeding from the battle-field, where the vultures are feeding upon our warriors who perished in trying to avenge my wrongs. And who is the cause of all this? —a mortal," she screamed, "a man by the name of Rāma; a mere youth who has been exiled from his father's court! But he carries a bow like a rainbow, and from it he sends forth blazing arrows, which are fatal as the poison of serpents. I saw the army falling before him like a crop of grain that is smitten by the rains of Indra. Oh Rāvaṇa! this Rāma has a beautiful wife of charming face and lovely form, and her complexion is bright as molten gold. Oh, my brother! It was because I wanted to bring this beautiful woman away to be your wife, that I was disfigured by the cruel Lakshmaṇa. O raja of the Rākshasas, avenge the death of your brothers upon Rāma and Lakshmaṇa, and take the beautiful Sītā to be your wife!"

Bending down the haughty demon laid his hand caressingly upon the rough head of Śūrpa-ṇahkā, and answered in tones of thunder, "I will indeed avenge my fallen brothers, and I will bring this dainty beauty to my own court."

Then ordering his golden chariot, which moved through the air at the will of the charioteer, he called one of his courtiers to accompany him, and while they moved on their way he gave his orders. He was met with expostulations and warnings, but he only replied: "The sovereign of the world is not to be contradicted. I did not ask your advice; I only commanded your assistance. You must assume the form of a golden deer, and going into the presence of Sītā you must attract her attention. Having done this, you are at liberty to go where you please, for I shall have no further need of you.

> "Doubt not the lady, when she sees
> This wondrous deer among the trees,
> Will bid her lord and Lakshman take
> The creature for its beauty's sake.
> Thy life, if thou the task essay,
> In jeopardy may stand.
> Oppose me, and this very day
> Thou diest by this hand."

THE ABDUCTION.

It was evening in the wilderness of Daṇḍaka. The day with her sandals dipped in dew was passing through the golden gates of the west, and the crescent moon and the evening star had come forth to bid her good-night. Rāma and his young wife stood at the door of their leafy tent looking in silence upon the glories of the western sky, when a beautiful fawn came out of the thicket and entered the plantain grove, which had been cleared of its undergrowth. In the evening light he shone like burnished gold flecked with spots of silver, and his tiny horns seemed to be tipped with sapphire, while his delicate mouth and fine nostrils were like the red lotus blossoms, and his dark eyes looked fearlessly into the face of the princess.

Sītā was delighted with his beauty, and appealed to Rāma to capture him for her. "We could keep it," said she, "in our leafy dwelling, and when our term of exile is finished we could take it with us to Ayodhyā.

But if you cannot capture it alive, bring at least its beautiful coat as a covering for our couch." The willing husband acceded to her request, but Lakshmaṇa offered a word of warning: "Do you not know, my brother, there was never a fawn of such brilliant hues? Surely it is an illusion furnished by demons. Be not so rash, oh prince, as to pursue it." But Rāma answered, "Be not alarmed—even if it proves to be a demon I will slay it, and bring the skin to the daughter of Janaka. During all the time she has been in this forest she has made only this one request. Do you think I will fail to comply with it? Stay with her, my brother, and guard her from all harm until I return." Then throwing his golden bow over his shoulder, he started in pursuit of the beautiful fawn. But gracefully eluding his grasp the pretty creature bounded into the thicket, cautiously pursued by Rāma. It often seemed to be upon the point of capture, but as often it evaded the hunter's touch and fled farther toward the inaccessible hills in the distance.

It was now growing dark beneath the trees, although it was still light above them, and at last the fawn paused as if wearied, while its little mouth quivered and foamed, seemingly with exhaustion. "Now," thought Rāma, "my game is secure," and again he attempted to lay his hand upon its graceful neck; but there was another bound, and this time it was far beyond the hunter's reach. Dismayed and out of patience and already far from home Rāma drew his bow and sent his unfailing arrow through the side of his victim. The fawn fell to the earth with a human shriek, and in the very tones of Rāma it called upon Lakshmaṇa for aid. The distant cry was heard by the listening pair at the door of the hermitage, and Sītā besought Lakshmaṇa to fly to her husband's aid. In vain he argued that it was a deceitful cry—that Rāma's power was such that he needed no aid; she would not listen to a refusal, and at last taunted him with cowardice and with motives which were even more unworthy. Stung by her severity he darted into the forest, leaving the beautiful princess alone amidst the rapidly falling shades of night.

A feeling of loneliness and terror came over her at once, but she would not call him back, and she was soon comforted by seeing a humble priest approaching her little dwelling. In one hand he bore a staff and in the other a scrip. On his forehead was a straight mark and on his fingers were large rings of sacred grass. His body was emaciated and his feet only partially covered by his torn sandals. He meekly approached her, asking for food, and supposing him to be a true hermit she paid him lowly reverence and gladly invited him to enter her little home and rest until her husband returned. "Beautiful lady," he said, "your smile is entrancing, and your radiant eyes illumine with brightness even the approaching darkness. How came so beautiful a gem to be in this rough setting? Why should so fair a lady be found in this gloomy forest?" Sītā innocently told him the story of their exile, when the mighty raja of the Rākshasas said to her, "I am Rāvaṇa, the terror of the world I have assumed this lowly form only to gain admission to your presence, for my power is known throughout the universe. Your beauty, oh, radiant one, eclipses in my eyes the beauty of all my own wives! Will you not be my rani—the chief of them all? Lankā, my beautiful city, is on an island of the sea. Built of palaces and filled with glories, it is as renowned as the city of Indra. There, O Sītā, you shall walk with me among the groves and feel no wish to return to this forest. You shall be the chief of all my wives, and five thousand beautiful handmaids shall attend you."

But she indignantly replied, "Know that I am the daughter of raja Janaka, and my husband is my deity. As a lioness attends a strong lion, so am I the constant attendant of the majestic Rāma! Do you, a pitiful jackal, wish to obtain a lioness, who is to you like a ray of the sun to a firefly?"

Then the demon was enraged, and he exclaimed, "Infatuated as you are, oh, Sītā, you cannot know of my power. I can torment the sun and pierce the earth through with my arrows. I can slay the King of Death himself in single-handed combat. Behold me in my own form." And assuming his own personality, he seemed as vast as a mountain and as terrible as Yama. His red eyes glared upon her, and his enormous body seemed to be covered with bristles of fire, and great earrings of molten gold gleamed in all his ears. With his ten horrible heads and twenty terrible arms he stood before her, like a black, angry cloud flashing with lightnings. With one pitiful cry of "Rāma! Rāma!" she fainted at his feet. Then with a fiendish laugh he lifted her from the ground and calling for his chariot he entered it, bearing his beautiful prey in his arms.

THE SEARCH.

The grass and ferns were heavy with the evening dew when Rāma turned from the Rākshasa that had in death revealed his true character, and started with a heavy heart toward his home. Soon he saw his brother hastening toward him, and upbraided him bitterly for leaving Sītā alone. Lakshmaṇa explained that he came only in obedience to the command of Sītā, who felt that her husband was in danger. Then they knew they were the victims of a plot, and hurrying in silence to the hermitage their fears were realized; for the beautiful Sītā was not to be found. They searched around the little tent and down by the crystal stream that went murmuring by, singing in its dreams, all unconscious of their agony. Then their lamentations were pitiful to hear. Rāma bewailed the cruel losses of his life, which had culminated in the loss of her who was dearer far than life itself.

"Tossing his mighty arms on high,
He sought her with an eager cry.
From spot to spot he wildly ran,
Each corner of his home to scan.
He looked, but Sītā was not there,
His cot was desolate and bare,
Like streamlet in the winter frost,
The glory of her lilies lost.
With leafy tears the sad trees wept
As a wild wind their branches swept.
Mourned bird and deer; and every flower
Drooped fainting round the lovely bower.
The sylvan deities had fled

The spot where all the light was dead.
He saw and maddened by his pain
Cried in lament agaiu, again,
'Where is she? dead or torn away?
Lost, or some hungry giant's prey?
Or did my darling chance to rove
For fruit and blossoms through the grove?
Or has she sought the pool or rill
Her pitcher from the wave to fill?'
His eager eyes on fire with pain,
He roamed about with maddened brain.
Each grove and glade he searched with care,
He sought, but found no Sītā there."[1]

Then beneath the dark foliage of the sandal trees the brothers swore by the stars of night to find their beloved Sītā and to slay him who had carried her away, whether he proved to be a man, a god, or a demon. In his own terrible agony Rāma requested his brother to direct the search, and taking only his bow with his quiver of arrows, among which was the wonderful arrow that Brahmā had given him to be used only in a dire emergency, he followed Lakshmaṇa. Neither of them thought of sleep. Through the dark and pathless forest they sought a charmed cavern in the depths of the wood, whose inmates, they thought, might give them the information they sought. At the foot of a mountain they found the entrance to the cave; day was now breaking, and there, resting upon the thick foliage of a laurel bush, lay a delicate wreath which Sītā had worn in her hair. Rāma caught up

[1] Book III, Canto 61.

the half-withered flowers, and while he pressed them to his lips his eye caught sight of a friendly vulture. The vulture told them that Rāvaṇa, the demon king, had hurried by a short time before, bearing a beautiful woman in his arms, and pointed out the way he had gone. They stayed for a few questions, and then performed the funeral rites of the vulture, who died before their eyes, having received a death wound from Rāvaṇa, in consequence of his vain attempts to rescue Sītā from the grasp of the fiend. Having performed this labor of love for their lost friend and thereby assured to him a higher birth and an entrance to heaven, they hastened onward.

SUGRĪVA, THE MONKEY KING.

After a long and wearisome journey, Rāma and Lakshmaṇa came to the beautiful lake of Pampa, with its wealth of water lilies and lotus blossoms. The sweet breath of the flowers mingled with the rich odor of the sandal trees, and multitudes of water birds with radiant plumage stood upon the green bank of the lake or hovered joyously over its crystal surface. Amidst the dense foliage on the other shore the wild cotton tree of Indía lifted here and there its leafless branches, glowing with heavy crimson blossoms, and over all the peaceful scene rested the benediction of the parting day. Here they remained through the night, the faithful Lakshmaṇa making a bed of lotus for his brother and bringing water from the lake to bathe his weary feet.

Rising early in the morning, they performed their customary ablutions in the clear waters of the lake, and pressed forward toward the mountain Ṛishya-mukha, where lived the monkey raja, Sugrīva.[1]

Sugrīva and his monkey counselors beheld their approach from a fort on the top of the mountain, and the raja said, "There are two men coming from the Pampa; they are dressed like devotees, but they carry arms. I fear they are enemies."

But Hanuman, who was the chief among his counselors, answered, "Be of good cheer, oh Sugrīva, for these are the sons of a raja, and they have come for our deliverance." Then Hanuman descended the mountain to meet the travelers, and escorted them into the presence of his king.

Rāma told his story to Sugrīva, and the monkey king replied, "Some days ago I was sitting here with my counselors, when a fearful darkness came over the whole mountain, and looking upward we saw the terrible Rāvaṇa passing over us. In his arms he held a beautiful woman, who was calling upon the trees and the sun to rescue her, and who, as they passed us, threw down her ornaments and her veil, which we have kept, hoping to identify her by them."

1 In the southern part of India there are multitudes of monkeys of great intelligence and shrewdness. Their successful trips over almost impassable barriers and their apparent organization have made a strong impression upon the superstitious natives, who seem to regard them as creatures half human and half divine. In the "Conclave of the Gods," when Vishnu promised to overthrow the demon, he commanded the other deities to assume the form of monkeys and come to his assistance. It is very probable, however, that the monkeys of Southern India have been confounded with a race of aboriginal natives who worshiped this animal as a god. In a recent letter to the author on this subject Sir Monier Williams says, "The monkeys of the great Epics are really the aboriginal tribes of India, who belong to a lower type of humanity, and were in ancient times very like monkeys or apes in appearance (as they are even now where the aboriginal type is preserved). In the same way, the powerful Dravidians, who conquered the aborigines and were a terror to the Aryan invaders, are called *demons*."

Sugrīva then sent for the ornaments and handed them to Rāma. He took the little silver bells that had tinkled round her graceful ankles and raised them to his lips amidst a flood of tears; the delicate veil he kissed over and over again, while all around him were deeply affected by the scene.

Hanuman built a fire, and Rāma and Sugrīva made a covenant of mutual friendship before it. Then the monkey king told the story of his own grievance as follows: "I am the younger son of a great monkey raja. One day, going out to hunt with my brother Bali, who had just ascended the throne, we found a demon, who fled into a cave. Bali directed me to stand at the mouth of the cave while he went in and killed the demon. I stood there until I saw a stream of blood issuing from the cavern. Still my brother came not out. So, supposing that the demon had slain him, I stopped up the mouth of the cave with a rock and went back to the city. The monkeys accepted me as their raja. In a few days, however, my brother returned, and was very angry with me for supplanting him in the raj. He took my wife to be his own and banished me to this mountain, where I have no raj, as you may see, but only a few faithful followers, who chose to share my exile."

Then said Rāma, "Cast aside, my friend, all fear of Bali; I promise to make you free. Put on your war dress and go to the gates of the palace and challenge your brother to single combat, and when he comes out against you I will slay him."

Then Sugrīva set out for the monkey city, accompanied by Rāma and Lakshmaṇa. When they arrived, the two brothers concealed themselves in the forest, while Sugrīva went forward and in tones of thunder challenged Bali to single combat. Tara, the wife of Bali, tried to prevent him from going out, but maddened by the repeated challenge of his brother he finally flung himself upon him, and they struggled until Rāma, seeing that the battle was going against Sugrīva, sent an arrow through Bali and killed him. All of the monkeys set up pitiful cries and howls of rage when they saw that their king was slain, and the moans of the female monkeys were piteous to hear. But Sugrīva was beside himself with joy when he learned that his brother had fallen before the arrow of Rāma.

The chosen monkeys placed the dead body of Bali upon a litter and taking it upon their shoulders carried it to the burning pyre, followed by the other monkeys, crying bitterly. The hypocritical Sugrīva occupied a prominent place among the mourners. After the funeral rites were completed, Sugrīva took again his own wife, Ruma, and also appropriated Tara, the widow of Bali. It was agreed by all the monkeys that Sugrīva should be their raja, and that Angada, the son of Bali, should be installed as the Yuva-rāja. Sugrīva was therefore installed as the raja of the whole kingdom of monkeys,[1] and as the rainy season

[1] J. Talboys Wheeler says, in his "History of India," "The narrative of Rama's alliance with the monkeys exercises a weird influence upon the imagination. . . . The mind is called upon to deal with nondescript beings, half monkey and half man; having long tails and walking upon all fours, and yet performing funeral rites for a deceased raja, and installing a successor upon the throne, with all the form and ceremony of human beings. It was a monkey raja, surrounded by his monkey counselors, who beheld the approach of Rama and his brother from the bastion of their fort on the mountain. The combats between

had now commenced, Rāma told Sugrīva to enjoy himself in his new capital until the rains were over, and then go with him in search of Sītā.

EXPEDITION OF THE MONKEY GENERAL, HANUMAN.

When the rainy season closed, and the land of India was luxuriant with the glories of her new foliage and delicate blossoms, a large force of monkeys was gathered together and sent out in search of Sītā. The troops were under the command of Hanuman, who was the shrewdest and most powerful of all the monkey generals. When he departed he asked of Rāma some token which he could give to Sīta if he found her, as a proof that he was indeed a messenger sent from her husband. Rāma gave him a ring which he had received on his wedding day from Janaka, the father of Sītā.

The expedition moved to the southward and searched the country in every direction without finding any clew to the location of the fair captive. After a month spent in this way they were returning to Sugrīva, discouraged and disconsolate, when one evening, as they had composed their weary limbs for the night, they saw upon a distant crag the chief of vultures, Sampati. One of the monkeys ventured to climb up the crag where he was sitting and inquired

Sugriva and Bali are the combats of monkeys. As regards the narrative, it certainly seems to refer to some real event among the aboriginal tribes: viz., the quarrel between an elder and a younger brother for the possession of a raj, and the subsequent alliance of Rama with the younger brother. It is somewhat remarkable that Rama appears to have formed an alliance with the wrong party, for the right of Bali was evidently superior to that of Sugriva, and it is especially worthy of note that Rama compassed the death of Bali by an act contrary to all the rules of fair fighting." (See Vol. II, pp. 323-324.)

reverently of him if he remembered having seen the demon king rushing through the air during the last few months. "Indeed," answered the vulture, "I remember it well, for I was upon the wing in search of food, and not a living creature was in sight. A terrible horror seemed to fill the very air, and not even a mouse ventured forth that I might appease my hunger. As I searched everywhere in vain I noticed that the sky was growing dark, as if a tempest were hovering above us, and glancing upward I saw the terrible Rāvaṇa. His fiery eyes glared upon me; but his attention was diverted from me by a pitiful cry from a beautiful woman whom he held in his arms, and hurrying into a thicket I escaped with my life." "That beautiful woman is the object of our search," said the monkey. "Can you tell me which way the demon went?"

"Yes, he went toward the island of Ceylon, and it is doubtless in his palace in the city of Lankā that you will find his captive," responded Sampati, as he smoothed his feathers and began to make himself comfortable for the night. "I have often soared above it, and it is the finest city in this part of the world; but the Rākshasas who inhabit it are even more dangerous and terrible then men are, and I would advise you monkeys to stay away and let them alone." But the adventurous messenger, overjoyed at the reception of the tidings, hastened to his commander with the information. As soon as the morning dawned Hanuman awoke his followers, and after a hasty breakfast of fruit and leaves in the branches of the trees the little fellows started bravely for the sea coast. But they beheld the island they sought fully sixty miles from the shore, nor were there boats or bridges to enable them to make the hazardous passage.

Hanuman called for volunteers to go to the island and obtain the desired information, but not one of the dismayed little soldiers raised a hand. At last Hanuman said, "As none of you dare to undertake it, I will go myself. But I shall jump all the way across these great billows, and land upon the island." Then there was a great cheering and chattering, for besides the admiration felt for their brave commander, every ape was greatly relieved to know that he would not be compelled to undertake the task. Hanuman then distended his form until it was as large as a mountain, and his body glittered like gold in the sunlight, while his face was as red as rubies. His arms were extended like the wings of a great dragon, and his tail was so long that the end of it could not be seen. He took his position upon the mountain Mandara (the fabled center of the earth) and cried in a voice of thunder,

"Swift as a shaft from Râma's bow
To Râvan's city I will go."

Then extending his long arms he drew in his neck, erected his ears, and raising himself upon the mountain sprang toward the south and alighted upon the island of Ceylon with a bound that made the island tremble. The demon king sent for his counselors and demanded of them why the earth was quivering beneath his capital city. They answered that it was an earthquake, but one who was bolder than the others ventured to hint that the earthquake had been sent by the gods on account of the detention of Sītā, and advised that she be restored to her friends before the island was entirely destroyed. But the haughty king replied that he had not sent for them because he needed any advice, and angrily dismissed his counselors.

LANKĀ.

Hanuman had alighted upon the summit of the Sabula mountain, and stood looking down upon the city of Lankā, which was a hundred miles in length and thirty in breadth. It was completely surrounded by numerous walls and canals, one within another. Inside of the great outer canal was a broad belt of thick forest, which was infested with wild animals. Inside of that was an impenetrable wall of iron, with a gate on each of the four sides, guarded by hundreds of Rākshasas. Lankā itself was beautified with lakes and parks and palaces of Oriental magnificence. In the center of the city rose the lofty domes of the palace of Rāvaṇa, and every parapet was crowded with armed demons, whose duty it was to guard their king, whether he was asleep or awake.

In order to reconnoiter without alarming the foe, Hanuman assumed the form of a cat. In this shape he slipped by the guards and through the gates with perfect impunity. The broad streets were set with gems, but such was the discipline of Rāvaṇa that no one dared to pick one up, even if it became loosened in its setting. The magnificent houses were open to receive the cool air of the evening, and within them he saw hideous Rākshasas, of every shape and form. Some of them were as tall as the trees and others were dwarfs. Some of them had only two legs, while others had three or four. Some had heads like serpents, others wore the features of donkeys. Some had heads like horses, while the faces of others were decorated with trunks like elephants.

While the monkey general in the shape of a cat was carefully observing these things, the shades of night settled down upon the city and the streets were deserted.

THE PALACE OF RĀVAṆA.

After the demons had fallen asleep, the strange scout slipped quietly into the palace of raja Rāvaṇa. This resplendent mansion was surrounded on all sides with a canal, from whose clear waters rose the green leaves and bright blossoms of the lotus, while the evening air was laden with their fragrance. Within this watery barrier the golden walls arose to such a height that the birds could not fly above them, and the pillars on each side of the gates were made of black crystal. The gates were guarded by thousands of Rākshasas, and over the walls floated the soft strains of music. "Surely," thought the little spy, "this raja Rāvaṇa must have been a very virtuous man in his former life, and for this reason he enjoys so much wealth now." Then he slipped through the gate and into the inner apartments of the palace, where he found fountains and pools of clear water, with masses of gorgeous tropical flowers around them.

The sleeping room of Rāvaṇa presented a scene of

barbaric splendor. The walls were blazing with gold and gems, while the floor was inlaid with black crystal. The royal couch was as beautiful as art could make it. The draperies were as soft and white as waves of milk. Golden jars filled with water stood in the corners of the room, and lamps of precious stones were hung from the ceiling. Hundreds of beautiful women were sleeping in various parts of the great room, and the demon king lay upon his royal bed, a crown of gold upon each black and terrible head, and his twenty hands laden with heavy jeweled rings. While he slept, Hanuman looked carefully around the room, but among all the beautiful women there he found no one that answered to the description of Sītā. Leaving the palace, he entered a luxuriant

AŚOKA GROVE.

He hastily climbed into the branches of one of the trees[1] and looking around him saw not far away a beautiful woman, whose eyes were red with constant weeping. She was sitting sadly upon the ground surrounded by hideous Rākshasa women. The fair girl reminded him of a beautiful doe surrounded by tigresses, which were ready at any moment to feed upon her delicate flesh. Her attendants were pleading with her to become the wife of Rāvaṇa, but she only replied by chanting in a sweet minor key the name of "Rāma!" "Rāma!"

While Hanuman still looked, the demon king himself appeared, attended by all the women of his court.

1 The Joneala Asoka is one of the loveliest trees of that tropical clime, its foliage being crowned with a profusion of gorgeous red blossoms.

The little spy then crept along the branches nearer to Sītā. When Rāvaṇa with his attendants came into the grove, she started and shivered with terror. The raja appealed to her to wipe away her tears and enjoy the luxuries of his court. "Do not fear me," he said, "for I am your slave and you need have no fear of being discovered by others, for no man can enter my palace. Let me send for women who will wash you with water and costly perfumes; who will dress your beautiful hair and adorn your lovely form with magnificent robes and the richest jewels of the east. You shall be the mistress of all my other wives and the queen of my heart."

But Sītā answered, "Oh, lord of Lankā, you are renowned throughout the world for your wealth, strength, and valor. Do not, I implore you, soil your reputation by wickedness. Restore me, I pray you, to my husband, Rāma, and entreat his forgiveness. My husband is my wealth. He is more to me than all the riches at your command."

He continued to plead with her until she turned upon him and threatened him with the anger of her husband. "Oh, wicked Rāvaṇa," she cried, "you have not long to live. Your golden Lankā will soon be a heap of ashes and your numberless army shall fall like ripened grain before the arrows of Rāma. There is as much difference between you and him as there is between a mouse and a lion, or a mosquito and a hawk. You are only a glow-worm, but he is the noonday sun. You are a grain of sand, but he is a precious stone."

Stung by her taunts, the demon's eyes flashed fire.

"Thy language," said he, "is more like that of a master than of a creature who is helpless in my hands. I will give thee, however, two months in which to decide the matter, and if at the end of that time thou consent not to become my wife,

"My cooks shall mince thy limbs with steel,
And serve thee for my morning meal."

He turned haughtily away and with his attendants returned to his palace.

INTERVIEW BETWEEN HANUMAN AND SĪTĀ.

At last she was left alone with her agony and terror; but while she moaned aloud in her suffering, she heard a voice in the trees above her sweetly chanting the name of "Rāma." Looking upward she saw only a diminutive monkey and concluded that the voice was an illusion. But the monkey said, "I am the slave of Rāma, and I have been sent by him to discover his bride;" then coming quickly down from the tree and bowing himself before her he proved his claim by presenting her with Rāma's signet ring. At the sight of the ring she wept for joy and catching hold of the precious jewel pressed it to her lips, then placed it upon her head in token of his sovereignty and afterwards clasped it to her heart. Hanuman proposed to carry her away upon his back, but she answered that so small a monkey could not carry her across the ocean. Thereupon he increased his size to more than giant proportions, and while she looked at him in wonder she said, "I do believe you could carry me; but I will never willingly touch the form of any man except my husband. Besides, if you took me away by stealth, the world would say that Rāma is a coward and is unable to punish Rāvaṇa." So she dismissed him with loving messages for her husband and with an admonition for him to hasten to her relief, as only two months remained for her to live unless he came. She sent to Rāma the only ring she still possessed and placed his upon her own finger, begging Hanuman to hasten his departure with her messages.

HANUMAN DESTROYS THE MANGO GROVE.

But Rāma's messenger was not content to leave the beautiful island without avenging in some way Sītā's wrong upon the demon king; so in the form of an immense baboon he rushed into a beautiful grove of mango trees, and tore off the rich fruit and foliage, breaking the branches until he destroyed every tree in the grove. The guards of Rākshasas were awakened by the noise, and instead of stopping to do battle with the invader, they rushed off and informed the king that a huge monkey had entered Lankā and was destroying all his trees.

When Rāvaṇa heard of this, he ordered an army of eighty thousand Rākshasas to capture the invader and bring him in chains before the king. But the valiant monkey after a short conflict sent the whole body of troops to the regions of Yama. When the king heard that his soldiers were all slain, he sent the giants of his army, but they too met the same fate. At last a shrewd Rākshasa captured the marauder with a powerful noose, and he was led into the council hall of Rāvaṇa.

Hanuman then defied the king to his face and declaring himself to be the ambassador of Rāma demanded the restoration of Sītā. But the king arose from his throne in a terrible rage and ordered that the monkey should be beheaded. His chief counselor, however, declared that they had no right to kill an ambassador, although, according to the Śāstras, they could mutilate him in one of three ways. He might be disfigured, or beaten with stripes, or his head might be shaved.

Then said Rāvaṇa, "I will not kill this monkey, but he shall not go unpunished; and as his tail is his principal ornament, I shall have it set on fire and burned."

THE BURNING OF LANKĀ.

The king's orders were quickly obeyed, and the monkey's tail was wrapped with inflammable fabrics, which were soaked with oil and set on fire. But Hanuman immediately reduced his body to a diminutive size and, slipping quickly out of the noose, sprang upon a wall, and before they could recapture him was lashing the roof with his flaming tail.

"He scaled the palaces, and spread
The conflagration where he sped.
From house to house he hurried on,
And the wild flames behind him shone.
Each mansion of the foe he scaled,
And furious fire its roof assailed,
Till all the common ruin shared.
Vibhīshan's[1] house alone was spared.

[1] The counselor who had saved his life.

From blazing pile to pile he sprang,
And loud his shout of triumph rang.

. . . .

Loud was the roar the demons raised
'Mid walls that split and beams that blazed,
As each with vain endeavor strove
To stay the flames in house or grove.
He saw the flames ascend and curl
Round turkis, diamond, and pearl,
While silver floods and molten gold
From ruined wall and lattice rolled.
As fire grows fiercer as it feeds
On wood and grass and crackling weeds,
So Hanuman the ruin eyed,
With fury still unsatisfied."

HANUMAN REJOINS THE MONKEY ARMY.

Leaving the blazing city to be cared for by its terror-stricken inhabitants, Hanuman rushed to the seashore and with a mighty leap landed in the midst of his own troops and triumphantly related the story of his exploits in Lankā. The army was placed in marching order and joyfully set out to carry the glad tidings to raja Sugrīva, chanting as they advanced the name of Rāma. When they arrived at the court Hanumau advanced into the royal presence, bowing himself before the monkey raja and also before Rāma, to whom he told the story of his adventures. He placed in Rāma's hand the ring which Sītā had given him, and delivered her messages, saying that unless she could be rescued within two months, Rāvaṇa would surely accomplish his murderous threat. Rāma received the jewel with great emotion and made a solemn vow that within two months the demon king should pay the penalty of his fearful crime.

CHAPTER XVI.

THE STORY OF THE RĀMĀYAṆA, CONCLUDED.

THE MONKEY EXPEDITION AGAINST LANKĀ — THE SOUTHERN SEA — THE OCEAN BRIDGE — INVASION OF LANKĀ — RĀVAṆA AND RĀMA IN SINGLE COMBAT — THE DEATH OF RĀVAṆA — RESTORATION OF SĪTĀ — SĪTĀ'S TRIAL AND VINDICATION — TRIUMPHANT RETURN TO AYODHYĀ — THE BANISHMENT OF SĪTĀ — THE SONS OF SĪTĀ — THE DEPARTURE.

ONE bright morning the tropical sun looked down upon an innumerable host of monkeys ready to march upon Lankā at the word of command. The raja had given the control of his troops into the hands of Rāma, who was the commander general of the expedition, while Lakshmaṇa and Sugrīva were his chiefs of staff. The vast army extended in length a thousand miles. When they were all arrayed in military order, the heroic monkeys sounded their conch shells, and the earth trembled beneath their exultant screams and the lashing of their tails.[1] The innumerable host poured over the mountains and through the great forests, and living upon the fruits and leaves of the

[1] See the Adhyatma version which is divided into seven books bearing the same titles as Valmiki's version. Its object is to show that Rama is a representation of the Supreme Spirit, and that Sita is a type of Nature.

trees they desolated the land like an army of locusts, leaving not even a flower in their track. They swept like a torrent over the fertile fields and flowery vales, until they reached the fair shores of

THE SOUTHERN SEA.

Here they called a halt, for before them the wild billows foamed with rage and the dark tide came sweeping in closer and closer to their feet with every throbbing pulse from the great heart of the ocean. Lankā lay in safety far beyond their sight, entrenched behind the pathless billows. While the chiefs were gathered in counsel upon the shore, another night came down upon them and the starlight touched with silver the heads of the dashing waves.

Wearied by the rapid march and perplexed by the hopeless situation, Rāma left the council of his chiefs and with his head bared to the cool night air walked slowly to the water's edge. As the dark breakers came rolling in he bent above them, invoking the aid of the fair goddess of the sea, when suddenly in the coral chambers beneath the surf there flashed a phosphorescent light, which slowly formed itself into a beautiful woman. Her white shoulders gleamed like pearl beneath the tide and her crimson lips were wet with the kisses of Neptune. Her heavy hair was bound with delicate sprays of the seaweed and her shell-tinted robe was fastened with branches of coral. In gentle tones she asked, "What wilt thou, Rāma, that I shall do for thee?" "Fair goddess of the sea," he cried, "a demon has stolen my wife away and crushed my heart beneath his feet. My beautiful bride is a prisoner on yonder isle—help me to bridge this pathless deep and avenge her wrongs with my gallant troops."

Again her silvery voice was heard amid the roaring of the surf: "Say to Nala that he shall build a bridge, and every stone he touches shall float upon my waves." Then turning away she waved her graceful hand, and the dark drapery of the waves hid her from his sight.

THE OCEAN BRIDGE.

As soon as the crimson light of morning kissed the mountain peaks and crowned the ocean waves with light, Rāma sounded upon his conch shell the call of "Attention. Promptly his troops were gathered at his feet, and he sent for Nala, the shrewdest general in his army. After giving him a few directions he turned to the rank and file and ordered them to bring to Nala all the material they could find, with which to build a bridge to the fair island of Ceylon, that they might march in triumph to its capital city. All the weariness of the long march was forgotten, and the order was received with screams and shouts of exultation. In a few minutes thousands of monkeys were running in every direction, and bringing to Nala rocks and the trunks of trees, with which to build the great bridge. Even mountains were torn up and hurled upon the waters, where beneath the magic touch of Nala every tree and stone and the great masses of earth floated together into one unyielding mass.

In the meantime the mother of Rāvaṇa began to see evil omens on every side, and calling to her other son, Vibhīshaṇa, she begged of him to advise Rāvaṇa to restore Sītā to her husband. But Rāvaṇa was so vain and self-conceited that he would receive no advice from his friends, and only abused his brother for interfering with his affairs. The bridge was at last completed, and one night the strange army marched over it and encamped on the island of Lankā, near the Sabula Mountain. Vibhīshaṇa, the brother of Rāvaṇa, deserted his people and went over to the camp of Rāma; whereupon the commanding general ordered water to be brought from the sea, and pouring it upon the head of Vibhīshaṇa declared him to be the raja of Lankā instead of his brother Rāvaṇa.

INVASION OF LANKĀ.

Rāvaṇa sat in state in his council hall upon a throne set with precious stones. Ten crowns of pearls and jewels were upon his ten heads and thousands of giants surrounded his court. A rich canopy of strung pearls was suspended over his throne and he held a wine cup in his hand, while beautiful girls amused him with dance and song.

But his counselors entered his chamber and informed him that Rāma had landed his troops and was preparing to attack the city. He immediately sent for the commander-in-chief of his armies and told him to gather the hosts of the Rākshasas and make ready for battle. At the sound of the bugle they were drawn up in military array before the demon king, who ordered them to meet the invaders at the gates of the city and bring him the heads of their chiefs. The army of demons marched out of the fortress to the strains of discordant music. Their cavalry was mounted on buffaloes, camels, lions, hyenas, wolves, and even hogs. Their arms consisted of swords, clubs, bows and arrows, spears, and many nondescript weapons.

In the meantime Rāma, having marshaled the ranks of the monkeys, placed himself at their head, and led them to the attack. Some of them had torn up the trunks of trees for weapons and some carried immense rocks in their arms, while others depended upon their teeth and nails, which they had sharpened like swords. They were drawn up in long lines of battle, with ten million monkeys in each line. Sounding their shells they marched to the fray shouting, "Victory to Rāma!" The fight was long and the issue doubtful, when Sugrīva, seizing a large tree, tore it up by the roots and hurled it upon Indrajit, the famous son of Rāvaṇa, who had once conquered Indra. The tree crushed his chariot and killed his horses and charioteer. The demon retreated and offered a sacrifice to Agni, when suddenly out of the fire came a golden chariot drawn by four horses, and Indrajit, seating himself within it, became invisible and discharged his arrows at Rāma and Lakshmaṇa, who could not see whence they came. At last he threw a noose made of serpents over the two brothers and caught them in its meshes. But Garuḍa, the bird upon which Vishṇu rides, came to the rescue, and when the serpents saw him they fled, leaving the brothers unharmed.

Finding that the tide of battle was going against his troops Rāvaṇa marched to the field in person at the head of powerful re-enforcements. His ten faces were black with rage and his heads appeared like rough mountains. His twenty eyes gleamed like fiery furnaces and his eyebrows and whiskers were composed of the shining bodies of black serpents. As the terrible conflict continued, Rāma and Rāvaṇa came face to face in the fight and were soon engaged in

SINGLE COMBAT.

The god Indra looked down from heaven, and seeing that Rāma was without a chariot, sent him his own, with armor and weapons, and also his charioteer. As the terrible duel progressed, growing more and more desperate every hour, the gods became so absorbed in the fight that they could not refrain from joining in the fray, even as the gods of Greece took part in the siege of Troy.

> "When the powers descending swelled the fight
> Then tumult rose; fierce rage and pale affright
> Varied each face; then Discord sounds alarms,
> Earth echoes, and the nations rush to arms.
> Now through the trembling shores Minerva calls,
> And now she thunders from the Grecian walls.
> Mars, hovering o'er his Troy, his terror shrouds
> In gloomy tempest and a night of clouds."[1]

Vishṇu and Indra with all their allies took sides with Rāma, while the evil spirits joined their forces with Rāvaṇa. The demon king rode in a magic car which was drawn by horses having human faces. The armies on both sides soon stopped fighting, for the whole interest of the troops was concentrated upon the terrible conflict between Rāma and Rāvaṇa, in which the

[1] Il., Book XX.

gods themselves took part. The demon king was at last driven from the field by his charioteer, but he furiously commanded him to return to the fight. The battle raged with undiminished fury for seven days and nights. Again and again Rāvaṇa was borne down by the missiles of Rāma, and his charioteer drove his master in a fainting condition to the walls of his castle. As soon as he recovered, however, he angrily bade him return to the contest.

"With wondrous power and mighty skill
The giant fought with Rāma still.
Each at his foe his chariot drove,
And still for death or victory strove.
The warriors' steeds together dashed,
And pole with pole re-echoing clashed.
Dense clouds of arrows Rāma shot
With that strong arm that rested not;
And spear and mace and club and brand
Fell in dire rain from Rāvan's hand.
The storm of missiles fiercely cast
Stirred up the oceans with its blast,
And serpent-gods and fiends who dwell
Below were troubled by the swell.
The earth with hill and plain and brook
And grove and garden reeled and shook;
The very sun grew cold and pale,
And horror stilled the rising gale."

As the fight grew more and more desperate, the combatants drew closer, and at last an arrow hissing from Rāma's bow cut off one of Rāvaṇa's heads; but like the hydra whose heads were severed by Hercules, another immediately grew in its place. Again and again he cut a head from the demon, only to see it renewed by the time he could draw his bow again.

"Then to his deadly string, the pride
Of Rāghu's race[1] a shaft applied.
Sharp as a serpent's venomed fang,
Straight to its mark the arrow sprang
And from the giant's body shred
With trenchant steel the monstrous head.
There might the triple world behold
That severed head adorned with gold;
But when all eyes were bent to view,
Swift in its stead another grew.
Again the shaft was pointed well,
Again the head divided fell;
But still as each to earth was cast,
Another head succeeded fast.
A hundred bright with fiery flame
Fell low before the victor's aim.
Yet Rāvan by no sign betrayed
That death was near or strength decayed;
The doubtful fight he still maintained
And on his foe his missiles rained.
In air, on earth, on plain, on hill,
With awful might he battled still.
And through the hours of night and day
The conflict knew no pause or stay."

Rāma, however, had the charmed arrow which had been given to him by Brahmā to use only as a last resort.

1 Raghu was the great-grandfather of Rama.

RĀVAṆA'S DEATH.

"Then Mātali to Rāma cried,
'Let other arms the day decide;
Launch at the foe thy dart whose fire
Was kindled by the Almighty Sire.'
He ceased, and Rāghu's son obeyed.
Upon his string the hero laid
An arrow like a snake that hissed,
Whose fiery flight had never missed.
By Brahmā's self on him bestowed
When forth to fight, Lord Indra rode.
. . . .
He laid it on the trusted cord
And turned the point at Lankā's lord;
And swift the limb-dividing dart
Pierced the huge chest and cleft the heart,
And dead he fell upon the plain,
Like Vṛitra[1] by the Thunderer slain.
The Rākshas host when Rāvan fell,
Sent forth a wild, terrific yell,
Then turned and fled, all hope resigned,
Through Lankā's gates, nor looked behind.
His voice each joyous Vanar raised,
And 'Rāma, conquering Rāma,' praised.
Soft from celestial minstrels came
The sound of music and acclaim;
Soft, fresh, and cool, a rising breeze
Brought odors from the heavenly trees;
And, ravishing the sight and smell,
A wondrous rain of blossoms fell;

1 The spirit of evil who was slain by Indra, "the Thunderer."

And voices breathed round Rāghu's son,
'Champion of gods, well done, well done.'"

Ere long the cry that the monarch had fallen was borne to his palace, and all his wives came out with disheveled hair and went to the battle-field, uttering bitter cries as they passed through the terror-stricken throng in the streets. When they came to the dead body of the demon, some of them fainted and others caressed the hideous creature as if he were still alive. Rāma was touched by their sorrow, and ordered Vibhīshaṇa to take the women back to the inner apartments of the palace and perform the funeral rites for his brother Rāvaṇa.

The dead raja was buried with elaborate ceremonies and all the pomp appropriate to an imperial funeral. As soon as the days of mourning were ended, Vibhīshaṇa was installed as raja of Lankā.

THE RESTORATION OF SĪTĀ.

When all the rites had been performed, Rāma formally demanded of the new raja the return of his wife. Vibhīshaṇa immediately ordered that a multitude of maids should attend upon Sītā; that they should dress her hair and adorn her person in a way that befitted her queenly estate. She had received the crown of youth from the aged devotee in the forest and was beautiful as a dream. Neither tears nor suffering had power to mar her bright face or change the delicate lines of her beautiful mouth.

His lovely queen was brought in imperial state to Rāma, attended by a long procession of musicians and dancing girls, her palanquin well-nigh covered with flowers. Rāma ordered the carriage to be opened and bade his wife descend, that her great beauty might be seen by the troops who had so valiantly fought for her rescue. Although this order was a violation of Hindū etiquette, which did not allow a wife to be seen unveiled, the loving Sītā obeyed without hesitation and stepped out in full view of the multitude. A low murmur of admiration passed through the throng as the beautiful vision dawned upon them. Sītā stood in the presence of her lord, with her loving eyes upon the ground, while with joined hands she reverently waited his summons to fly into his arms. The thought of his loving welcome had been her only comfort in the terrible hours of her captivity, and her loyal heart hungered for the warm love and caresses which had been her life in the years that were gone.

But no word of affection, no look of love, greeted the restored captive. With folded arms and stony eyes he thus addressed her:

> "Lady, at length my task is done,
> And thou, the prize of war, art won.
> . . . .
> If from my home my queen was reft,
> This arm hath well avenged the theft;
> And in the field has washed away
> The blot that on my honor lay.
> . . . .
> But, lady, 'twas not love for thee
> That led mine army o'er the sea.
> . . . .
> I battled to avenge the cause
> Of honor and insulted laws,

My love is fled, for on thy fame
Lies the dark blot of sin and shame.
And thou art hateful as the light
That flashes on the injured sight;
The world is all before thee; flee!
Go where thou wilt, but not with me.

. . . .

For Rāvan bore thee through the sky,
And fixed on thine his evil eye;
About thy waist his arm he threw,
Close to his breast his captive drew,
And kept thee, vassal of his power,
An inmate of his ladies' bower."

At these cruel words the smooth cheek paled with agony, the beautiful eyes filled with tears, and the delicate frame quivered beneath his scorn like an aspen leaf swept by a terrible tempest.

SĪTĀ'S TRIAL AND VINDICATION.

The beautiful woman stood trembling in the presence of the man she had so long worshiped, and who had chosen to reward her devotion by public humiliation and accusation. At last amidst her sobs she answered:

"Canst thou, a high-born prince, dismiss
A high-born dame with speech like this?
Such words befit the meanest kind,
Not princely birth and generous mind.
By all my virtuous life I swear
I am not what thy words declare.
If some are faithless, wilt thou find

No love or truth in womankind?
Doubt others if thou wilt, but own
The truth which all my life has shown.
If when the giant seized his prey
Within his hated arms I lay
And felt the grasp I dreaded, blame
Fate and the robber, not thy dame.
What could a helpless woman do?
My heart was thine and still was true."

Then turning to his brother Lakshmaṇa, who had always been her loyal friend, she commanded him to prepare for her a funeral pile, declaring that its fire was her only refuge in her dark despair. Said she, "I will not live beneath the weight of the shame and injustice which have been heaped upon me; I will end my woes by entering the fire, and thou, my brother, in preparing it for me wilt prove my best and truest friend."

"His mournful eyes the hero raised
And wistfully on Rāma gazed,
In whose stern look no ruth was seen,
No mercy for the weeping queen.
No chieftain dared to meet those eyes,
To pray, to question, or advise.
The word was passed, the wood was piled,
And fain to die stood Janak's child.
She slowly paced around her lord,
The gods with reverent act adored.
Then, raising suppliant hands, the dame
Prayed humbly to the lord of flame:
'As this fond heart by virtue swayed

From Rāghu's son has never strayed,
So universal witness, fire,
Protect my body on the pyre.
As Rāghu's son has idly laid
This charge on Sītā, hear and aid.'
She ceased and, fearless to the last,
Within the flames' wild fury passed."

Lakshmaṇa and others looked anxiously at Rāma, expecting to see some sign of relenting in his stony face; but he was the victim of his own false ideas concerning woman's purity and honor and stood looking on with folded arms, while the flames wreathed the fair form of his wife. The beautiful victim quivered in anguish, and cries of reproach came from the troops. When it was too late to save her from her fate, Rāma seemed to relent, and he cried, "Alas! I have reproached her for nothing—I shall never find so faithful a wife again." But the cruel pyre blazed on amidst the cries and lamentations of the multitude, when lo! the god of fire came forth from the flames, bearing Sītā in his arms, a beautiful living queen.

"Fair as the morning was her sheen,
And gold and gems adorned the queen.
Her form in crimson robes arrayed,
Her hair was bound in glossy braid."

Giving her to Rāma Agni said: "Take her as your wife. She is without a stain. I know the hearts of all, and had she the shadow of a stain upon her chastity she could never have passed in safety from me." Then Rāma placed his arm around her, and ashamed to confess the great wrong that he had done her, complacently said, "I knew my beloved Sītā was chaste and true, but I put her to the test of the fire, lest men should blame me. Now I am free from all censure." His troops applauded him, and Sītā, with that womanly forgiveness which is so nearly akin to the divine, nestled again in her husband's bosom.

TRIUMPHANT RETURN TO AYODHYĀ.

The time of his exile was now drawing to a close, and Rāma ordered that the great golden chariot[1] which had been used by Rāvaṇa should be made ready for their triumphal departure. But Sugrīva and all of the monkeys, and Vibhīshaṇa, and even the inhabitants of Lankā, begged that they might be allowed to witness his inauguration at Ayodhyā. Rāma therefore commanded that all of the monkeys and all of the Rākshasas should enter the golden chariot. Then the great car, laden with millions of monkeys and demons, with Rāma and Sītā in the seat of honor, arose in the air and flew rapidly to the northward. When they arrived at the beautiful mountain of Ćitra-kūṭa, Rāma sent Hanuman to the city in order to inform his brother Bharata of his approach.

When the younger brother received the glad news he summoned his counselors together and issued a joyful proclamation to the people: "Cast aside all sorrow and grief and prepare to receive Rāma. Let the whole city be adorned and let worship be offered to every god. Let every horse and elephant and chariot be

[1] This was the self-moving car Pushpaka, which the demon king had stolen from the god of wealth.

gotten ready, and let every man go out to meet Rāma on his return to Ayodhyā."

When the people heard that Rāma was indeed returning, the whole city rejoiced and began to array itself for the festival. The streets were swept and sprinkled with perfumed waters and strewn with flowers. At the foot of every tree was placed a golden jar of sacred water, filled with the beautiful branches of the mango tree or sprays of the feathery tamarind and wreathed with tropical flowers. The houses were also decorated with floral designs and with flags. Then the great procession was formed, and with flying banners and strains of music the whole army went out to greet Rāma. Upon his head Bharata carried his brother's golden sandals, above which was held the royal canopy. Two men attended the sandals, fanning them with snow-white fans. Bharata was surrounded by all the ministers and counselors of the raj and by a multitude of people from the city. When Rāma and his attendants met them, the forest resounded with shouts of welcome. The two brothers embraced each other affectionately, and through the long lines rang the shout of "Victory to Rāma!"

Rāma bowed at the feet of Kauśalyā, and the glad mother took her son once more in her arms and blessed him with her warm caresses. Rāma dismissed the chariot Pushpaka, and bade it return to its rightful owner, Kuvera, (the god of wealth) from whom it had been taken by Rāvaṇa. Then Rāma and his brothers were bathed with perfumed waters and anointed with fragrant oils, and laying aside their devotee's dress of bark put on a costume of yellow silk, with many jewels. The ladies of the court attended to the toilet of Sītā, and she, too, was arrayed in exquisite garments.

The great procession then started to return to Ayodhyā, and Rāma directed the monkeys to choose whatever conveyance they pleased. Some of them, therefore, mounted the chariots or suspended themselves from the edge above the wheels, and others curled their tails around the tusks of the elephants and rocked to the swaying motion of the animals, while others still clung to the manes of the horses. When all was ready the strains of music again pealed through the forest, and the great procession went back to the capital city.

Rāma was installed as the raja amid the great rejoicing of the people, and the city wore its gala robes, while the streets resounded with glad music for many days and nights. "Long live Maha-raja Rāma," was the joyous cry that rang through the air at all hours of the night, and "Long live Maha-raja Rāma," was the glad refrain that greeted the light of the morning. Day after day musicians haunted the windows of the palace, chanting the praises of the imperial pair, and the years went softly by, wearing the sandals of peace and the bright robes of happiness.

"No widow mourned her murdered mate,
No house was ever desolate;
The happy land no murrain knew,
The flocks and herds increased and grew.
The earth her kindly fruits supplied;
No harvest failed — no children died.

Unknown were want, disease and crime,
So calm, so happy was the time."

BANISHMENT OF SĪTĀ.

At last, however, it began to be whispered in the capital that a woman who had spent months of her life at the court of the demon king was unfit to be the queen of Ayodhyā. One of his ministers who was bolder than the others found courage to say to Rāma, "There is poverty among your subjects, oh, Maharaja! because of your sin in taking Sītā back." The cloud of discontent continued to gather around the royal pair, and occasionally the rumors were brought to the ears of the king. He knew that his wife was as pure as the snow upon the distant peak of the Himālaya; he knew that she was as far above immorality as that icy coronal was above the dust in the vale at its feet. The god of fire had brought her out of the flames because of her unconquerable chastity, and had presented her to him as pure gold is brought from the crucible. But this divine Rāma, the mere chanting of whose name is still supposed to bring absolution from all sin, had not the manliness to stand by his loyal wife in the hour of her greatest need.

She had gladly left a court of luxury to follow in his exile the man she worshiped. For his sake she had bravely met the terrors of the jungle, and but for her loyal love to him she would not have been exposed to the terrible hand of the demon king. But his danger was passed; prosperity now flowed upon Rāma in one broad golden river, and his vanity craved even a stronger adulation from his subjects.

He was the model of all the Hindū divinities, the noblest and bravest of all the gods of their mythology; but he turned treacherously against the brave woman whose life had been one long scene of devotion to him. She was soon to become a mother — soon to give him an heir to the throne; but without deigning to give her any explanation, he sent her away to face the dangers of the jungle, under the pretense that she was to visit the sages there. She was accompanied only by Lakshmaṇa, who was ordered to explain the situation to her and then leave her alone in a thicket which was near the mountain of Ćitrakūṭa.[1]

Here came the banished wife and paused in terrible agony not far from the cot which she had made so happy for her exiled prince. Her faithful brother had wept bitterly when he told her of the cruel orders of her husband, and besought her to try to reach the hermitage of Vālmīki. But she knew not which way to turn to find the humble home of the devotees. Overwhelmed with suffering she wandered over a sandy plain, on which the tropical sun blazed like a fiery furnace. Her tender feet were torn with thorns and burned to blisters, while ever and anon her frame quivered with a new, strange agony that she had never known before. Physical suffering is hard enough to bear, but cannot be compared with the sufferings of a loyal heart which is being trampled to death by the

1 There is also a legend to the effect that Rama sent his faithful brother into exile, and J. Talboys Wheeler remarks that "We might almost infer from the current of national tradition that Rama as he advanced in years became jealous and peevish, like Henry the Eighth."—(Hist. of Ind., Vol. II, p. 405.)

object of its worship. But she had given him so much of tenderness, and Rāma knew the faithful love of his wife so well, that he was not afraid to outrage her purest and most sacred feelings, assured that the wounded heart would gladly creep back to his, whenever in his own royal pleasure he saw fit to treat her decently. The exiled wife still struggled on her unknown way, her throat parched with thirst and her delicate skin scorched by the blazing sun, until the birds in pity dipped their pinions in the waters of the Ganges and fanned her feverish face, that she might not faint with the heat. The royal tiger, ashamed of the cowardice and treachery of Rāma, left his cool bed in the jungle and walked beside her to protect her from the hungry wolves in the wilderness. But at last she fell fainting by the way and was found in a swoon by Vālmīki the sage, who lifting her tenderly in his arms carried her to his hermitage, and gave her into the care of his noble wife.

THE SONS OF SĪTĀ.

The very night that she was taken into the humble home of the devotees, Sītā gave birth to two beautiful boys whom she named Lava and Kuśa. But no word of inquiry was sent from Rāma to learn the fate of his wife. Living in luxurious splendor himself, he did not ask whether Sītā had found a place of refuge or had been devoured by the wild beasts of the jungle.

The two sons of Sītā were carefully educated by Vālmīki. Before they were twenty years of age they had attained to physical and mental manhood. The devoted mother lived in her noble boys and poured upon them the wealth of affection which had been so cruelly despised by Rāma. They in return almost worshiped their beautiful mother, doing everything in their power for her comfort and happiness.

As the years passed by Rāma began to feel uneasy, not on account of his cruelty to Sītā, but because he had slain Rāvaṇa, who was the son of a Brāhman. To slay a Brāhman was a grievous sin to the Hindūs, he therefore resolved to perform the horse sacrifice and thereby obtain absolution for his crime, in order that he might not forfeit any of the rewards in future births.

The horse was procured and given his liberty with the usual ceremonies, and Rāma's younger brother Śatru-ghna followed him with an army. As he wandered away without control he at last came to Ćitrakūṭa, where the sons of Sītā were hunting. Lava had just sent his unfailing arrow through the heart of an antelope, when his eyes fell upon a magnificent horse which appeared to be entirely uncontrolled. He captured the beautiful animal and was leading it away, when he was attacked by the whole army. Turning upon them, however, he called his brother, who was a little further in the jungle, and the two gallant boys soon put the whole army to flight. When Rāma heard what had occurred, he angrily ordered Lakshmaṇa to go out with another body of men and recover the horse. But his troops also were defeated by the wonderful prowess of Lava and Kuśa, and he himself was left for dead upon the field.

At last Rāma went in person at the head of an army, determined to conquer an enemy who threatened to become invincible. Having reached the place of the former defeat he went alone to meet the two young men, and ascertain if possible who they were. Soon he saw two splendid specimens of manhood coming toward him with a fearless step and an imperial bearing, which told him they were of royal birth. The youths bowed reverently before him, and Rāma inquired of them whose sons they were. "Our mother's name," answered Lava, "is Sītā, but we do not know who our father is. We have been brought up and educated by the good sage Vālmīki, who lives near us."

When Rāma realized that his own sons stood before him, he was overcome with emotion and before he could speak Vālmīki appeared upon the scene and begged of him to be reconciled to his wife.

He then stated to Vālmīki that he knew Sītā to be the soul of purity and was rejoiced to find that his sons had become such noble men. "But," said he, "it is necessary to prove the chastity of Sītā," and turning to his assembled troops, which had been brought forward by his command, he complacently announced to them that Sītā would again demonstrate her innocence by undergoing the fiery ordeal, and ordered Vālmīki to bring his wife into his presence.

THE DEPARTURE OF SĪTĀ.

But the grandest and purest devotion that ever lived in the heart of woman may be murdered by persistent outrage. Rāma had by his own conduct deliberately killed the great love which his faithful wife had borne for him so many years. For the first time in her life Sītā refused to obey his call, declaring that she had no wish to look upon his face again. But her old friend Vālmīki, who had been a father to her in her time of need, urged her to lay aside her personal feelings in the matter, and for the sake of her children to forgive their father. Unable to resist the entreaties of Vālmīki and his noble wife, she at last consented. Bathing herself in perfumed waters and wearing silken garments, she was brought to the place of sacrifice.

She still wore the crown of eternal youth which had been given her in the forest, and the mother of these stalwart sons appeared before her husband in all the youth and beauty of the bride whom he had won so many years before. Exclamations of wonder and admiration passed from lip to lip, and Rāma gazed as if spellbound upon this vision of loveliness, which entranced his senses as in bygone days. She heard again his voice, but her murdered heart could not leap again for joy. She stood before him again with downcast eyes, which she would not raise toward her treacherous husband. But instead of invoking the god of fire, as before, she said, "Oh, Earth, if I have never turned my thoughts toward any man but Rāma; if my truth and purity are known to thee; I beseech of thee to open a passage for me and receive me into thy bosom, for I will never again behold the face of any living creature."[1] On hearing these terrible words, a thrill of horror ran through the multitude, and they waited spellbound for the last scene in the great drama. The earth thus appealed to slowly heaved and opened, while the terror-stricken throng looked on in breathless

[1] See the Adhyatma version.

silence. Out of the newly formed abyss arose a splendid throne, adorned with gold and studded with gems; it was set with pearls and rubies and supported by four of the sacred serpents. Then the beautiful goddess of the earth came from the chasm, wearing a robe of molten silver, and taking Sītā by the hand she said, "I come, Sītā, in obedience to thy command. Thou art worthy of the purest affection of immortals. I have brought this throne for thy conveyance to the regions of happiness." Haviug thus spoken she led Sītā to the throne, and took a seat beside her; the glad earth swallowed them up, and the gods sang the praises of Sītā and threw masses of beautiful flowers upon the spot where she had disappeared. But the terror-stricken spectators, turning their eyes upon Rāma, beheld him groveling upon the ground in agony. At length the aged and heart-broken king returned to the palace, taking his sons with him. But the virtues and sorrows of Sītā will be sung in the beautiful land of the Hindū by lips which are yet unborn, and the notes of the song will echo through the crags of the Himālayas and be borne to the sea upon the musical waves of the Ganges.

CHAPTER XVII.

THE MAHĀ-BHĀRATA.

THE COMPANION OF THE RĀMĀYAṆA — A COLOSSAL POEM — DERIVATION OF THE NAME — HISTORICAL VALUE OF THE MAHĀ-BHĀRATA — THE RELIGION OF THE GREAT EPIC — LITERARY STYLE — THE AGE OF THE MAHĀ-BHĀRATA — TRANSLATION OF THE WORK.

ANOTHER Indian Epic of colossal proportions is the Mahā-bhārata. It is the companion piece of the Rāmāyaṇa, and naturally follows it in the arrangement of Sanskṛit literature. Although some portions of it were doubtless written before the other poem, it was probably completed a hundred years later than the Rāmāyaṇa.

The Mahā-bhārata is the most gigantic poetical work known to literature. It consists of two hundred and twenty thousand lines, while the Iliad and Odyssey combined contain only about thirty thousand. It is divided into eighteen Parvans, or sections, nearly every one of which would make a large volume.

It is claimed in the introduction that the word Mahā-bhārata is "derived from its large size and great weight, because the poem is described as outweighing all the four Vedas and the mystical writings taken together."

The word, however, really comes from mahā, meaning great, and bhārata, relating to Bharata, and the title of the poem signifies "The Great War of Bharata."

THE HISTORICAL VALUE OF THE MAHĀ-BHĀRATA.

Some historians claim that the legends of the Mahā-bhārata are but little better for historical purposes than the dreams of a madman, but it must be admitted that even the wildest fictions illustrate the ideas and the moral standards of the times in which they were produced. The literature of the Hindūs is largely found in their two great epic poems, the Rāmāyaṇa and Mahā-bhārata.

These masses of tradition and fable are the national treasuries from which their bards have borrowed the themes for their ballads, and their genealogists have taken the materials for their so-called histories. Hindū art is indebted to them for her subjects, and the Hindū drama constantly illustrates the characters of the two poems. Much of the matter of the Purāṇas has been taken from these storehouses of literature, and the later Brāhmans have also drawn from them the subjects, and largely the matter, of their religious discourses. To reject these stories, then, as unfit to serve in any way the purpose of the historian would be to lose valuable hints concerning the inner life of this ancient people. It is, indeed, questionable how far they represent the real facts of the period to which they refer, but they certainly must reflect to a considerable degree the feeling and the judgment of the age in which they were composed.

The mass of Oriental literature found in these two

great Epics comprises all that their own writers have left us of the social, political, and religious history of India. A familiarity with these two poems, therefore, is indispensable to a knowledge of the Hindūs, as their influence upon the people is stronger and more universal than Europeans and Americans can fully appreciate. They are held sacred as the repositories of their faith, and are cherished as the treasures of the historian.

We might have expected that the traditions of the royal house of Bharata would throw some direct light upon the Āryan conquest of India; but the attention of the earlier warrior bards seems to have been concentrated upon the fratricidal contest between the two rival branches of the royal family. Legends have indeed been preserved concerning the early rajas, but the Kshatriya bards declared that the rajas of Bharata were descended from the moon, and that one of them had conquered Indra, the ruler of the gods. The Brāhmanical compilers of these stories promptly admitted both statements, but in order to establish the superiority of their own caste they asserted that the moon itself was begotten by a Brāhmanical sage, and that the raja conquered Indra with the assistance of the Brāhmans.

It is with such material as this that the historian has to deal. Nevertheless, there is an apparently authentic tradition to the effect that the Kauravas, who were the sons of the blind raja Dhṛita-rāshṭra, engaged in a long and bitter rivalry with their cousins, the Pāṇḍavas, who were the sons of raja Pāṇḍu, and that it was this rivalry between the two branches of the royal house that led to the great war from which the Mahā-bhārata derives its name. The instruction which was given to these princes throws considerable light upon the so-called education of that age, and the whole story illustrates the relations that existed between Āryan settlers and the original inhabitants.

This Epic contains vivid pictures of the social position of the Hindū woman before the Mohammedan conquest. The habit of seclusion, and the acknowledged inferiority of their wives are to a certain extent natural to the Eastern nations, and prevailed even in the earliest times. Still, there are passages in both Epics which clearly establish the fact that the women of India were under less social restraint in former days than at present and enjoyed considerable liberty, of which they have been deprived by the influence of Mohammedanism.

These strange traditions are not to be accepted, of course, as literal narratives, but they are to be studied carefully, that we may catch the historic value of their pictures, the meaning of their allusions, the significance of their surroundings, and, above all, the spirit of the individual and national life which they depict.

THE RELIGION OF THE GREAT EPIC

is in the main a spiritualistic pantheism, in which one spirit is represented as peopling heaven under various personifications and becoming incarnate upon the earth in a multitude of different characters. But the work of compilation covered so long a period that the poem exhibits almost all of the multitudinous forms of Hindūism; at times its heroes are models of strictness in their adherence to the rules of priestcraft, and again they display the greatest laxity of conduct and a marked opposition to the ritual of the ecclesiastics. But upon one point at least it is always a unit, and that is the assertion of its own sanctity.

Vyāsa, the supposed author or compiler, says, in his exordium to the work: "The reading of the Bhārata is sacred; all the sins of him who reads but a portion of it shall be obliterated without exception. . . He who in faith shall persevere in listening to the recital of this sacred book shall obtain a long life, great renown, and the way to heaven." To this day it is devoutly believed that only to listen to portions of either poem is a deed of such merit that it will insure prosperity in this world and happiness hereafter; that it will bring wealth to the poverty-stricken and children to the barren woman. Patriotism, as well as religion, has shed a halo of sanctity over these great Epics, which are regarded by the Hindū as a national possession and cherished by him as the peculiar heritage of his race.

LITERARY STYLE.

The Mahā-bhārata, unlike the Rāmāyaṇa, is not a single poem; it is an immense collection of Hindū mythology, legend and philosophy. The main narrative is merely a thread connecting a vast number of traditions and myths, the arrangement of which resembles somewhat that of the Arabian Nights.

In consequence of its miscellaneous origin and the

protracted period of its composition, the style of the work is exceedingly varied; but the language is usually simple and natural in its construction. The progress of the story is checked by no limitations either of time, space, or numbers; it is full of fabulous chronological and historical details, and its assertions are generally of the wildest character. Space is measured by millions of miles, and time by millions of years. In the descriptions of battle scenes, horses, men, and elephants are all said to number millions. Yet the fictions of the two Epics are still essential to the religious creed of the Hindūs. It is true that the educated classes look upon the more extravagant myths as allegorical. but the great mass of the people receive them as literally true.

The speeches which have been preserved in the Mahā-bhārata are not characterized by the fiery eloquence which breathes from the lips of Homer's heroes; on the contrary, they often seem childish and puerile. Still, there are occasional scenes which are characterized by vigorous and dignified thought. Homer's heroes, however assisted by their tutelar deities, are always men; but in the Indian Epics every great man is a god, and his foes are demons.

The deification of their heroes is supposed to be largely the work of Brāhmanical compilers, who sought by this means to bring into their own ranks the most distinguished men of the Kshatriya class. The regard of the Indian soldiery for their favorite commanders still finds expression in an act of worship. The gallant John Nicholson was revered by his men as a demigod, and was even compelled to punish them for their superstitious devotion. Therefore, it is natural that in the Indian Epics the boundaries between the divine and the human should be quite indefinite. Deities or semi-divine persons are constantly appearing upon the scene, while gods, animals, and men are liable at any time to change places.

In the Iliad and Odyssey the supernatural is perhaps almost as prevalent, but it is introduced and maintained with more consistency, and hence adds to the sublimity of those poems, instead of detracting from them, as is frequently the case with the Hindū Epics. But in portraying scenes of domestic love and loyalty, the Sanskṛit writings cannot be surpassed, even by the eloquence of the Grecian classics. Human nature is world-wide, and the warm heart of the Hindū pours out his love in the luxuriant poetry of his own tropical clime. We also find the highest portrayal of woman's truth and purity, even though she is often held in a position entirely unworthy of her great devotion. The sacredness of love and the holiness of domestic ties are as beautiful in the lines of the Hindū poet as in the grander numbers of Homer.

THE AGE OF THE MAHĀ-BHĀRATA.

This work appears to have been the slow growth of three or four centuries. It is supposed that the earliest part of it was written before the Rāmāyaṇa; for it describes a conflict between rude colonists at a time which is nearer to the earliest settlements of the Āryans, while the Rāmāyaṇa represents a more advanced civilization. But the principal narrative of the Mahā-bhārata is so completely covered by later additions that it is hardly possible to analyze critically the chronology of the composition. When the story of the great war had become a national tradition, subsequent compilers did not hesitate to insert in the text the legends of the later wars waged by the Āryans against the aborigines during their progress toward the southeast.

There are evidences of at least three compilations or collections of these scattered legends and songs of India. They were gathered and arranged by different authors at various times during a period covering three or four hundred years. Sir Monier Williams assigns the first orderly completion of the Mahā-bhārata in its Brāhmanized form to about the second century B. C.[1] But he points out the fact that while many of the legends are Vedic and of great antiquity, many others are comparatively modern and have probably found a place in this collection during the Christian era. The primitive elements of the text seem to belong to early times; but its comparatively modern form and other indications have induced scholars to assign portions of the work to the early centuries of our own era.

Weber and Lassen agree in their interpretation of a passage in the Mahā-bhārata to the effect that early in the Christian era three Brāhmans visited a community of Christians, and that on their return "they were enabled to introduce improvements into the hereditary creed, and more especially to make the worship of Kṛishṇa Vāsudeva the most prominent feature of their system."[2] If these Orientalists are correct in

[1] See Ind. Wis., p. 319.
[2] Hardwick, Vol. I, p. 182. See also Notes from Weber and Lassen.

their rendering of this passage, it proves beyond a doubt that some parts of the Mahā-bhārata were written during the Christian era. Prof. Weber, also, who is a man of critical judgment and profound scholarship, says, "The final redaction of the work in its *present* shape . . . . *must* have been some centuries after the commencement of our era."[1]

We may also cite the testimony of the distinguished native scholar, Kāśhinath Trimbak Telang, M. A., who states that "we have reason to believe some parts . . . of the Mahā-bhārata to have been in existence prior to the sixth century after Christ, and that some parts of the thirty-seventh chapter were probably extant in the time of Pata*n*jali; viz., the second century before Christ."[2]

J. Talboys Wheeler claims that a part of the story of Duryodhana was "borrowed from the Koran of the Mussulmans." If he is correct in this supposition, it brings some portions of the Mahā-bhārata down into the Christian era at least as far as the seventh century.

TRANSLATION OF THE WORK.

We have not as yet a complete translation of this great treasury of Hindū literature, but many portions of it have been given to the English-speaking world and some of them have been repeatedly translated. The task of analyzing and fairly representing the work as a whole by European scholars has been greatly facilitated by the discovery of a manuscript translation of

1 Hist. Ind. Lit. p. 188.

2 See Bhagavad-gita, p. 140. The time of Pata*n*jali is still a debated question, but Prof. Max Müller places him *after* the third century of the Christian era.

the more important portions, which was probably made by the late Prof. H. H. Wilson. This valuable document was placed some years ago in the Calcutta library, under the head of Bhagavad-gītā, but it was at last found to contain the bulk of the Mahā-bhārata. The discovery was made by J. Talboys Wheeler, who prepared a critical and valuable digest of the whole paper, consisting of nine folio volumes.

Sir Monier Williams, Dr. Muir, Rev. H. Milman, and others have also made careful translations of some portions of it, and other parts have been rendered into English by a prominent native scholar. We have, besides, more than one careful analysis of the whole poem.

In the two following chapters we shall give as briefly as possible the principal story of the Mahā-bhārata. A full translation of the whole of this colossal poem would fill about seventeen volumes, but we shall present merely an outline of what purports to be the historical portion.

The events here recorded are represented as taking place in an age previous to the one in which the poet wrote, the heroes of the great war having lived and died perhaps a thousand years before their deeds were placed upon record. These events, which took place (if at all) in the early Vedic period of Indian history, have been very much colored and changed by the opinions of the succeeding age. The religion which flourished at the time of the great war had to a great extent passed away, and a new one had been established before the poems were composed. Hence, the heroes of the Mahā-bhārata are more or less deified by the fancy of the Brāhmanical compilers, and the student of modern times can only guess at the amount of historical fact which may have been transmitted orally from one generation to another during this long period.

CHAPTER XVIII.

LEGENDS OF THE MAHĀ-BHĀRATA. THE GREAT WAR.

THE KAURAVAS AND PĀṆḌAVAS—THE TOURNAMENT—THE SVAYAMVARA—THE HOME-COMING—DRAUPADĪ MARRIES FIVE HUSBANDS—THE COUNCILS OF WAR—PREPARATIONS FOR THE GREAT WAR—THE CHALLENGE GIVEN AND ACCEPTED—RULES OF WARFARE.

IN early times the royal house of Bharata was represented by two rajas, who were brothers. Raja Pāṇḍu was a mighty warrior, the hero of many conquests, and his kingdom, the raj of Hastināpur, was as great and glorious as it had been under the reign of raja Bharata. He was the father of five princely sons, who were called the Pāṇḍavas. The name of the eldest was Yudhi-shṭhira. Bhīma, the second son, was distinguished for his voracious appetite, it being the family custom to serve as much food to him as was eaten by his four brothers. The next was gallant Arjuna, tall, handsome, and kingly in his bearing. The two youngest sons were Nakula and Sahadeva. The royal brother of raja Pāṇḍu was the blind king Dhṛitarāshṭra, who was the father of a family called Kauravas, after their ancestor Kura.[1] The eldest son was named Duryodhana, but the bravest was Duḥśāsana.

[1] It is said that Gandhari, the wife of the blind raja, once hospitably entertained a great sage, whereupon he offered her any boon that she might

Raja Pāṇḍu died while yet comparatively young, and the blind king took the surviving widow of his brother and her five sons into his own palace. He tried to nurture in the young princes a genuine respect and affection for each other, but a spirit of rivalry and jealousy seemed to exist between them from the first hour in which they shared the same home. A famous preceptor named Droṇa was engaged to educate them in the use of arms, but he was so indiscreet as to exhibit a preference for the Pāṇḍavas, especially in the case of Arjuna, who was evidently his favorite. This manifest preference of the preceptor added fuel to the flames of jealousy, and Duryodhana, the eldest of the Kauravas, was especially vindictive against Arjuna, who under the instruction of Droṇa became the most famous archer of his time.

THE TOURNAMENT.

After years of careful instruction and faithful practice, the royal pupils were all experts in the departments they had chosen. Bhīma, the young man of the voracious appetite, applied his herculean strength to the dexterous use of the club, Nakula was master of the art of taming and managing horses, and the others had been taught to handle skilfully the sword and spear.

Droṇa then approached his royal patron and said to him, "Your own sons and the sons of your brother Pāṇḍu are now expert in the use of weapons, and they

choose, and she requested that she might become the mother of a hundred sons. Accordingly she gave birth to a lump of flesh, which the sage divided into a hundred and one small pieces, placing each piece in a jar, where they ultimately became children.

are prepared to meet any foe upon the battle-field." The Maha-raja replied, "Let a place be prepared on the great plain outside the city where your pupils may engage in a mock combat and display their skill before all the chiefs and the people of the raj." So Droṇa ordered that preparations be made for a great tournament without the city, and had the vast space assigned for the sport protected by barriers. On one side of the ground galleries were built for the Maha-raja and his chieftains; on the other were placed galleries for all the ladies of the royal house of Hastināpur.

The morning of the tournament dawned without clouds. The great trees in the amphitheater stood like tall columns supporting the heavy roof of foliage above them, and were decorated with bright flags. Long garlands of rich tropical flowers were festooned around the galleries, loading the air with their fragrant breath. At an early hour the populace from all parts of the raj filled the great plain, pressing as closely as possible around the barriers of the amphitheater. Soon the blind raja was led in and escorted to his place on a throne which had been erected for him and covered with the fairest blossoms of the land. At his right hand sat his faithful uncle, Bhīshma, who managed the affairs of the raj for the king, who had been his care from childhood. On the left of the Maha-raja sat Vidura, his half-brother, who was appointed to explain to him the scenes that took place on the plain below them. The ladies of the royal house occupied the other galleries, which were bright with the sheen of silken garments and the radiant light of jewels flashing amidst the flowers. But the most highly favored of the ladies were Gāndhārī, the mother of the Kauravas, and Kuntī, the mother of the Pāṇḍavas. Their womanly hearts were throbbing with joyous anticipation over the gallant deeds of their princely sons, and they waited anxiously for the opening of the tournament.

When all was ready Droṇa, the preceptor, entered the arena clad in garments of the purest white and offered the incense of praise to their gods. Then came the princes lightly girded for exercise and bearing their bows in their hands. Bowing low at the feet of their preceptor they awaited his commands. As they stood there in the glory of their young manhood, a loud cheer went up from the multitude, for their training had developed every muscle, and their fine physiques and princely bearing won the hearts of the people. Their skill was tested in shooting arrows—first on foot; then galloping around the amphitheater on horses they still struck the mark with wondrous precision. Afterward they exhibited their archery from chariots or the backs of elephants, always winning loud huzzas from the spectators. Then there were brilliant mock fights with the sword and buckler.

Droṇa at last called upon his favorite pupil, Arjuna, and the young chieftain stepped forth as stalwart and handsome as one of the gods. He entered the arena clad in golden mail and gracefully bearing in his hand a bow inlaid with pearl. The multitude greeted him as another Indra, and the glad heart of his mother who sat in the gallery above him throbbed with exultation. There had been set up the figure of an iron boar, and Arjuna sent five arrows into its mouth at one bending of the bow. Then mounting his chariot he was driven swiftly along, while he shot his arrows with such marvelous rapidity and dexterity as to bewilder the cheering spectators. In his sword-play the weapon flashed so rapidly in the sun that men fancied the lightnings were playing around him. Then arming himself with a noose, he threw it so dexterously that every horse or deer at which it was hurled was brought down. At last, having finished his exercises, he gracefully saluted his preceptor, who embraced him amidst the wild applause of the multitude.

The Pāṇḍavas, of course, had been exulting in the triumph of their brother; but Duryodhana was wild with jealous rage, and when they came to the exercise of clubs the fighting became real, and the scene was terrible. These young athletes gave a practical exhibition of their envy and jealousy, and the blood flowed freely on both sides. At one end of the great arena Duryodhana engaged with Bhīma, and the contestants rushed furiously upon each other.

"With ponderous mace they waged the daring fight.
As for a tender mate two rival elephants
Engage with frantic fury, so the youths
Encountered, and amidst the rapid sphere
Of fire their whirling weapons clashing wove
Their persons vanished from the anxious eye.
Still more and more incensed their combat grew,
And life hung doubtful on the desperate conflict;
With awe the crowd beheld the fierce encounter
And amidst hope and fear suspended tossed,
Like ocean shaken by conflicting winds."

The glad cheers of the multitude gave way to cries of horror, but some of the spectators caught the spirit of the fray and ran wildly to and fro, shouting each for his favorite in the fight. Droṇa sent his son to separate the combatants, but no one heeded him; then Droṇa hastened to them, but his words had no influence, and he was compelled to lay hands upon them and separate them by main force, and send them to their home. The multitude went away in sorrow; the flowers drooped and wilted in sadness, and the loving mothers grieved in solitude, for blood had been shed in anger. This tournament which had opened so joyously was the beginning of those long feuds and terrible contests which stained for many years the escutcheon of the noble house of Bharata.

The blind king, thinking to dispel the ill will between the two factions, at last divided his raj and gave to the Pāṇḍavas the most distant portion of it. So the Pāṇḍavas took leave of their beloved preceptor, Droṇa, and bidding farewell to their kindred took their mother with them and went into a strange land. On the banks of the beautiful river, Jumna, they built a fort and collected their subjects together under the rule of the eldest brother Yudhi-shṭhira. The new raja soon won the hearts of his people by his wisdom and kindness. He promptly punished evil-doers, and those who had been wronged went to him for aid, as children go to a loving father. His fame as a wise and beneficent ruler extended throughout India, and he built a fair city called Indra-prastha. But before it was finished the brothers attended the Svaya*m*vara of the princess Draupadī, which proved to be one of the most important events of their lives.

THE SVAYAMVARA.

One of the institutions of India in early times was the Svaya*m*vara; it resembled the tournament of the Middle Ages, wherein the victor was crowned with the laurel wreath by the Queen of Love and Beauty. But in the Hindū contests the prize was a lovely bride—usually the daughter of a royal house.

The raja Draupada, who reigned over the kingdom of Pa*n*ćāla, was blessed with a beautiful daughter. The fair princess was as radiant and graceful as if she were descended from the gods. Her dark eyes beamed with intelligence, and her cheeks glowed with the rich crimson blood of her race. The fame of her loveliness spread even beyond that of her father's name, and the rajas of the neighboring kingdom came to ask her hand in marriage. But her proud father determined that no ordinary ruler should win his beautiful solitaire; therefore, when she came to a marriageable age he announced a great Svaya*m*vara, in which the neighboring rajas were invited to take part, and announced that the prince who performed the greatest feats of archery should be rewarded with the lady's hand. It was said that all the rajas from the four quarters of the earth would be present to compete for the hand of the lovely princess Draupadī. The five Pāṇḍavas had been greatly interested in the accounts they had heard of the lady's beauty and decided to join the illustrious throng of competitors; but they disguised themselves as Brāhmans and appeared upon the brilliant scene in the garments of the priesthood. When they reached the city they found a vast number of rajas encamped there with their hosts of troops and attendants, and a multitude of horses and elephants. There were also Brāhmans, Kshatriyas, traveling merchants, and a great throng of spectators.

Outside of the city a great plain had been enclosed with barriers and supplied with glittering pavilions for the benefit of the most distinguished guests, and the long galleries were draped with bright flags and decorated with masses of flowers. At one end of the amphitheater stood a tall pole which upheld a golden fish, and just below the fish a large wheel was rapidly revolving, so that any arrow striking the fish must first pass through the spaces in the revolving wheel.

The rule of the Svaya*m*vara was that whoever discharged an arrow through the wheel at the first shot and struck the eye of the golden fish should be the husband of the princess Draupadī.

The assembled throng spent many days in sporting and feasting before the time arrived for the contest, but at last the memorable morning dawned upon the fair city of Kampilya.

At the rising of the sun the whole city was awakened by the joyous strains of martial music. At an early hour the great galleries and vast pavilions of the amphitheater were thronged with distinguished guests, while the multitude gathered in dense masses around the inclosure.

"Without the barriers pressed the countless crowd.
Skirting the distance multitudes beheld
The field from golden lattices, or thronged
The high housetops, whose towering summits touched

The clouds, and like a mountain of the gods
The sparkling peaks streamed radiant through the air.
A thousand trumpets brayed, and slow the breeze
With incense laden wafted perfume round."

The well-armed troops of the raja maintained perfect order, and the people were entertained with the preliminary exercises of dancers, jugglers, actors, athletes, wrestlers, and swordsmen.

Delicate refreshments were served to the guests and cup-bearers sprinkled the throng with the choicest perfumes of the East. At last the beautiful princess was led to the floral throne in the arena, the soft sheen of her rich garments mingling with the blaze of her jewels. But richer than her costly robes was the crimson of her lips, and brighter than her gems was the light of her beautiful eyes, as she held in one graceful hand the garland of flowers destined for the victor. Low murmurs of admiration rang through the vast throng, and choirs of Brāhmans chanted her praises in softly modulated notes. In the deep silence that followed the strains of the song the brother of the princess announced that he who sent the arrow through the flying wheel and struck the eye of the golden fish should have the princess for his wife, and he invited the rajas and great chieftains who were present to come forward and try their skill.

"Quick from their gorgeous thrones the kings uprose,
Descending to the conflict, and around
The lovely Draupadī contending pressed,
Like the bright gods round Śiva's mountain bride.
Love lodged his viewless arrows in their hearts,

And jealous hatred swelled their haughty minds.
Each on his rivals bent a lowering glance,
And, friends till now, they met as deadliest foes."

The rajas looked in dismay at the golden fish beyond the flying wheel and then at the huge bow and heavy arrow that was to be used. The more prudent suitors retired from the field, but at last one raja who was braver than the others stepped forward and lifting the bow tried to bend it, but failed in the attempt and retired at last amidst the derisive laughter of the spectators. One after another the great rajas then made the attempt, but no one of them succeeded.

"No hand the stubborn bow could bend—they strained
Fruitless each nerve, and many on the field
Recumbent fell, whilst laughter pealed around.
In vain they cast aside their royal robes
And diamond chains and glittering diadems,
And with unfettered arm and ample chest
Put forth their fullest strength—the bow defied
Each chief, nor left the hope he might succeed."

At last a young man of princely bearing, wearing the garb of a priest, came forward. As he lifted the great bow the eyes of the princess brightened, for she had seen his handsome face and admired his godlike form.

A cry of astonishment rang through the assembly upon seeing a Brāhman enter the competitive list at a Svayamvara. The Brāhmans feared that such an act would offend the rajas so that they would not bestow the customary gifts, and they pleaded with him to withdraw from the contest. But the new competitor was Arjuna, the hero of the Pāṇḍavas, and heedless alike of praise or blame

"He grasped the ponderous weapon in his hand
And with one vigorous effort braced the string.
Quickly the shafts were aimed; swiftly they flew;
The mark fell pierced; a shout of victory
Rang through the vast arena; from the sky
Garlands of flowers crowned the hero's head,
Ten thousand fluttering scarfs waved in the air,
And drum and trumpet sounded forth his triumph."[1]

The beautiful princess came gladly forward and crowned the handsome victor with the garland she held in her hand, and permitted him to lead her away, according to the rules of the Svaya*m*vara. The cheering of the multitude, however, was quickly drowned by the voices of discontent that came from the discomfited rajas. "Is raja Draupada to invite us to a Svaya*m*vara and then give his daughter to a Brāhman?" they cried. "Down with the guilty race of Draupada!" and they gathered angrily around the king with naked swords and threatened to burn the princess alive unless she chose a Kshatriya for a husband. But at the first onset upon the raja Draupada they were met by the Pāṇḍavas. The herculean Bhīma tore up a tree, using it effectively as a club. Arjuna, too, rushed upon his foes like a wild elephant, and

[1] Williams' trans. This description reminds one of the scene in the Odyssey where Ulysses

"Then notched the shaft, released, and gave it wing;
The whizzing arrow vanished from the string,
Sung on direct, and threaded every ring." (Book 21.)

the royal suitors, vanquished in archery and conquered in fight, were glad to leave the fair princess in the hands of the gallant youth who had fairly won her and retire from the field in sullen anger.

THE HOME-COMING.

At evening the Pāṇḍavas arrived at their home, accompanied by Arjuna's beautiful prize, and one of the sons hastened to his mother's apartment exclaiming, "We have made a fine acquisition to-day." The mother supposing they had brought home some trophies of war answered, "Share it equally among yourselves, my sons." Then Yudhi-shṭhira exclaimed, "Oh, mother, what have you said? Arjuna has to-day won a beautiful damsel at the Svaya*m*vara." Arjuna led the fair princess into his mother's presence, but the whole family were in grievous trouble; for the words of a parent thus spoken could not be set aside without bringing sad misfortune. The five brothers, it is true, were all in love with Draupadī, but Yudhi-shṭhira said to Arjuna, "You have fairly won her, and we will marry her to you according to law." Arjuna modestly replied, "You are the eldest brother; to you belong the trophies of war, and this damsel is worthy of being espoused by you."

Then the eldest brother said, "It is the raja Draupada who has the disposal of his own daughter, and we will leave the matter to him."

DRAUPADĪ MARRIES FIVE HUSBANDS.

In the meantime, the raja had been greatly troubled with the thought that his daughter had been won by a Brāhman; but learning that the young men were the sons of the raja Pāṇḍu, he was much pleased with the thought of being allied to the royal house of Bharata. He therefore invited the Pāṇḍava princes to a great feast, and after the festivities were over he asked Yudhi-shṭhira if it was his will as the elder brother of the family that the princess should be married to Arjuna, who had fairly won her at the Svay-*am*vara. The young prince answered that he thought it would be proper to ask the counsel of the great sage Vyāsa.

The sage being summoned to the council had the matter presented to him, whereupon he gravely replied, "Many years ago there lived a maiden lady who besought the gods to send her a good husband, and at last the god Śiva appeared to her and announced that she could have no husband in that life, but in her next transmigration she should have five husbands. But the lady replied, 'I do not want five husbands, I want only one.' 'I cannot help it,' answered Śiva, 'you have petitioned me five different times for a good husband, and each time your petition has been answered by a decree that you should have one husband, therefore in the next life you shall have five good husbands.' Time passed on and the maiden lady died, but only to be born again as Draupadī, the beautiful Hindū princess, who is the only daughter of the raja Draupada. The gods have therefore decreed that the princess shall wed all of the brothers."

Yudhi-shṭhira replied, "What Vyāsa has said is just, and, moreover, we hold our mother's word to be right and true when she commanded that we should all share the prize which Arjuna had won." The raja then gave his consent to this strange union. The princess was therefore arrayed in the richest fabrics of the Eastern looms, and adorned with many jewels. She was first married to the eldest brother and then to each of the others in the order of their ages.[1] The ceremony was celebrated with all the pomp and magnificence pertaining to royalty, and both families were greatly strengthened by the alliance.

THE COUNCILS OF WAR.

A long mythical account is given of the feuds and adventures of the following years. Yudhi-shṭhira was invited to visit the Kauravas, and while there played dice with an accomplished gambler and lost all of his wealth, his kingdom, his brothers, his wife, and finally his own liberty. Draupadī was finally restored to them, but by the terms of the game they were all banished to the jungle for a series of years. Their exploits and adventures are interminable, even the stories told by them during their exile being given; a part of the Rāmāyaṇa is recited; the story of the deluge as found in the Śatapatha-brāhmaṇa (see page 81) is also repeated and many other digressions are made.

After the years of their banishment had expired, a council of princes was called by Virāṭa and a consul-

[1] Polyandry is still practiced among the hill-tribes in the Himalaya range near Simla; it also prevails among the Todas and the Nayar tribes in Malabar, and among some of the tribes of the Pacific islands, Africa and Australia. Cæsar charges the ancient Britons with the same practice. (See De Bello Gallico, V, 14.)

The custom of polyandry must also have existed in very early times among the Vedic Aryans, there being a hymn in the Rig-veda which represents a maiden as the prize of a chariot race, which was won by the two Asvins. (See R.-v., Mand. 1, Hymn 119, Verse 5.)

tation was held as to what course the Pāṇḍavas ought to pursne. Having honorably complied with their agreement, they were entitled to their portion of the raj, which had been held during their exile by the Kauravas, but Duryodhana, who had become the virtual master of his blind and aged father, refused to give it up.

To this council Kṛishṇa was invited;[1] also their father-in-law, the raja Draupada, and indeed all the allies of the Pāṇḍavas. The courtly company was gathered in the magnificent council hall of raja Virāṭa, whose daughter had just been wedded to the son of Arjuna. Thc great hall was transformed into a floral bower, and the rich perfume of tropical blossoms filled the gorgeous room.

When all the chieftains were seated, the situation was freely discussed, and it was decided to send the family priest of raja Draupada to Hastināpur as a messenger of peace, demanding, however, that the Kauravas make a fair treaty and restore to the Pāṇḍavas their own territory. Having little faith in the success of their ambassador, the Pāṇḍavas and their allies proposed to make war in case of a refusal.

But even before the priest had started, Duryodhana had determined to go to war rather than relinquish his ill-gotten territory. With this purpose in view he visited Kṛishṇa, "the rude and amorous warrior of the Yādava tribe," in order to gain his assistance. Arriving at his residence, he was told that Kṛishṇa

[1] J. Talboys Wheeler says, "The great mass of details which associate him (*Krishna*) with the Pandavas bears every trace of being a series of mythical interpolations of the Brahmanical compilers, who sought to deify the hero." (Hist. of Ind., Vol. I, p. 246.)

was asleep, but the haughty raja of the provinces did not stand upon courtesy; entering Kṛishṇa's sleeping room he took a seat at the head of his bed to await his awakening. Before the chief of the tribe awoke, however, Arjuna entered the room with the same object in view, modestly taking his seat at the foot of the bed. On awakening, therefore, the eyes of Kṛishṇa rested first on Arjuna. But Duryodhana pressed his own claim as being paramount, on the ground that it was he who first entered the room. At last Kṛishṇa said to them, "I will put myself alone into one scale and all the warriors of my army into the other, and you can choose between the two; but if you choose me, remember I shall not fight, though I will give counsel." Arjuna at once decided to take Kṛishṇa alone, and Duryodhana was pleased to receive all the warriors of Kṛishṇa's army, though the chief himself was on the side of the foe.[1] Duryodhana returned to Hastināpur in time to receive the Brāhman envoy from raja Draupada.

The blind Maha-raja called a council to listen to the message, and when the chieftains were gathered together the Brāhman spoke as follows: "An envoy is the tongue of the party by whom he is sent, and if he fails in the discharge of his trust, he is guilty of an act of treachery. Have I, therefore, your permission to repeat the message sent by the Pāṇḍavas?" The assembled chieftains answered with one accord,

1 Wheeler points out the impossibility of any such interview taking place, Hastinapur being seven hundred miles in a direct line from Dvaraka, and shows the mythical character of the interpolation, which was evidently inserted to promote "the worship of Krishna as a deity." (Hist. of Ind., Vol. 1, pp. 246-248.)

"Speak plainly the words of the Pāṇḍavas, without extenuation and without aggravation." Then said the Brāhman, "The Pāṇḍavas send their salutations and speak thus: 'Raja Dhṛita-rāshṭra and raja Pāṇḍu were brothers, as all men know. Why then should the sons of Dhṛita-rāshṭra inherit the whole raj, while the sons of Pāṇḍu are shut out? You, Duryodhana, from the time of your childhood up to this day have taken every opportunity to injure us. You caused false dice to be made and then invited us to a gambling match; by foul play you dispossessed us of all we had and compelled us to wander like vagabonds for twelve years. We have fulfilled the conditions, and if you now restore to us our rightful share of the raj, we are ready to forget the wrongs we have endured; but if you reject our rightful claims, the blood of all the slain will be upon your head, and rest assured that Arjuna alone will devour your armies as a fowl devours grain.'"

Bhīshma replied in effect: "All you have said may be just and reasonable, but in boasting of the valor of Arjuna you have said too much. He may indeed be worthy of all your praises, but I warn you not to repeat them in our presence."

The fiery Karṇa then bounded to his feet and rebuked the aged Bhīshma for admitting that there was anything reasonable in the demands of the Pāṇḍavas, and declared that not a foot of land would be yielded up. There were animated discussions of both sides of the question, and a number of envoys were sent to and fro between the contending parties. But Duryodhana remained obdurate, and disdaining the counsel of his aged father furiously demanded war, and at the final council closed a defiant speech with the words: "What, then, are all the beggarly Pāṇḍavas that you should think to frighten me with them? Never will I stoop and humble myself to them, say what you will."

PREPARATIONS FOR THE GREAT WAR.

Duryodhana called another council of war immediately after the departure of the last envoy of the Pāṇḍavas, and required the members of his council to make a solemn covenant with him that they would never yield to the foe, but would fight as long as life lasted. He then summoned his whole army and marched to the plain of Kuru-kshetra,[1] where he fired their hearts with vindictive speeches, and drew up his battle line with barbaric pomp and magnificence. He stationed his army behind a beautiful lake in the center of the plain, and dug a deep trench on the flank of his troops, fortifying it with towers, upon which he placed great jars filled with poisonous serpents and scorpions, and reservoirs of burning sand and boiling oil. The venerable Bhīshma was enthroned with elaborate ceremonies as the generalissimo of all his armies, and was brought into the field wearing the robes of royalty, with the sacred canopy held over his head.

The Pāṇḍavas also marshalled their forces, choosing for their commander-in-chief Dhṛishṭa-dyumna, the brother of their wife Draupadī, and marched with

[1] In modern times, this plain (now called Panipat) is celebrated as having been the scene of three decisive battles which sealed the fate of upper India: in 1526 when Baber on his invasion of India completely defeated the imperial forces; in 1556 when his grandson, Akbar, on the same battle-field conquered Hemu, the Hindu commander, and finally on the 7th of January, in 1761, when the sovereign of Cabul shattered the unity of the Mahratta power, thereby preparing the way for British rule.

strains of martial music to the beautiful plain, as yet unstained with blood. They were drawn up in solid phalanxes on the western side of the clear waters of the lake, while the hosts of the Kauravas were encamped upon the eastern shore. The tropical sun looked down upon the gay trappings of horses and men, upon glittering spears and burnished shields. The richly caparisoned elephants were mounted by chieftains clad in brilliant armor and holding conch shells, upon which they sounded the signal of advance. Beside the camp of the Pāṇḍavas the river Sara-swati flowed gently along between banks bordered with coroneted palms, while the many-colored lotuses rising above its bosom burdened the air with their fragrance.

THE CHALLENGE GIVEN AND ACCEPTED.

When the troops on both sides were ready for battle, Duryodhana called one of his kinsmen and ordered him to carry a challenge into the other camp. He was received by the Pāṇḍavas according to the courtesies of war, and addressed them as follows: "You have sworn, oh, Pāṇḍavas, that when your exile was ended you would wage a war against us, and the time has come for you to fulfill your oath. You have been deprived of your raj; your wife Draupadī has been grievously insulted, and you have been driven into exile. Why then do you sit unconcerned when you ought to rush into battle with your hearts on fire?

"Where is the sleepy Bhīma, who threatened to drink the blood of Duḥśāsana, who waits for him here? We are assured that whoever comes out to battle against us, be he man or elephant, will never escape with his life, and though you are our brethren, you know no more of our power than the frog who lives in a river knows of the caves beneath it. In order to obtain a raj, men should have good fortune as well as strength. Of what use was the bow of Arjuna at the gambling match where you staked yourselves to become our slaves?"

This speech elicited an angry response and eager acceptance; but before the two armies were hurled against each other the following rules of warfare were agreed upon:

1. There shall be no strategy or treachery.

2. When we are not fighting there may be free and friendly intercourse between the two camps.

3. The fugitives, the suppliants, and the charioteers shall not be slain.

4. Horsemen shall fight only with horsemen and footmen with footmen.

5. When warriors are fighting with words only, no one shall take up arms against them.

6. No man shall take up arms against another without giving him warning.

7. When two combatants are engaged with each other no third man shall interfere.[1]

The rules of warfare being decided upon, night came down upon the plain and wrapped the expectant armies in a sleep which was lighted by dreams of victory. But when the moon came out in the troubled

[1] These peculiar rules of warfare are evidently an interpolation of later date. The great war was not fought upon these principles, and they are at variance with the barbarous character of those times, as well as with the fierce hatred which prevailed between the parties. It is probable, therefore, that the first onset between the two armies took place immediately after the insulting challenge of Duryodhana had been accepted.

sky her pale face was stained with blood, and the low roll of distant thunder was heard. Dark clouds wept over the coming contest, and their tears were tears of blood.

But the fearful omens vanished before the rays of the morning sun. Drums were beaten, trumpets and war shells were sounded, and gorgeous banners waved upon the air. The rajas on either side wore golden armor and stood in their chariots radiant with the gems which gleamed on their hands or flashed in the setting of their golden mail. On the one side the troops were drawn up in the form of a crescent, while on the other they stood awaiting the battle in the shape of an enormous bird with outstretched wings. Elephants, cavalry, and endless hosts of infantry[1] swayed to and fro like the rushing waves of a boundless sea. The chieftains arranged their magical arrows in their quivers, and everything was ready for the attack.

[1]It is claimed that princes from the remotest parts of India were gathered under these banners. The troops employed are said to have numbered millions, billions, trillions, and even more reckless figures are advanced. If all the present inhabitants of the earth were multiplied a thousand times over they would still fall short of the fabulous numbers which the Hindus claim were engaged in this "Great War." Even the elephants and chariots are counted by tens of millions. Chariots are said to have been broken or burned by an arrow, and the great war elephants are represented as being conquered and killed by a single blow from the hand of any one of the warriors.

CHAPTER XIX.

LEGENDS OF THE MAHĀ-BHĀRATA. THE GREAT WAR, CONCLUDED.

THE BHAGAVAD-GĪTĀ — THE ATTACK AND REPULSE OF THE KAURAVAS — THE THIRD DAY — FALL OF BHĪSHMA — A NIGHT SCENE — WAR OF EXTERMINATION — RAJA YUDHI-SHṬHIRA — THE DESTRUCTION OF THE TRIBE OF YĀDAVAS — DEATH OF KṚISHṆA — ABDICATION AND PILGRIMAGE OF THE RAJA — ASCENSION.

THE great plain glittered with radiant armor and the bright trappings of war horses, while the impatient armies awaited the signals of their chieftains and a terrible conflict was momentarily expected. At this point in the account a later hand has interpolated a long series of discourses by Kṛishṇa, called the Bhagavad-gītā, which will be treated in another chapter. According to some writers the foe considerately waited until this "Divine Song" was finished, and then the attack was made by Bhīshma, who advanced with the troops of the Kauravas.

The mighty host poured over the plain with their lances gleaming in the sunlight and gorgeous banners waving above them. The gallant Karṇa led his faithful bands close behind the battalion of his commander. The monarch, in golden armor, rode upon his great war elephant, whose gorgeous trappings were in harmony with the glittering uniform of the king. As they marched to the front the war shell of Bhīshma sounded its defiant challenge above the strains of martial music and the whole army was hurled upon the foe.

"The sons of Pāṇḍu marked the coming storm
And swift arrayed their force. The chief divine
And Arjuna at the king's request
Raised in the van the ape-emblazoned banner,[1]
The host's conducting star, the guiding light
That cheered the bravest heart, and as it swept
The air, it warmed each breast with martial fires."

Arjuna led his battalion in person. Standing in his chariot, covered with gleaming mail and sternly grasping his massive bow, Gāṇḍīva, he was looked upon by his men as the messenger of fate.

"Now, as on either hand the hosts advanced,
A sudden tumult filled the sky; earth shook
Chafed by the winds, the sands upcurled to heaven
And spread a veil before the sun.
. . . .
And ever and anon the thunder roared,
And angry lightnings flashed across the gloom,
Or blazing meteors fearful shot to earth.
Regardless of these awful signs, the chiefs
Pressed on to mutual slaughter, and the peal
Of shouting hosts commingling shook the world."

1 Arjuna had entreated the monkey demigod Hanuman to lend him his aid, but Hanuman replied that if he would put a picture of a monkey on his banner it would answer every purpose.

The battle became general at the first attack and in a moment the air was thick with whizzing arrows, while the whole plain resounded to the beating of the drums, the sounding of the war shells, the neighing of the horses, and the roaring of elephants. In the first terrible charge it seemed as if heaven and earth had come together. Swords and spears flashed like lightnings in the sunlight, and every stroke was followed with blood, which stained the gleaming armor before it reached the sod of the plain. A cloud of dust soon dimmed the light of the sun, and beneath its pall the shouting combatants struggled in deadly conflict.

At last the son of Arjuna, seeing that the battle was going against the Pāṇḍavas, made a personal attack upon Bhīshma and his staff. He succeeded in cutting down the ensign on his chariot, and in his reckless charge left many a foe helpless upon the field. But the night came down upon the fearful scene, and the warriors retired to their camps without any decisive gain to either side. The next day, however, after many hours of hard fighting, the Pāṇḍavas were victorious, Arjuna in a brilliant charge driving the foe from the field. Rising still higher in his chariot he exclaimed:

"'Fear not, my friends, still, still your fame maintain!'
So speaking, on he dashed with whirling wheel
Through the deep streams of blood, with carcasses
And shattered weapons choked, and thundering drove
Against the Kuru ranks. Around his course
In clouds the arrows flew, and darkened earth

And heaven, and hid the combatants from sight.
Precursor of nocturnal shades; for now
The sun behind the western mountain sunk,
And gloom profound ensued, nor friend nor foe
Could longer be distinguished. Droṇa then
Commanded conflict. cease, and Arjuna
Restrained his now re-animated troops.
Each to his tent withdrew. Amidst his peers
The glorious Arjuna unrivaled shone
As gleams the moon amongst the stars of heaven."

THE THIRD DAY

dawned bright and beautiful upon the blood-stained field. The Pāṇḍavas drew up their army in the form of a half moon, and attacked at once the center and both flanks of the foe, throwing them into complete disorder, then rapidly re-formed and charged again. The slaughter of the day was terrible; the plain was strewn with heaps of dead and weapons of every description. There were headless bodies[1] and riderless horses, and the dust of the plain was laid with blood; but the Pāṇḍavas again put to flight the Kauravas, who fled before them like frightened deer. Duryodhana at last reproached his commander-in-chief, Bhīshma, with his repeated disasters, and complained that he was indifferent to the great slaughter of his own troops. The furious chieftain responded to his complaints with the defiant sounding of shells and the braying of trumpets. His disheartened followers responded bravely to his call, and in a fiercely fought battle the Pāṇḍavas

[1] In the original it is stated that the bodies of the slain rose up without their heads and gave battle to each other.

were repulsed. They rallied, however, under the "ape-emblazoned banner" of Arjuna, and the Kauravas were again defeated, while shouts of victory and the triumphant notes of shell and bugle arose from the hosts of Pāṇḍu.

FALL OF BHĪSHMA.

Five days longer the terrible contest went on with varying result, but the advantage was mainly with the Pāṇḍavas.[1] At last, stung by the reproaches of his king, and receiving an intimation that the resignation of his command would be acceptable, Bhīshma declared that upon the morrow he would either be victorious or would be left dead upon the field. On the tenth day of the war, therefore, he challenged Arjuna to single combat, and after many hours of desperate fighting he received a mortal wound from the hand of his favorite pupil.[2] Droṇa was then given the position of commander-in-chief, and the fighting became, if possible, more desperate.

"Forgot his years—the veteran chieftain fired
With rage, the energy of youth resumed;
Amidst the Pāṇḍu ranks he smote resistless,
And many a headless corse and mangled limb

1 The wildest descriptions are given of the victories of these warriors. Arjuna is described as killing five hundred warriors at once; as covering the plain with dead and filling the rivers with blood. Bhima is represented as annihilating with a single blow of his club a monstrous elephant with all the officers mounted upon it, and many foot soldiers beside, while the younger Pandavas, from their chariots, were cutting off thousands of heads and sowing them like seed upon the ground.

2 Bhishma is said to have been so evenly pierced in every part of his body by the arrows of Arjuna, that when he fell mortally wounded from his chariot, he rested upon the points of the arrows and lay thus for many weeks. The whole episode is probably an interpolation.

And car deserted marked the warrior's path.
Fast flew his arrows with unerring aim,
And heaven loud echoed to his rattling bow.
The soil was saddened with the crimson stream
Of the vast numbers, men and steeds and elephants,
Whom Droṇa's shafts to Yama's halls consigned."

The fight between Dhṛishṭa-dyumna and Droṇa was a long and doubtful conflict. At length Kṛishṇa suggested that if Yudhi-shṭhira would assure Droṇa that his son, Aśvatthāman, was dead, the old warrior would lose all heart and become an easy prey to his opponent. Yudhi-shṭhira, however, refused to tell the base falsehood required of him. Kṛishṇa then directed the Pāṇḍavas to kill an elephant that was named Aśvatthāman, and Droṇa was told that Aśvatthāman was dead. Not believing it he fought fiercely, and his fatal blows fell with terrible effect upon both the cavalry and infantry of the foe.[1] Feeling anxious, however, about his son, he called to Yudhi-shṭhira to know if he were indeed dead. Yudhi-shṭhira answered: "Aśvatthāman is dead—not the man, but the elephant." Knowing that he was about to tell the whole truth, Kṛishṇa and Arjuna sounded their war shells furiously as soon as the first words were uttered, so that Droṇa heard only the message of death. Believing that his son had indeed fallen, he laid down his arms and willingly received the fatal blow. The death of the great commander was the turning-point in the terrible conflict.

[1] The original states that the infuriated commander slew ten thousand cavalry and twenty thousand infantry at this critical juncture, and would have destroyed the whole army of the enemy had he not been restrained by the gods, who reminded him that he was a Brahman.

A NIGHT SCENE.

The days went by with blood-stained feet, and multitudes of brave men had been lost on both sides. The gallant son of Arjuna—a mere stripling—had fallen while fighting bravely against a cordon of Kuru chieftains. His grief-stricken father had sworn vengeance upon the slayers of his son, and the terrible conflict grew more and more desperate. And now at set of sun there was no stay to the spilling of blood, as heretofore. The troops fought on while darkness gathered around them. Friends instead of foes sometimes fell beneath the strokes of the warriors, but still no trumpet called retreat. The pale moon came up and looked upon the awful scène, but as her light silvered the spears and helmets, it lighted up also dark pools of blood and the headless forms of the slain. Then she grew paler still and shuddering with horror drew back her face behind the clouds of night.

But the furious avenger of the fallen boy ordered lighted torches to be brought, and soon every warrior was carrying a gleaming flambeau in one hand and his sword in the other, while the chariots of the commanders fairly blazed with lurid light. The whole plain was illumined with the fitful fire, and the golden armor of the rajas shone in the light that fell upon the living and the dead. Their jeweled arms sparkled beneath the glare as if in mockery of the groans of dying men, and their swords gleamed in the firelight as they drank the blood of the foe. Hour after hour passed away in the terrible work, until midnight hushed the voices of anger and Arjuna called his wearied troops to rest.

Then the exhausted horseman laid his tired head upon his steed and slept upon the field; the foeman lay upon his arms, and the riders of elephants reposed upon their faithful bearers.

A WAR OF EXTERMINATION.

Now that their commander-in-chief, the venerable Droṇa, was numbered with the dead, the tide of battle went steadily against the Kauravas, but they bravely gathered their shattered troops and made a gallant rally under the leadership of Karṇa. The fighting was again desperate, but after leading the armies of the Kauravas for two days the new commander was slain in single combat with Arjuna, his death being caused by the dishonorable conduct of his opponent, who acted under the advice of Kṛishṇa. On the evening of the seventeenth day of the great contest Śalya was placed in command. The eighteenth and last morning of the great war dawned bright and clear above the field, whose blood-stained soil was rough with the bodies of her dead. The brave Kauravas once more charged upon their triumphant foe, but the charioteer of Śalya was slain, and his death was quickly followed by a single combat between Bhīma and Śalya. They fought with jeweled maces, while the remnants of both armies anxiously waited for the result.

"Soon as he saw his charioteer struck down,
Straightway the Madra monarch grasped his mace
And like a mountain firm and motionless
Awaited the attack. The warrior's form
Was awful as the world-consuming fire,

Or as the noose-armed god of death, or as
The peaked Kailāsa, or the Thunderer
Himself, or as the trident-bearing god,
Or as a maddened forest elephant.
Him to defy did Bhīma hastily
Advance, wielding aloft his massive club.
A thousand conchs and trumpets and a shout,
Firing each champion's ardor, rent the air.
From either host, spectators of the fight,
Burst forth applauding cheers: 'The Madra King
Alone,' they cried, 'can bear the rush of Bhīma;
None but heroic Bhīma can sustain
The force of Śalya.' Now like two fierce bulls
Sprang they towards each other, mace in hand,
And first as cautiously they circled round,
Whirling their weapons as in sport, the pair
Seemed matched in equal combat. Śalya's club,
Set with red fillets, glittered as with flame,
While that of Bhīma gleamed like flashing lightning.
Anon the clashing iron met and scattered round
A fiery shower; then fierce as elephants,
Or butting bulls they battered each the other.
Thick fell the blows, and soon each stalwart frame,
Spattered with gore, glowed like the Kinśuka,
Bedecked with scarlet blossoms; yet beneath
The rain of strokes, unshaken as a rock,
Bhīma sustained the mace of Śalya, he
With equal firmness bore the other's blows.
Now like the roar of crashing thunder-clouds
Sounded the clashing iron; then, their clubs
Brandished aloft, eight paces they retired,

And swift again advancing to the fight
Met in the midst, like two huge mountain crags
Hurled into contact. Nor could either bear
The other's shock; together down they rolled
Mangled and crushed, like two tall standards fallen."[1]

The Kauravas after continual reverses rallied their scattered forces for a final charge, which led to a complote rout and general slaughter. Only three or four of their chiefs remained alive, and not a single soldier of their eleven armies had survived the campaign. The victors in the fight were but little better off; at the end of the terrible contest only the five Pāṇḍavas and two of their adherents still lived. Of the many millions said to have been engaged only eleven warriors survived the contest.

RAJA YUDHI-SHṬHIRA.

The elder brother of the Pāṇḍavas was duly crowned as king of the entire raj. Great pomp and magnificence attended the ceremony, but the willow was entwined with the laurel, and the cypress of death was wreathed with the roses of victory. The aged Dhṛita-rāshṭra mourned his fallen sons, and the new raja was sad at heart. In the triumphal processions in his honor the low wail of suffering was mingled with the strains of martial music; for his victory had been won at a fearful cost, and the royal canopy above his head seemed draped with mourning. But he submitted to the splendors of the ceremony, and sat upon the royal tiger's skin before the sacrificial fire with

[1] William' trans. Ind. Wis., p. 406.

Draupadī, the wife of all the Pāṇḍavas. With no sign either of sorrow or joy he distributed the usual gifts, and in his public address he announced that he lived only for his people and to promote the happiness of the blind king, whose sons had been slain in battle. The days went by amid splendid pageantry whose royal magnificence was often disturbed by the requiems for the dead. At last the new raja, with a retinue of attendants, sought the counsel of the aged Bhīshma, who still lay upon his arrowy bed on the forsaken battle-field. (See note to page 308.)

Passing over the broken arrows, wrecked chariots, and unburied forms of their kinsmen, they found the suffering patriarch patiently awaiting his release. He delivered a long discourse to Yudhi-shṭhira on his duties toward the living, and then bade them farewell. The arrows left his body, his skull divided, and his spirit, bright as a meteor, ascended through the top of his head to the skies. Then they covered him with beautiful garlands of flowers, and carried him to the sacred waves of the Ganges. The purifying waters were sprinkled over his silent form, and the oblations for the dead were done.

Returning to his kingdom, the raja resumed the duties of his government, but the splendors of his position brought no rest to his burdened heart—no peace to his troubled spirit. When he slept the horrors of the battle-field intruded upon his vision, and in his waking hours his hands seemed stained with blood. At last he determined upon the performance of an Aśva-medha, the greatest and most difficult rite that a raja can perform, by the accomplishment of which he was believed to have asserted his sovereignty over the whole earth.

In deference to his age, the blind Dhṛita-rāshṭra was placed upon a throne of gold above the one occupied by Yudhi-shṭhira, but the old king could not forget his slain sons, nor did he wish to share the honors of the government with their murderers, even though they treated him with the deference which was due to his years and infirmity. The aged monarch therefore left the kingdom, taking his faithful wife and a few other friends with him, and established a modest home on the banks of the Ganges. The soft monotone of the sacred waves was the sweetest of music to the blind raja. Afar from the cares of government and away from the haunts of men, he sat upon the green banks of the river and listened hour after hour to the musical murmur of the waters as they hurried by.

In after years the Pāṇḍavas, with Draupadī, made a visit to the aged king, and gathered there upon the sacred river they talked in low, sad tones of the horrors of the war and the brave men lost. The sage Vyāsa then said to them: "Go all of you into the river and bathe, and each shall behold the kinsman for whom he has been sorrowing." So they all went down to the beautiful stream and chose a bathing place for themselves and their families.

At eventime, when the sun was floating slowly away in a sea of gold and crimson light, they entered the clear waters of the river. Then the waves beat higher, and the foam-crested billows rolled like an angry sea in a storm. The last rose-tinted rays faded from the western sky and darkness settled down upon the foaming river, when from the restless bosom of the tide arose living knights in armor. Bhīshma and Droṇa appeared in their chariots, and the starlight gleamed softly upon their golden armor. Then came the heroic son of Arjuna and the five sons of Draupadī; after them, all the heroes of the war, mounted upon horses or chariots and carrying their banners and weapons. But peace rested upon the ensign of the risen host, and voices were heard chanting their praises. The glad wife embraced her restored husband; the mother sought her boys; sisters rejoiced over their brothers, and in the glad hour of reunion the fifteen years of loneliness and pain were forgotten.[1] The night passed away in the fulness of joy, but when the morning dawned the risen warriors mounted their horses and chariots and rode away in the gray light of the coming day, and the loyal widows went down and drowned themselves in the river that they might join their husbands in the land beyond the tomb.

Then the raja and his brothers and their wife Draupadī took leave of the blind king on the shores of the Ganges, and returned to the capital city. They never saw his face again, for in a few days the news came that there had been a terrible fire in the jungle and that Dhṛita-rāshṭra and all of his family had perished in the flames.

[1] For many centuries the sacred books of the Hindus had steadily taught the transmigration of the soul, and this sudden change to the very opposite, viz.: the doctrine of the resurrection, is additional proof that portions of the Maha-bharata were written after the story of the risen Christ had penetrated India. The author is supported in this opinion by Richard Collins, M. A., of the Philosophical Society of Great Britain.

DESTRUCTION OF THE TRIBE OF YĀDAVAS.

The burning of the jungle with its fatal results brought terror to the hearts of the Pāṇḍavas, for they looked upon it as a bad omen for the future—the beginning of horrors. In a short time sad tidings came from Dvārakā, the capital of Kṛishṇa, who was the chief of the tribe of Yādavas. The fair city was situated upon the ocean shores and the vine-laden valleys around it were beautiful as a poet's dream. But the rich clusters of fruit were perverted from their legitimate use and the fermented juice of the grape became the curse of the city by the sea. Kṛishṇa and his brother Bala-rāma are spoken of in the Mahā-bhārata as "the wine-loving Bala-rāma and the amorous Kṛishṇa."

The capital was often the scene of disgraceful dissipation, for the tribe of Yādavas (cow-herds) were never noted for their morality. Dvārakā was visited, it is said, by a fearful apparition, which showed itself at the doors of all the houses. The people declared that it was death in human form, for its color was black and yellow, and its head was shorn, and all of its limbs were distorted. They who saw it were paralyzed with fear or convulsed with trembling. Then a great wind arose and trees were uprooted and carried away by the power of the tempest, while the terrified rats swarmed into the houses by thousands and even gnawed the hair and beards of the sleeping inmates. The frightened owls also sought the companionship of men and crowded into their habitations, while other birds cried in terror during the long hours of the night.

At last Kṛishṇa issued a proclamation that on the

morrow all the people of the city should go down to the seashore and pay their devotions to the deity of Dvārakā. But as if in defiance of this proclamation the apparition of a black woman, clothed in black garments, walked slowly into the streets. From house to house she wandered, looking in at the windows and grinning at the inmates, her great yellow teeth projecting beyond her distorted lips. If any one attempted to seize her she vanished out of his hands with a low mocking laugh and showed her hideous head far away. Then the charioteer of Kṛishṇa harnessed his master's horses, but they bounded into the air and bore the chariot far out over the foaming sea, where they disappeared forever from sight.

Hoping to put an end to these terrible omens and avert further disaster, the people gathered upon the shores of the sea to propitiate the god of Dvārakā. Some took up their abode in tents upon the sand, while others sought the shelter of trees; but they carried with their provisions a great abundance of wine, and the expedition which was intended as an act of devotion became a scene of disgraceful revelry. All the chieftains of the Yādavas were there, and the wine flowed freely. Soon insults began to take the place of jesting; angry words were followed by angry blows.

At last Kṛishṇa ordered a friend to repeat a story which represented one of the chieftains as a thief and a murderer, whereupon the insulted chief drew his sword, and calling upon his friends to aid him they slew the man who told the story and also a son of Kṛishṇa, with many other warriors. The melee now became general, for Kṛishṇa sprang into the fight and slew the murderers of his son. But the combatants were all so frantic with anger and with wine that they fell indiscriminately upon each other, striking blindly at friend and foe alike. Drunken fathers slew their sons; brothers fought together until one was slain, when the survivor sought a fresh victim. The strife went on until the whole tribe of Yādavas were killed except Bala-rāma and Kṛishṇa and one other chieftain, the sons and grandsons of Kṛishṇa being amongst the slain. His charioteer came presently to his master and told him that his brother, Bala-rāma, had gone out of the crowd at the beginning of the trouble; the chief therefore with his one surviving friend went to find him.

They found him sitting in the dense shade of a banyan tree, whose gnarled roots were reaching hungrily down from the branches to find nourishment in the earth. Kṛishṇa commanded his charioteer to go hastily to Hastināpur and tell the Pāṇḍavas of the trouble, and request the raja Yudhi-shṭhira to send Arjuna with all speed to Dvārakā. He also ordered his companion to go immediately to Dvārakā and to save the women and children from the hands of the drunken populace. The chieftain started upon his errand of mercy, but he was attacked by a drunken fisherman, who slew him on his way.

THE DEATH OF KṚISHṆA.

When Kṛishṇa approached his brother, who was sitting with closed eyes and leaning against the trunk of the banyan tree, he found that he was already dead, and exclaiming, "I saw all the Kauravas perish, and now I have seen all of the Yādavas slain," the mourner sat down near the dead body of his brother and gave himself up to troubled thoughts. But a hunter passing near saw him and mistaking him for a wild animal shot him, killing him instantly. "Thus died the mighty Kṛishṇa."

The city of Dvārakā was now a city of widows and orphans; the wail of wondering children was mingled with the lamentations of the women.

Each one of the sixteen thousand wives of Kṛishṇa appeared to think that her wifely duty consisted in making louder demonstrations of grief than the others, and when Arjuna entered the city he was distracted with the terrible howlings within her walls; for the mourning wives came to meet him with disheveled hair and violent outcries. As soon as Arjuna could command himself, he went to the scene of the drunken melee where the Yādavas had slain each other. With the assistance of the Brāhmans who had survived the disaster he gathered a great quantity of fuel and burned the bodies of the dead, not neglecting the usual funeral oblations. Then he sent parties out in various directions to search for the bodies of Bala-rāma and Kṛishṇa, which when found he caused to be burned "with much precious odors" and "sprinkled water for their souls." Four of Kṛishṇa's widows burned themselves upon the funeral pile, and all the others assumed the dress of devotees and retired to the jungle.[1] Arjuna took the treasures of the city and the

[1] The number of his wives is elsewhere given definitely as sixteen thousand one hundred and nine. It is also stated that his wives bore him one hundred and eighty thousand sons, but in this immediate connection nothing is said of this large family of fatherless children, except that his sons and grandsons were killed in the drunken melee.

remnant of her people—a few Brāhmans and a multitude of women and children—home with him, and settled them in Indra-prastha. Scarcely had they left the scene of revelry and crime, when the waves of the sea arose and swept the devoted city down into her bosom. Fishes swam through the gilded saloons of Dvārakā, and the sea mosses twined around cornice and pillar, while the moaning waves sang the requiem of fallen splendor and the billows chanted the dirge for the dead.

ABDICATION.

The reign of Yudhi-shṭhira was one long drama of sorrow—one dark scene of tragedy. The stain of fraternal blood was on his ivory throne and on the costly draperies of his palace. Even with the strains of martial music were mingled the minor chords of grief, and the drum-beats seemed muffled as for a funeral dirge. For thirty-six years he struggled bravely to overcome the disaster and gloom that met him on every side, but at last he decided to abdicate the throne which had been obtained at such fearful cost, and make a pilgrimage to Indra's heaven, in the rocky heights of Mount Meru.[1] When his loyal brothers heard of this high resolve, they determined to share

[1] The mournful grandeur of the raja amidst the magnificence of his court suggests the touching scene in Book XIII of the Odyssey, when Ulysses after ten years of war and ten years more of wandering reaches the goal of his ambition upon the shores of Ithaca. Bitterly the hero bewails his disappointment:

> "Then on the sands he ranged his wealthy store,
> The gold, the vests, the tripods numbered o'er;
> All these he found, but still in error lost
> Disconsolate he wanders on the coast,
> Sighs for his country and laments again
> To the deaf rocks and hoarse-resounding main."

his fate, and with Draupadī followed him to the great wilderness. The people pressed after, remonstrating and pleading with the raja to return, but finding him immovable they bade the wanderers farewell and returned to the city. His wife and brothers and a faithful dog were now his only courtiers. The imperial canopy was the blue heaven above him and his kingdom the wilderness around him.

"Then the high-minded sons of Pāṇḍu and the noble Draupadī
Roamed onwards, fasting, with their faces towards the east; their hearts
Yearning for union with the Infinite, bent on abandonment
Of worldly things. They wandered on to many countries, many a sea
And river. Yudhi-shṭhira walked in front, and next to him came Bhīma;
And Arjuna came after him, and then, in order, the twin brothers.
And last of all came Draupadī, with her dark skin and lotus eyes—
The faithful Draupadī, loveliest of women, best of noble wives—
Behind them walked the only living thing that shared their pilgrimage—
The dog. And by degrees they reached the briny sea; . .
They reached the northern region and beheld with heaven-aspiring hearts
The mighty mountain Himavat.[1] Beyond its lofty peak they passed

[1] Himalaya.

Towards a sea of sand, and saw at last the rocky Meru, king
Of mountains. As with eager steps they hastened on, their souls intent
On union with the Eternal, Draupadī lost hold of her high hope,
And faltering fell upon the earth."[1]

One by one the others fell, leaving only Bhīma, Yudhi-shṭhira, and the dog. The eldest walked on unmoved by the fate of the others, with his calm, inflexible face fixed toward the summit, but Bhīma questioned him as to the reason of their fall. He answered that it was because of their sinful thoughts. That Draupadī fell because of her excessive love for Arjuna; the others on account of pride or vanity. At last Bhīma fell also and was told that he suffered death on account of his selfishness.

ASCENSION.

Only Yudhi-shṭhira was now left, and he walked persistently onward still followed by the faithful dog. At last he was met by Indra, who hailed him as a prince and invited him to ascend to heaven. Then the king looked back upon his fallen brothers and pleaded,

"Let my brothers here
Come with me. Without them, O god of gods, I would not wish to enter
E'en heaven; and yonder princess Draupadī, the faithful wife

[1] William's trans. Ind. Wis., p. 412.

Worthy of endless bliss, let her, too, come. In mercy
hear my prayer."

Indra replied that the spirits of Draupadī and his brothers were already in heaven, and that only the king himself could be permitted to ascend in his bodily form. Yudhi-shṭhira then implored that his dog might be permitted to go with him to Paradise, but Indra indignantly asserted that "Heaven was no place for men accompanied by dogs." The king, however, firmly refused to go into the radiant home of Indra unless his dog could bear him company. "You have abandoned Draupadī and your brothers, why not forsake your dog?" the god demanded. To this the king replied: "I had no power to bring them back to life; how can I abandon those who no longer live?"

Finding that Yudhi-shṭira was determined not to leave him, the dog, who had been the king's father in a former birth, assumed his human form and the two went together into Paradise. There beneath the golden dome and amidst the jeweled thrones he found Duryodhana and all the Kauravas, but neither his brothers nor Draupadī were present. Addressing Indra he declared that he could not stay in heaven without the presence of those he loved, and besought the god that he might share their fate in hell. A radiant messenger was therefore sent from the throne of Indra to conduct the king to the lower regions.

He entered a dense forest composed of trees which bore terrible thorns and swords instead of leaves. With naked feet he walked over pavements made of razors with the edges upturned to meet the culprit.

He passed over the foul and mutilated bodies of those who had preceded him, while hideous shapes flitted through the darkness and hovered with outstretched hands above him. Onward, still onward, he urged his way with cut and mangled feet, until he came to the place of burning, where the forms of his brothers were seen in the pitiless flames with multitudes of others.

Draupadī turned her suffering eyes to him and reaching out her burning hands she pleaded with him to save her. The beseeching voices of his brothers, also, were borne to his ear, and in a moment the heroic heart had chosen to share their pain. Turning to his angel guide, he bade him go and leave him there with those he loved. Brave soul! It was the last trial of his loyal heart, and the terrible illusion vanished.

He was bidden to go and bathe in the sacred waters of the Ganges, and as he entered the cooling waves heaven was opened above him, and there in the land of undying flowers he was greeted by the gentle Draupadī. Advancing from curtains of azure, with her dark eyes gleaming with light and love, she gave him one delicate hand and led him to a royal throne gleaming with jewels and draped with flowers. On beyond a floral grove he saw the glad faces of his brothers amid the roses, and turning he made a joyful salutation to Indra, the god of battles.

Beside the main story of the Mahā-bhārata which we have here given, there is an interminable mass of myth and legend, consisting mainly of fairy tales of little or no literary value. For instance, in the original poem there are hundreds of pages devoted to the adventures of the horse which Yudhi-shṭhira allowed to wander at his will during the prescribed year of preparation for the Aśva-medha sacrifice.

But there is occasionally a gem of sentiment which ought to be preserved, such as the victory of love over death in the beautiful legend of Sāvitrī and Satyavān. This little poem is well worthy of the attention which has been given it by various scholars. Of all the myths of the Mahā-bhārata it is perhaps the purest and most touching. We give a prose version of it in the following pages.

CHAPTER XX.

LEGENDS OF THE MAHĀ-BHĀRATA, CONCLUDED. SĀVITRĪ AND SATYAVĀN.

THE KING'S DAUGHTER — SĀVITRĪ'S CHOICE — THE MARRIAGE — LOVE CONQUERS DEATH.

LONG years ago there lived in palace halls the mighty king of Kekaya. Gallant and brave in person, just and beneficent in the administration of the laws of his realm, he was the hero of his people and they rendered to him a loyal obedience.

But King Aśva-pati carried a desolate heart amidst the magnificence which surrounded him, for the gods had written him childless. Through long years of faithful fasting and penance his prayers had been unanswered. But one glad day the goddess of the sun arose from his sacrificial fire; beautiful and bright she came in the form of glorious womanhood, and rising through the crimson flame stepped into the royal presence, saying: "What wilt thou, mighty raja, that I shall do for thee? I have listened to thy prayers; I have watched thy penance, and seen the bounty of thine offerings. During all the years of thy reign the poor have found in thee a valued friend, and now, oh, king! I wait to do thy bidding; tell me now the dearest wish of thy heart." And Aśva-pati answered: "Oh, beautiful goddess, 'tis for my barren line that I do penance and have performed my vows lo! these many years. Give me an heir for my throne and kingdom; give me children to grace my royal hearthstone." Then the radiant goddess smiling said: "I knew thy wish, oh king, and there shall be born a daughter unto thee—not a son, but a fair girl—the loveliest that the stars have ever shone upon;" and, smiling still, the beanteous vision vanished in the sacrificial flame.

Time passed on with flying feet, and ere long a child was given to the royal house and courtiers brought their praise unto the palace gates, while the streets of the city were ringing with joyous music and everywhere the glad news went that the queen had borne a daughter—a babe of loveliest mould. The child was named Sāvitrī and the happy father made a royal birthday feast; the poor were fed and the city was decorated with bright flags and long festoons of flowers. Every porch and pillar was made bright and fragrant with floral vines, and the great vases in front of the palace were filled with branches of orange and mango trees.

The little one who met with such a royal welcome grew more beautiful as the years went by, and when she reached the fair heights of womanhood she was a vision of grace and loveliness. The lithe figure of this Indian maid was like a dream of beauty and grace, and the rosy light of health flashed through the olive shades of her face. The crimson lips smiled over pearly teeth and the great dark eyes were luminous with light and love. But still no raja dared to ask the hand of the princess in marriage. Her loveliness and truth, her queenly independence had awed them into silence.

At last her father gave to her a princess' right to choose for herself a lord, and gave his royal word that the man she chose should be welcomed by her sire. A royal train moved through the provinces and visited every court, for Sāvitrī with her ministers and maidens would take the air and travel for the princess' health. They received everywhere a royal welcome, but she loved best the trees and groves; hence, they wandered through the fragrant woods and gathered fruits and flowers there.

One day they found a hermit, aged and blind, who with his faithful wife sat in the dense shade of a teak tree, whose abundant leaves gleamed in the sunshine above them and protected them from its heat. The gentle princess stayed to give them a few kindly words and enjoy the wild flowers around the hermitage. While she listened to their story a young man came from the thicket bearing the sacred wood to be used in the evening sacrifice. He stopped in wonder and admiration before Sāvitrī, and her eyes rested a moment upon his manly form and honest face. It was Satyavān, the hermit's son, who stayed to serve his aged parents in their banishment, The princess had dawned upon his vision like a dream of heaven, and like a dream she vanished from his woodland home, leaving her memory to haunt his steps and make his loneliness more terrible. In the still hours of the night he heard her voice and saw the lovely face which had become part of his being.

SĀVITRĪ'S CHOICE.

One day the Maha-raja sat in his council hall with the sage Nārada. They were talking in low tones of the affairs of state when the king's daughter was announced. With her dark eyes glowing with light and happiness she stepped into the royal presence and bowed meekly before her father, who laid his hand lovingly upon her dark hair, as he bent down and caressed his child. Nārada looked in admiration upon the princess and said to the king, "Thy daughter is very fair. Thou shouldst give her in marriage to the raja of some goodly kingdom." "For this purpose she has been abroad," replied the king. Then turning to his daughter he said, "My child, hast thou chosen thy lord?" But she answered not. Standing before the sage with her face crimsoned with blushes, her eyes mutely appealed to her father to stay his questions. Reading her wish, he said, "Fear not, my child, to speak before the sage Nārada; he is thy father's best and truest friend; but tell me if thou hast found the object of thy search." Then she answered: "Father, I have been long away; I have visited the courts of princes; I have offered sacrifice in the sacred groves, and I have found in one of these the banished king of Chalva, who lost his throne and kingdom because of blindness. An usurper reigns upon his throne, and his faithful queen stays with him in the woodland cot. Their loyal son ministers to their wants; he brings them fruit and game for food; he feeds their sacrificial fire and pulls the sacred kusa grass to make their couch both soft and warm; he brings fresh water from the passing brook and gives them love and tenderness in their daily need. Father, I have chosen him, this banished prince, to be my lord."

Then said Nārada, "Not he, my child,—thou canst not choose the banished Satyavān. He is both brave and noble; a grander youth ne'er trod a kingly court, but o'er his head there hangs a fearful fate. He is doomed to die, and in a year the gods decide that he must go." Her blushes fled and her cheeks grew strangely pale as she answered: "Whether he live long or die to day, whether he be full of grace and wisdom, or graceless stand before me, my heart hath chosen once—it chooseth not again, and I have my father's royal pledge that he will ratify my decision."

Then said the king, "Remember, child, the sad lot of Hindū widowhood, and choose again. The noblest raja in the land would gladly call thee wife. Let not this banished youth who has only a year to live take my peerless Indian gem into his rough woodland home."

The dark eyes were raised again to his and in their liquid depths he read her answer even before her lips replied, "A loyal heart can choose but once, and a loyal sire will not revoke his promise."

Then the raja sighed, "As thou wilt, dear child, but for thine own sake I would have had thee make a wiser choice." One quick look of gratitude flashed from the wondrous eyes, then bending her blushing face to kiss her father's hand and reverently bidding the sage farewell, she left the council hall.

THE MARRIAGE.

Having given his royal sanction to his daughter's choice, the king ordered that preparations should be made for the coming nuptials. Though the bride should dwell in a lonely hermitage she would still be a king's daughter, and her robes even in the woodland should befit her noble birth. It was an imperial pageant that went forth to the humble dwelling of the hermit. There were the priests and sages and courtiers, and the royal family, mounted upon the war elephants with their costly trappings.

Amid the strains of martial music the train went forth from the palace gates. No courier had been sent to give warning of their coming; therefore the king ordered a halt when near the hermitage, and he himself went forward to hold council with the blind lord of the humble home. Courteous salutations were passed between them, and after extending the modest hospitalities that still were his, the blind king asked what brought the Maha-raja to his door. "I have come," said he, "to ask of you that you will ratify my daughter's choice; she hath chosen your son Satyavān to be her lord."

Then answered the banished king, "In the days of my proud position it was my ambition to link my house with yours by ties of blood, oh, noble king! but now that my kingdom is lost and I am but a dethroned and banished sovereign, I could not take the lovely princess from her palace home to share our humble fate."

But the raja replied, "You and I are both too old

to think that happiness is dependent upon luxury. We know that love can hold her sylvan court in humblest bower, and your son is the lady's choice. She has chosen to dwell in modest guise with him she loves rather than share the splendors of another. Shall we deny her wish?" "Nay, never," said the banished king. "Her gracious wish is mine, and great honor she brings to our fallen house. May the blessings of Indra rest upon her beauteous head!" and calling Satyavān he told him why the raja came. The bewildered prince could scarcely believe the lovely princess had chosen him. His words were few; but his eyes were eloquent with the joy his lips refused to voice.

Then the royal train was ordered into view, and there beneath the massive trees were gathered priest and sage with golden jars filled from the waves of the sacred Ganges. Beyond the great trees where the hermitage stood were thickets of rose laurel, whose fragrance filled the air; on the other side a silver brook was hastening by to find rest in the bosom of a clear lake, beneath the fragrant cups of lotus blossoms and white lilies. Here in Nature's temple, beneath her shining dome and beside her sacred pools, with legal rites the two were bound in holy marriage; and Love stayed by and held his court where the royal lovers pledged their faith.

The raja and his queen bade their child a fond farewell, and when they passed from sight the princess took from her hands and arms the costly jewels that she wore and laid aside her silken robes; then on her delicate form she placed the rough garments that befitted her new station as a hermit's wife. Thus she proved the great love that brought her here; she could not wear a finer robe than he; she could not see her little hands decked with gold and gems while his were roughened with honest toil. She had chosen to share the fortune of the man she loved, and no ray of barbaric splendor should suggest to him that she cared for things he could not furnish. The gray-haired mother looked smilingly on and loved the loyal wife, whose gracious ways and loving words soon won the heart of the banished king as well.

The little family dwelt in their forest home in sweet content and the days went by on silver feet. To Satyavān it seemed that life's ills all were done, and he rested in the heaven of his happiness feeling that the gods could do no more. But Sāvitrī carried in her loving heart a fearful dread—a counting of the days when the death decree should be fulfilled. When the sun went down in the sea and the soft folds of night cooled the fevered earth she knew that one day less remained to Satyavān.

LOVE CONQUERS DEATH.

At last the days had nearly fled—the little wife grew strangely still; her gentle, loving deeds were still her own, but her songs were hushed in tearful prayers. When the time was nearly come she sat beneath a great tree like a beautiful statue and neither ate nor drank. For three long days and nights she sat thus, mutely imploring the gods to save from death's decree the man she loved. During all the year she had carried the fatal secret in her own faithful heart. She could not pain the others with the weight of her terrible woe, and they wondered now at the severity of her penance; but they thought she craved some great gift of the gods, and they could not deny her wish.

The fateful day dawned at last and found her weak and faint, but she would not taste of food. Only one plea she made—that she might go with Satyavān when he went out into the forest to cut the sacred wood for the evening sacrifice.

Tenderly he remonstrated, "The way is rough and thy little feet are tender; the mother's side is a safer place for thee." But still she pleaded, "I cannot let thee go unless I am with thee," and Satyavān looked down into the depths of her tearful eyes, that looked back love and tenderness into his own. Then said he, "Surely thou shalt go and make the dark wood glad with thy sweet presence."

Cheerily he set out ax in hand through the wilderness, making a path for the little feet that patiently followed his own. The morning was wondrously bright; flower-laden trees stood here and there along the pathway; gigantic climbers grew in the thickets in great profusion, interlacing the smaller trees and even piling their gorgeous blossoms upon their heads. The sunlight lay upon the surface of the little lake near their home, and bright water birds hovered above the reeds and rushes, or settled down amidst the white lilies and fragrant lotus cups near the water's edge. Away in the distance the Himālayas lifted their snowy brows into the blue heavens and reflected the sun's rays from their icy peaks. "Is it not beautiful?" said Satyavān, pointing to the landscape around him, or directing her attention to the strange wild flowers springing from the mosses at their feet. And smiling the little wife replied, even while the fearful dread around her heart almost stayed its beating.

Afar from home, they gathered fruits and flowers for the evening sacrifice, and all the while the anxious wife watched with aching heart every look and motion of her lord. He struck the tree to gather sacred wood, and blow after blow of his ax echoed through the forest. At last he reeled in sudden pain and cried, "I cannot work;" then falling at her feet he fainted there. Quickly the beloved head was laid upon her lap, and eagerly she strove by chafing the temples and tired hands to bring the life tide back. She knew it was the day of fate, but still she could not yield.

Suddenly at her side she saw a fearful shape, that was neither god nor man—tall and dark with visage grim, he looked down pitilessly upon them both. His garments were crimson as if with blood; his cruel eyes glowed like burning coals in their deep sockets. In one hand he bore a long black noose and bent over Satyavān. As the spectre leaned above her husband, the trembling princess laid the head tenderly upon the ground, and springing up reverently folded her hands in supplication, and prayed to know who he was and why he came. He answered, "I am Yama, the god of death, and I am come to bear away the soul of Satyavān." "But," pleaded the wife, "'tis thy messengers that bear away the souls of men. Why is it, mighty chief, that thou hast come?" "Because Prince Satyavān was the grandest, noblest of his race," replied the god, "and none save Yama's self was worthy to bear his soul away," and bending lower still he fitted the dreadful noose and drew out the soul of Satyavān;[1] then silently he strode away toward the southland with his prize, leaving the poor body pale and cold, with life and grace and beauty gone.

But the stricken princess followed him. With her hands folded in supplication she hastened on behind this fearful King of Death. At last he turned. "Go back," said he, "why dost thou follow in my steps? No mortal e'er has dared to come whither I shall go. Go back and perform the funeral rites for thy dead lord."

But she replied: "Wherever my lord is borne, there I shall surely go; he is my life, my all; I cannot leave him, and I must go with thee. By reason of my wifely love thou wilt let me come." And still she followed on until the King of Death himself felt pity for the faithful wife, and turning back he said: "Return, my child, to life and health. Thy wifely love is good, but the kingdom of Yama is not the place for thee. Still, I will grant thee any boon that thou dost crave, except this life that I am bearing away." Then said Sāvitrī, "Let the blind and banished king, my husband's father, have both his sight and throne restored." "It shall be so," returned the god. "I grant thee this because of thy purity and fidelity; but now turn back; our way is long and dark, thy little feet are already weary, and thou wilt die upon the road."

"I am not weary," said Sāvitrī, "I cannot tire

1 According to Hindu theology the soul of a dead man is about the size of the human thumb. At death a hole should be dug northeastward of the fire where the soul can wait until the gross body is burned, and then emerging be carried with the smoke to heaven.

while I am near to Satyavān. Wherever he is borne, there the loyal wife must go." And the tireless feet toiled patiently on behind the King of Death until he turned again and said: "Darkness is coming on, soon thou canst not find thy way alone. I will give to thee another boon—anything except this life, and then thou must return." Quickly the princess thought of her own sire, whose only child now followed Death—thought of his lonely home and coming age, and she said, "Give to my father princely sons to bear his royal name. This is the boon I crave, oh, mighty one." "So shall it be," returned the king, "and now I have granted thy wishes, go back to life and light." But she only answered plaintively, "I cannot go, great king. I cannot leave my lord. Thou hast taken him and my heart is in thy hand. I must surely come with thee."

Darkness came slowly down in the dense forest, and her tender feet were torn with thorns and cut with the sharp stones of the rugged path. Hungry wolves and jackals pressed around her, while night birds spread their black wings above her and startled the silence with their cries. Trembling with terror and faint with grief and hunger, she still pursued her way. Her tear-blinded eyes could no longer see the terrible shape she followed, but she heard his footfalls and almost felt his fearful strides, for it seemed that every step came down upon her bleeding heart.

At last they came to a cavern, dark and damp as death itself, and here again Yama turned upon the pitiful figure in the darkness behind him, and this time he fiercely demanded, "Art thou still upon my track? If thou wert not so true and good, I would take thee in my arms, and my worms should feed upon thy beauty; but thou art truth itself, and I will give to thee, poor child, one more boon. In pity for thy grief I will give thee anything thou wilt—except this life within my hand." Then answered Sāvitrī, "Give me children—the sons of Satyavān. Let me bear to him brave, loyal heirs of his goodness and his truth."

Death grimly smiled. Should he be conquered yet by this little Hindū wife? But he answered: "Yama hath promised thee, and I must grant thee even this." Then with rapid strides he entered the great vault of the cavern, while the startled bats and owls flapped their dark wings and made the place more hideous with their cries. But still he heard the patter of patient feet behind him, and his burning eyeballs blazed in the darkness upon poor Sāvitrī.

"Go back," he said. "Thou shalt return; I will bear no longer with thy persistent following!" "I would go back, oh, mighty Yama, if I could," wailed the weary wife, "but in your hands you carry my own life. 'Tis only my helpless frame that follows thee, and now I am so weak with grief and fear that I must come nearer to Satyavān;" and the tired head drooped upon the dark, cold hand of Death, close to the life she craved. The pitiless king felt the soft touch of tear-wet cheeks and clinging hair, and again his cruel heart was softened by her faithful love. "Thou art innocence itself, and tenderness and truth," said Yama. "Thou hast taught me lessons new of woman's fidelity. Ask any boon thou wilt, and it shall be thine."

Then at his feet she fell in grateful joy and tenderly caressed them. "This time, oh, king," she cried, "thou hast excepted nothing, and I ask not wealth, nor throne, nor heaven itself. I crave my heart, my life—give me my Satyavān!" The fire in his eyes beamed more softly, and the light in them was almost tender as he said: "Fair queen, thou art the brightest gem of womankind. Here, take thy Satyavān. Saved by his peerless wife, he long shall live and reign with her, and his line shall be upheld by princely sons who shall call thee mother. Go now, my child, time hasteth, and long hast thou been with me." Then turning gloomily away, he went down—down into the darkness of the cavern. But the glad wife, holding her precious treasure close to her heart, retraced her steps back through the darkness of cavern and wood, her torn feet climbing the ascending pathway, fearing nothing, knowing nothing, save that in her arms she carried her beloved.

It was dark in the forest, where the dense foliage almost shut out the light of noontime, but it was lighter here where only little groves of sacred fig trees and thickets of flowering shrubs obscured the vision, and traces of gold and crimson still lingered round the setting sun. Thankful for the light, she hastened to where the body lay, and raising the head pressed it tenderly again to her bosom, and gently wooed the life tide back to heart and pulse. Soft and warm his hand became, and his lips moved to speak a tender word that had died upon them when Yama came. The evening light was gone, and darkness came down with velvet touch around them, but the glorious stars came out and the southern constellations flashed like crown jewels above the living prince and his loyal wife.

CHAPTER XXI.

THE BHAGAVAD-GĪTĀ.

EVIDENTLY AN INTERPOLATION—AGE OF THE GĪTĀ—ITS ORIGIN—"THE DIVINE SONG"—SELF-ADULATION OF KṚISHṆA—DIVINE FORM OF KṚISHṆA.

LEAVING the Mahā-bhārata proper, we will now turn our attention to the Bhagavad-gītā, which although it now forms a part of the great Epic is independent of it.

While the armies of the great war were drawn up in close proximity to each other, impatiently awaiting the order to charge, Kṛishṇa is represented as delivering to Arjuna a long philosophical and religious discourse, called the Bhagavad-gītā, or "Divine Song."

It is clearly an interpolation, like many others[1] which have been placed in the Mahā-bhārata by the more modern compilers, and scholars can only wonder why the Brāhmans who placed it in the text could not see the impropriety of throwing in a long discourse of

[1] The charioteer of the blind Maha-raja is represented as entertaining his master during the exciting battle—not by a description of the fight, but with a long dissertation upon the geography of the earth, and especially of India. The venerable Bhishma, after receiving a mortal wound, is not permitted to die, but must lie for many weeks upon the points of upturned arrows, in order to deliver to the king a lengthy speech on the duties of rajas, etc. No effort has been spared by the later compilers to convert the story of the great war into a medium for Brahmanical teaching, and sometimes their interpolations are so skilfully interwoven with the older text that it is almost impossible to separate them.

eighteen chapters on the very eve of an exciting battle. Only the vivid imagination of a Hindū would guess that any man, god, or demon would, when drawn up in his chariot, between the combatants, spend the entire day in philosophical discourse when his impatient troops were marshaled in battle array, with drums beating, banners flying, and soldiers shouting, while even the horses were apparently eager for the fray, and, indeed, according to Telang, after the signal had been given and the battle had actually begun.

AGE OF THE BHAGAVAD-GĪTĀ.

The author of this work is unknown, but he was evidently a Brāhman, and nominally a Vaishṇava. It was inserted into the Mahā-bhārata at a comparatively early period, but there is considerable discussion among scholars in reference to its exact age. Dr. Burr says that "at the time of its first translation into English an immense antiquity was claimed for the Bhagavad-gītā, but it is now generally admitted to be an interpolation into the Mahā-bhārata, and to have been produced subsequently to the rise, not only of Christianity, but of Kṛishṇaism itself." Richard Collins, in a paper read before the Philosophical Society of Great Britain, takes the position that the Bhagavad-gītā was written *after* the third century of the Christian era. Prof. Max Müller places it in what he terms the "Renaissance period of Indian Literature," the commencement of which he gives at about A. D. 300, while Sir Monier Williams speaks of it as being "a comparatively modern episode of the Mahā-bhārata," and assigns the author to one of the early centuries of the Christian era. We might also quote Prof. Weber, of Berlin, Prof. Lassen, and Dr. Lorinser, who assign it to about the third century A. D.; but a repetition of authorities is useless, as it is abundantly proved to belong to the Christian era.

ORIGIN OF THE GĪTĀ.

This work appears to belong in Sanskṛit literature to the family of Upanishads. Its philosophy, its strong pantheism and radical doctrines of transmigration, and its literary style all point to the one conclusion that it has been derived largely from the Upanishads. This view is well supported by the version of the Gītā which was published in Bombay in 1782. There is a stanza in this edition which says: "The Upanishads are the cows; Kṛishṇa, the milkman; Arjuna, the calf; and the milk is the nectar-like Gītā." This statement sufficiently illustrates the tradition among the Hindūs that the work is derived largely from the ancient Upanishads, and contains the essence of their teaching.[1]

THE "DIVINE SONG"

begins with the regrets of Arjuna at seeing his brethren arrayed in lines of battle, waiting the word of command to enter upon a fratricidal war. Addressing his charioteer, Kṛishṇa, he says:

"Beholding these my relatives arrayed
Before my eyes in serried line of battle

1 The native scholar Kashinath Trimbak Telang is naturally inclined to think that the Gita may have been a part of the original Maha-bharata, although he says "it is with a feeling of painful diffidence that we express ourselves regarding the soundness of any conclusion whatever." (Int. Bhagavad-gita, p. 5.)

Preparing for the deadly fray, my limbs
Are all relaxed, my blood dries up, a tremor
Palsies my frame, the hairs upon my skin
Bristle with horror. All my body burns
As if with fever, and my mind whirls round
So that I cannot stand upright nor hold
The bow, Gāṇḍīva, slipping from my hand.
I cannot—will not—fight. O mighty Kṛishṇa,
I seek not victory, I seek no kingdom.
What shall we do with royal pomp and power,
What with enjoyments or with life itself,
When we have slaughtered all our kindred here?"[1]

Kṛishṇa makes a long reply to this, in which he exhorts Arjuna to do his duty as a soldier, regardless of results. He repeatedly urges him to fight without wasting regret over the necessary slaughter of his relatives.

"Better to do the duty of one's caste,
Though bad and ill-performed and fraught with evil,
Than undertake the business of another,
However good it be. For better far
Abandon life at once than not fulfil
One's own appointed work; another's duty
Brings danger to the man who meddles with it.
Perfection is alone attained by him
Who swerves not from the business of his caste."[2]

The imperative duty of loyalty to one's caste, which is here inculcated, is repeated in various portions of the poem.

[1] Williams' trans. Ind. Wis., p. 139. [2] Ind. Wis. p., 140.

The first section of the Bhagavad-gîtâ, or Divine Song, dwells chiefly on the Yoga system, or intense concentration of the mind upon one subject, claiming that the end and aim of asceticism is to enable man to embrace the doctrine of pantheism and realize that God is everything and everything is God.

Arjuna is exhorted to fulfil the duties of his warrior caste, and proceed to kill his relatives, on the ground that death is merely a transmigration from one form to another.

"The wise grieve not for the departed, nor for those who yet survive.
Ne'er was the time when I was not, nor thou, nor yonder chiefs, and ne'er
Shall be the time when all of us shall be not. As the embodied soul
In this corporeal frame moves swiftly on through boyhood, youth, and age,
So will it pass through other forms hereafter—be not grieved thereat.
The man whom pain and pleasure, heat and cold affect not, he is fit
For immortality. Whatever is not cannot be; whatever is
Can never cease to be. . . . Know this—the Being that spread this universe
Is indestructible. Who can destroy the Indestructible?
These bodies that enclose the everlasting soul, inscrutable,
Immortal, have an end; but he who thinks the soul can be destroyed,

And he who deems it a destroyer, are alike mistaken; it
Kills not, and is not killed; it is not born, nor doth it ever die;
It has no past nor future—unproduced, unchanging, infinite; he
Who knows it fixed, unborn, imperishable, indissoluble,
How can that man destroy another, or extinguish aught below?
As men abandon old and threadbare clothes to put on others new,
So casts the embodied soul its worn-out frame to enter other forms.
No dart can pierce it; flame cannot consume it; water wets it not,
Nor scorching breezes dry it—indestructible, incapable
Of heat or moisture or aridity, eternal, all-pervading,
Steadfast, immovable, perpetual, yet imperceptible,
Incomprehensible, unfading, deathless, unimaginable."[1]

The transmigration of souls is here clearly taught. Kṛishṇa in another paragraph charges Arjuna with cowardice, and asks: "How comes it that this delusion which excludes from heaven and occasions infamy, has overtaken you in this place of peril? Be not effeminate . . . . It is not worthy of you. Cast off this base weakness of heart and arise."

Arjuna still pleading the humane side of the question, Kṛishṇa repeatedly teaches that the slaying of his relatives is an innocent act, from the fact that the soul cannot die. "The destruction of that inexhaust-

[1] Ind. Wis., p. 141.

ible principle none can bring about, therefore, do engage in battle, O son of Bharata . . . . . for to one that is born death is certain, and to one that dies birth is certain . . . . therefore you ought not to grieve for any being. You ought not to falter, for there is nothing better for one of the warrior caste than a righteous battle—an open door to heaven. But if you will not fight this righteous battle, then you will have abandoned your own duty and your fame, and will incur sin. All beings, too, will tell of your everlasting infamy, and to one who has been honored infamy is a greater evil than death."[1]

SELF-ADULATION OF KṚISHṆA.

The second division of the poem teaches the pantheistic doctrines of the Vedânta more directly, Kṛishṇa in the plainest language claiming adoration as being one with the great universal spirit pervading, and also constituting, the universe. For the twofold purpose of enforcing his arguments and compelling Arjuna to fight, and also to glorify himself, Kṛishṇa proceeds as follows: "I have passed through many births, O Arjuna! and you also. I know them all, but you do not know them. Even though I am unborn and inexhaustible in my essence; even though I am lord of all beings, still I take up the control of my own nature and am born by means of my delusive power. Whensoever piety languishes and impiety is in the ascendant, I create myself. I am born age after age for the protection of the good; for the destruction of evil-doers and the establishment

1 See Bhagavad-gita, Telang's trans., p. 46.

of piety . . . . I am the sacred verse. I, too, am the sacrificial butter, and I the fire, I the offering. I am the father of this universe; the mother, the creator, the grandsire; the thing to be known, the means of sanctification, the syllable Om;[1] . . . the goal, the sustainer, the lord, the supervisor, residence, the asylum, the friend, the source, receptacle, and the inexhaustible seed. . . . . I am the thunderbolt among weapons; the wish-giving cow among cows. . . . . Among serpents I am Vāsuki; among Nāga snakes I am Ananta. . . . . Among demons, too, I am Pralhada. . . . . I am the wind among those that blow."[2] There are many pages of the wildest self-praise, after which Kṛishṇa informs Arjuna that "there is no end to my divine emanations," the extent of which has been only partially described.

DIVINE FORM OF KṚISHṆA.

He then exhibited himself in his divine form, having many eyes and mouths and faces and weapons. Arjuna stood before him with bowed head, his hair standing on end, and with joined hands he said: "Oh, god! I see your body, the gods, as also all the groups of various beings: and the lord Brahman seated on his lotus seat, and all the sages and celestial snakes, I see you, who are of countless forms, possessed of many arms, stomachs, mouths, and eyes on all sides. And, oh, lord of the universe! oh, you of all forms! I do not see your end, or middle, or beginning. .

1 The syllable Om is said to comprise all the deities of heaven, earth, and sky.

2 Bhagavad-gita, Telang's trans., pp. 58-89.

"I see you bearing a coronet and a mace and a discus—a mass of glory, brilliant on all sides, difficult to look at, having on all sides the effulgence of a blazing fire or sun, and indefinable. . . . . I see you void of beginning, middle, end—of infinite power; of unnumbered arms, having the sun and moon for eyes; having a mouth like a blazing fire, and heating the universe with your radiance. For this space between heaven and earth, and all the quarters are pervaded by you alone. Looking at this wonderful and terrible form of yours, oh, high-souled one! the three worlds are affrighted. For here these groups of gods are entering into you. . . . . Seeing your mighty form, with many mouths and eyes; with many arms, thighs, and feet; with many stomachs, and fearful with many jaws, all people, and I likewise, are much alarmed, oh, you of mighty arms! Seeing you, oh, Vishṇu! touching the skies, radiant, possessed of many hues, with a gaping mouth and with large blazing eyes, I am much alarmed in my inmost self, and feel no courage, no tranquillity.

"Seeing your mouths, terrible by reason of the jaws and resembling the fire of destruction, I cannot recognize the various directions; I feel no comfort. Be gracious, oh, lord of gods! who pervadest the universe. And all these sons of Dhṛita-rāshṭra, together with all the bands of kings and Brāhmans, and Droṇa, and this charioteer's son likewise, together with our principal warriors also, are rapidly entering your mouths, fearful and horrified by reason of the ruggedness and distortion of your face and jaws. And some with their heads smashed are seen to be stuck in the spaces between the teeth. As the many rapid currents of a river's waters run towards the sea alone, so do these heroes of the human world enter your mouths blazing all around. As butterflies with increased velocity enter a blazing fire to their destruction, so, too, do these people enter your mouths, with increased velocity only to their destruction. Swallowing all these people, you are licking them over and over again from all sides with your blazing mouths. Your fierce splendors, oh, Vishṇu! filling the whole universe with their effulgence, are heating it. Tell me who you are in this fierce form. . . . . Be gracious! I wish to know you, primeval one, for I do not understand your actions."

Then Kṛishṇa said: "I am death, the destroyer of worlds, fully developed, and I am now active about the overthrow of the worlds. Even without you, the warriors standing in the adverse hosts shall cease to be. Therefore, be up; obtain glory, and, vanquishing your foes, enjoy a prosperous kingdom. All these have been already killed by me. Be only the instrument. Droṇa and Bhīshma and other valiant warriors whom I have killed do you kill. Be not alarmed. Do fight, and in the battle you will conquer your foes."[1]

Arjuna stood in his chariot, clad in golden armor and wearing the bright coronet which had been given him by the god Indra. On either side of him were the opposing armies, while arrows were flying through the air. But the hero of the great war, "trembling, with joined hands, bowed down and sorely afraid, and

[1] Bhagavad-gita, Telang's trans., pp. 98-130.

with throat choked up again spoke to Kṛishṇa after saluting him." He still pleaded the humane side of the question, but in vain.

Then follow many pages of questions and long discourses on the spiritual phases of Brāhmanical teaching, at the end of which Arjuna decides to fight and declares that he is ready to do the bidding of Kṛishṇa, and thereupon enters the battle.

Thus it will be seen that the "Divine Song" is quite foreign to the style and also to the subject matter of the Mahā-bhārata, so much so, indeed, that Sir Monier Williams claims that its proper place in the arrangement of Sanskṛit literature would be at the close of the subject of philosophy. It contains many sentiments which have evidently been borrowed from the Upanishads, and like some of the more modern writings of this class the Bhagavad-gītā is largely an effort to reconcile the various systems of philosophy by combining them with one another.

The next important division of Sanskṛit literature which claims our attention, is the Purāṇas. These works are still later and belong to mediæval times, but they are important as showing the development of Kṛishṇa worship. It is claimed that they were designed to teach the doctrines of Hindūism in their simplest form.

CHAPTER XXII.

THE PURĀṆAS.

EXTENT OF THE PURĀṆAS—SIGNIFICATION OF THE NAME—THEIR TEACHING—COMPARATIVELY MODERN ORIGIN—THE HARIVAṆŚA—THE BRAHMA PURĀṆA—THE PADMA OR GOLDEN LOTUS—THE VAISHṆAVA OR VISHṆU—BIRTH OF KṚISHṆA—WIVES AND CHILDREN OF KṚISHṆA—DEATH OF KṚISHṆA—THE ŚAIVA—ŚRĪ BHĀGAVATA—THE MĀRKAṆḌEYA—THE AGNI—THE VĀYU—THE BHAVISHYA—THE BRAHMA VAIVARTA—THE LINGA—THE VARĀHA—THE SKANDA—THE VĀMANA—THE KŪRMA—THE MATSYA—THE GARUḌA—THE BRAHMĀṆDA.

AMONG the later forms of Hindū literature are the Purāṇas, which present a comparatively modern field for investigation. They are eighteen in number, besides several smaller productions of a similar kind called Upa or Minor Purāṇas, the general character of which is very much like the larger works.

The Mahā or principal Purāṇas contain about sixteen hundred thousand lines, and when we consider that each minor work also contains many chapters, we realize something of the labor required to examine, index, and translate this enormous mass of literature.

The Hindūs themselves claim (in the Padma Purāṇa), that these books "consisted originally of one thousand million stanzas, but four hundred thousand of them were thought sufficient for the instruction of man, the rest being preserved by the gods." These four hundred thousand stanzas, however, are equal to sixteen hundred thousand lines, and the student certainly has reason to be grateful that the gods kept the greater portion of this literature for their own private benefit.

The theology and cosmogony of these books are largely drawn from the earlier writings; the doctrines which they teach, the institutions which they describe, and a part of the legends which they relate belong to a period long prior to their own compilation.

SIGNIFICATION OF THE NAME, AND OBJECT OF THEIR COMPILATION.

The name Purāṇa signifies old traditional story. These narratives are said to have been compiled by Kṛishṇa-dvaipāyana (the dark-colored and island born), the arranger of the Vedas and the Mahā-bhārata. The object of their compilation seems to have been the checking of the tide of Buddhism by stimulating the worship of Vishṇu and Śiva. In the Mahā-bhārata these deities had been regarded as but little more than great heroes, while in the Purāṇas they are represented as rival gods.

This department of Sanskṛit literature claims to teach mythology and cosmogony, geography and astronomy, chronology and grammar, and sometimes even anatomy and medicine, as well as to give the genealogies of kings; but the main object is evidently the exaltation of Brāhma, Vishṇu and Śiva, in their various manifestations. The Purāṇas are sometimes called a fifth Veda, having been designed to teach the Vedic doctrines to women and the lower caste men, who cannot understand the more complicated works.

THEIR TEACHING.

The pantheism of the Purāṇas is one of their invariable characteristics, but the particular divinity who is at once the source, the substance and the absorber of all things, varies according to the individual choice of the worshiper. According to Sanskṛit writers, these books treat of the "creation and renovation of the universe, the division of time, the institutes of law and religion, the genealogy of the patriarchal families, and the dynasties of kings." The historians were eager, therefore, to learn their contents.

Sir William Jones and others began the Herculean task by the employment of Hindū professors, or pandits, to extract such passages as seemed most likely to give the information sought; but the pandits themselves were not very familiar with the Purāṇas, and the extracts being necessarily left to their choice, European scholars had no means of knowing whether they had made wise selections or not. Another difficulty was the tendency on the part of the pandits to furnish the matter which was described and paid for, whether it could be found in their sacred books or not.

A good illustration of the risk incurred by European scholars in this kind of second-hand study is the well-known case of Lieut. Wilford, who was so cunningly deceived by the pandits (see page 5), and the most charitable conclusion that one can come to in the matter is that M. Jacolliot was victimized in the same way. Our translators soon recognized the fact that there was only one way to arrive at the truth, and the close, earnest work of many years has been productive of magnificent results.

It is true that so far as chronology and direct historical statements are concerned the Purāṇas are of little or no value, but their myths and legends form correct pictures of the times to which they belong. They give us a view of the mythology and religion of this peculiar people, and indirectly reveal much of their true history. They were probably at first the traditionary tales of the poets, who were at once the eulogists and historians of the family. But with the genealogies many myths were blended, and these materials were woven into connected form by later writers. To the mythology, also, systems of cosmogony, geography and astronomy were added. After this the contending sects added to them a mass of absurd fictions, calculated to glorify Kṛishṇa, Śiva, or any other deity who happened to be the favorite of the writer.

COMPARATIVELY MODERN ORIGIN.

The Purāṇas are the work of different generations and of varied circumstances, the nature of which must be conjectured from internal evidence. Probably none of them assumed the form in which we find them earlier than the time of Śankara Āćārya, who flourished about the eighth or ninth century. Of the Vaishṇava teachers, Rāmānuja lived in the twelfth century, Madhwāchārya in the thirteenth, and Vallabha in the sixteenth, and the different Purāṇas seem to have accompanied or followed the innovations of these men, and to have advocated the doctrines they taught.[1]

They are acknowledged by all scholars to be the most modern of the sacred books. Says Wilson: "I believe the oldest of them not to be anterior to the eighth or ninth century of our era, and the most recent of them to be not more than three or four centuries old."[2] Sir Monier Williams says: "The oldest we possess can scarcely date from a period more remote than the sixth or seventh century of our era."[3]

THE HARI-VAṄŚA

is a voluminous work, consisting of sixteen thousand three hundred and seventy-four stanzas, or more than the Iliad and Odyssey combined. It is a supplement to the Mahā-bhārata. "But," says Wilson, "it may be more accurately ranked with the Purānic compilations of least authenticity and latest origin." It is chiefly occupied with the adventures of Kṛishṇa, but it records the particulars of the creation of the world and the dynasties of kings. The compilation is careless and inaccurate, but has been carefully translated into French by M. A. Langlois. It represents Kṛishṇa as frightening away all the inhabitants of Vraja by converting the hairs of his body into hundreds of wolves to harass and alarm them.

It recounts the story of the protection of the cowherds in a storm by Kṛishṇa, who lifted a mountain

[1] Vish. Pur. Int., p. 10. [2] Rel. of Hin., Vol. II, p. 68. [3] Ind. Wis., p. 493.

and held it over their heads until the storm passed over. This narrative is repeated with some variations in several of the Purāṇas. In the Bhāgavata he is represented as protecting the gopīs from the wrath of Indra by holding the elevated mountain on his finger. It appears from this Purāṇa that Indra was enraged with the gopīs and tried to destroy them with a deluge on account of their love for Kṛishṇa, who spent his time with them and finally married a thousand of them.

The Hari-vaṉśa also contains an epitome of the Rāmāyaṇa and many other legends, which are repeated with more or less variation in the different Purāṇas.[1]

THE BRAHMA-PURĀṆA.

The greater portion of this work is devoted to legendary and local descriptions of the greatness and sanctity of particular temples and individual deities. It treats especially of the holiness of Utkala, the country which includes the low range of sand hills, where stands the celebrated temple of Jagan-nāth. It also gives due honor to the worship of the sun and of Mahades.

The adoration of Vishṇu as Jagan-nāth began to flourish in its greatest vigor after the twelfth century of the Christian era. The worship of the sun is also comparatively modern, the great temple known as the Black Pagoda being built A. D. 1241. The internal evidence which the work presents therefore makes it very probable that the Brahma-purāṇa was

[1] Unless otherwise indicated extracts from these works will be made from Wilson's translations.

composed in the fourteenth or fifteenth century after Christ. It must have been after the worship of Jagan-nāth predominated, and before Śiva and the worship of the sun had fallen into disrepute.

THE PADMA-PURĀṆA.

"That which contains an account of the time when the world was a golden lotus (padma) and of all the occurrences of that time is therefore called Padma by the wise." It treats of the primary creation by means of the cosmic egg, as in Manu; the fanciful formation and divisions of the earth; the genealogies of princes; it also explains the means by which moksha, or final emancipation from conscious existence, may be attained. All of these subjects are mingled with myths and legends innumerable, besides an opitome of the Rāmāyaṇa, and many other stories belonging to the earlier Hindū literature.

It admonishes the worship of Bali on the first of the moon's increase. It inculcates the worship of Kṛishṇa as Gopala, the cowherd. Considerable space is also devoted to Rādhā, the favorite mistress of Kṛishṇa, and the holiness of the forest which was the favorite haunt of Kṛishṇa and Rādhā. According to Wilson, the fifteenth century of the Christian era is the highest antiquity that this work can claim.

THE VAISHṆAVA OR VISHṆU-PURĀṆA.

This work contains only about seven thousand stanzas, although it is claimed to be much larger. There are at least seven copies of it extant, and in none of them is there anything to indicate that any portion is wanting. It was evidently written after the Gupta kings, who reigned in the seventh century, as it makes an historical mention of them. It also alludes to the Bauddhas, who were in existence as late as the twelfth century.

These and other facts prove the compilation of this work to have taken place somewhere between the seventh and twelfth centuries, and the approximate date is placed by Wilson at A. D. 1045. Being devoted to Vishṇu, it represents him as the Supreme God. He is spoken of as purusha (spirit), pradhāna (crude matter), and vyakta (visible form).

The course of elementary creation in the Vishṇu-purāṇa, as well as in the others, appears to be taken largely from the Sānkhya philosophy, which was the doctrine of evolution as believed and taught by a certain school of Hindū philosophers more than two thousand years ago. This system claims that pure spirit cannot originate in impure matter, and denies that anything can be produced out of nothing.

The following aphorisms contain a brief exposition of its doctrines. "There cannot be the production of something out of nothing, that which is not cannot be developed into that which is. The production of what does not already exist (potentially) is impossible, as a horn on a man; because there must of necessity be a material out of which a product is developed; and because everything cannot occur everywhere at all times, and because anything possible must be produced from something competent to produce it.[1] Thus

[1] This Sankhya creed is highly suggestive of the doctrines of Epicurus, as expounded by Lucretius, who argues that the world and other

curds come from milk, not water. A potter produces a jar from clay, not from cloth. Production is only a manifestation of what previously existed."[1] But in the Purāṇas the agency operating on passive matter is confusedly exhibited in consequence of the all prevailing doctrine of pantheism and the partial adoption of the Vedānta philosophy which is based upon pure pantheism. Its creed is simply stated in the Ćhāndogya Upanishad as follows: "All this universe indeed is Brahma; from him does it proceed; into him it is dissolved." The Vedānta system has some similarities to the idealism of Plato, and indeed the Hindū Vedāntist fought the Sānkhya theory of evolution very much as did the Grecian philosopher. It is in strict accordance with the Vedānta philosophy and the Purānic doctrine of pantheism that Vishṇu is represented as being "the cause of creation, existence, and end of this world; who is the root of the world and consists of the world."

The creation is referred to, as in the other Purāṇas, as coming from the egg which rested upon the bosom of the waters. This is a widely diffused opinion of antiquity,[2] and it is supposed by Bryant and Faber that the cosmic egg so often alluded to represented the ark floating upon the water. The Vishṇu-purāṇa also

material objects were formed by the coalescing of atoms and primordial seeds. The Epicurean theory was severely criticised by Cicero, who claimed that if a concourse of atoms could produce a world, it ought also to produce temples, houses, cities, and other things which are formed much more easily than worlds. (See De Natura Deorum, II, 37.)

[1] Ind. Wis., p. 89.

[2] Traces of this theory occur amongst the Syrians, Persians, and Egyptians; besides the Orphic egg amongst the Greeks and that described by Aristophanes, a part of the ceremony in the Dionysiaca consisted of the consecration of an egg, which according to Porphyry signified the world.

speaks of the successive creations so often alluded to, and the repose of the Supreme God during the intervals upon his mighty serpent couch in the midst of the deep. It also presents the raising of the earth from the water by the tusks of the great boar, and the churning of the sea of milk for the recovery of the lost ambrosia. It describes at great length the various worlds, heavens, hells, and planetary spheres, and gives the same description of the seven circular continents and concentric oceans that is found in the Mahā-bhārata.

It describes also the arrangement of the Vedas and Purāṇas by Vyāsa, and gives the rules of caste, in which the Purāṇa follows to a great extent the Code of Manu. Book IV. of this immense volume is occupied with lists of kings and dynasties. Book V. corresponds with Book X. of the Bhāgavata-purāṇa, and is devoted to a life of Kṛishṇa. Kṛishṇa is represented as the eighth child of his mother (the first six having been the offspring of a demon) and as originating in a black hair taken from the head of Vishṇu. His mission is to destroy the demon Kaṇsa, who tries to forestall him by killing him in his infancy. This is prevented, however, by his father, who carries him away in the night and exchanges him for another child. Book VI. describes the gradual deterioration of mankind during the four ages and the destruction of the world by fire and water at the end of a Kalpa.

BIRTH OF KṚISHṆA.

On the day of his birth the horizon was radiant with light and happiness, and the waves of the sea joined their music with the songs of the spirits and nymphs of heaven, who danced with joy. The gods walking through the sky showered down flowers upon the earth and the holy fires glowed with gentler flame.

As soon as the child was born, with the complexion of lotus leaves, having four arms and the mystic mark upon his breast, his father and mother implored him as a god to forego his four-armed shape, lest Kaṉsa should know of his descent and slay him.

Vasu-deva, taking the child, went out the same night into the darkness and rain and carried him to a place of safety, while Śesha, the many-headed serpent, followed the father, and spreading his hoods over them protected the infant from the rain. When they passed through the river, with its dangerous rapids and swift current, the waters were stilled and rose not above the knee of Vasu-deva. Coming to the bed of a sleeping mother, who had just been delivered of a daughter, he quickly exchanged the children, and taking the little girl hastened homeward. When the mother, Yaśodā, awoke and found her child (as she supposed) was a son as black as the dark leaves of the lotus, she was greatly rejoiced.

The female infant was placed in the bed of Devakī, and the demon Kaṉsa destroyed it, thereby releasing the goddess who had been born as the babe. Taunting him with his helplessness, and decorating herself with heavenly garlands, she vanished from his sight. King Kaṉsa being greatly troubled, called his chiefs together, and issued a decree that every male child in whom were found signs of unusual vigor should be destroyed.

Kṛishṇa is afterward represented as plunging boldly

into the lake of the serpent king, and conquering him by setting his foot upon the terrible head which had hitherto been unbended. The dying serpent feebly pleads for mercy, and Kṛishṇa allows him to live, but commands him to depart immediately with all his family and followers into the sea. It will be observed that there are some resemblances to the gospels in this Purāṇa, which dates from the eleventh century of the Christian era.

THE WIVES AND CHILDREN OF KṚISHṆA.

According to this authority the first wife of Kṛishṇa was Rādhā; afterward he married Jāmbavati, the daughter of a bear. This marriage was the result of a terrible contest with the father of the bride. Kṛishṇa fought the bear twenty-one days and at last conquered him. The bear then exclaimed, "Thou, mighty being, art surely invincible by all the demons and by the spirits of heaven, earth, and hell. Much less art thou to be vanquished by creatures in human shape, and *still less by such as we who are born of the brute creation.*" Then humbly prostrating himself at the feet of his conqueror, he presented to Kṛishṇa his daughter Jāmbavati as an offering suitable to a guest, and the bridegroom led her away in triumph.[1] Kṛishṇa then married three beautiful girls, and afterward espoused the two daughters of the king of Magadha. He also seized and carried off by violence the beautiful princess Rukminikī.

In Hindū mythology Rāvaṇa, the demon king of Ceylon, was born again as Śiśu-pāla, one of the char-

[1] Vish. Pur., p. 427.

acters of the Mahā-bhārata. He was betrothed to Ruminikī, but Kṛishṇa forcibly carried away the bride and made her his own. Afterward Bhīshma declared that the usual prize awarded to the greatest and strongest of their number was due to Kṛishṇa; but Śiśu-pāla publicly objected to having the award made to a cowherd, who was also a murderer, and after some bitter language on both sides Kṛishṇa "whirled his ćakra furiously at Śiśu-pāla and severed his head from his body." He afterward married not only Ruminikī, but also still later sixteen thousand and one hundred other wives at a single ceremony. We quote from the Vishṇu-purāṇa: "Sixteen thousand and one hundred was the number of the maidens (included in the last marriage), and into so many forms did the foe of Madhu (Kṛishṇa) multiply himself that every one of the damsels thought that he had wedded her in his single person, and the creator of the world—the assumer of universal shape—abode severally in the dwelling of each of these, his wives."[1] It is declared that these wives bore to Kṛishṇa one hundred and eighty thousand sons, and the Bhāgavata-purāṇa gives the names of about eighty members of this numerous family.

DEATH OF KṚISHṆA.

The Vishṇu-purāṇa agrees with the Mahā-bhārata concerning the principal incidents connected with the death of Kṛishṇa. The destruction of his tribe is recounted, and also the particulars of the drunken melee in which the fratricidal Yādavas slew each other. It is here again declared that Kṛishṇa was slain by the

1 Vish. Pur., p. 528.

arrow of a hunter who mistook him for a wild animal, but an additional incident is given to the effect that Kṛishṇa was sitting with one foot resting upon his knee, and the arrow entered the sole of his foot, which was the only vulnerable spot upon his body.

This Purāṇa enumerates twenty-eight hells, one of them being called the Kṛishṇa, or black hell, which is reserved for sinners who live by fraud, or who trespass upon other people's lands. The book closes with a prophecy of the Kali age, when all evil shall be destroyed.

ŚAIVA.

Śaiva gives the genealogies of the patriarchs and descriptions of the universe, mingled with praises of Śiva and the myths and legends of which he is the hero. It also teaches the efficacy of Yoga[1] and the glories of Śiva-pura, or the dwelling of Śiva, with whom the yogi, or devotee, is to be united.

ŚRĪ BHĀGAVATA

is a work of powerful influence in India, controlling the opinions and feelings of the people more than any other of the Purāṇas. It is called Bhāgavata, on account of its being devoted to the glorification of Bhagavat or Vishṇu. It gives a cosmogony which,

[1] The Yoga is considered a branch of the Sankhya system of philosophy, but it appears really to be a sort of penance for the purpose of concentrating thought with the greatest intensity upon the syllable Om, which is sometimes defined to be Brahma, and again, as the representative of all the gods of earth, air, and sky. The most unnatural and painful postures are assumed by devotees, and sometimes persisted in for years. It also includes twistings and contortions of the limbs, suppressions of the breath, and utter absence of mind. The variety and intensity of the various forms of suffering which are self-inflicted upon the devotees, would surpass all credibility if they were not attested by trustworthy evidence.

although in most respects similar to that of the other Purāṇas, is more largely mixed with allegory and mysticism, deriving its tone more from the Vedānta than the Sānkhya philosophy. It contains a variety of legends of a miscellaneous description intended to illustrate the merit of worshiping Vishṇu. There is also an account of the deluge, in which Vishṇu is represented as descending in the form of a fish to guide the ark.

It narrates the history of Kṛishṇa in much the same way that the Vishṇu-purāṇa does, and acknowledges its indebtedness to that work, showing conclusively that it is subsequent to the Vishṇu-purāṇa. The Bhāgavata closes with a series of encomiums on its own sanctity and efficacy to salvation. Mr. Colebrooke says of the work: "I am inclined to adopt an opinion supported by many learned Hindūs, who consider the celebrated Śrī Bhāgavata as the work of a grammarian (Vopadeva) supposed to have lived six hundred years ago."[1] Prof. Wilson and other Orientalists agree with Colebrook in ascribing the Bhāgavata to Vopadeva.

THE MĀRKAṆḌEYA,

containing nine thousand verses, is "That Purāṇa in which, commencing with the story of the birds that were acquainted with right and wrong, everything is narrated fully by Mārkaṇḍeya as it is explained by the holy sages in reply to the questions of Muni." The celestial birds (who were Brāhmans in a previous birth), are represented as answering the following

1 As. Res., Vol. 8, p. 467.

questions: "Why was Vasu-deva born as a mortal?" "How is it that Draupadī became the wife of the five Pāṇḍus?" "Why did Baladeva do penance for Brāhmanicide?" and "Why were the children of Draupadī destroyed when they had Kṛishṇa and Arjuna to defend them?" The account of the creation is also repeated by the birds. This Purāṇa is not easily placed with any degree of certainty, but is supposed to belong to the ninth or tenth century.

THE AGNI.

The Agni or Agneya treats of primitive and subsequent creations, the genealogies of demigods and kings, the reigns of the Manus, the histories of the royal dynasties, and other matters of a very different character. As it is evidently a compilation, its date is of very little importance. It is not unlikely, however, that chapters have been arbitrarily supplied during the last few centuries. For the Agni an ancient Purāṇa called the Vāyu is often substituted.

THE VĀYU.

The Vāyu-purāṇa is so named in consequence, it is said, of having been communicated by Vāyu, the deity of the wind, to the assembled sages. It treats of the families of sages and kings, followed by a cosmogony terminating with the destruction of the world at the end of each Kalpa. While it teaches the doctrine of pantheism, it also allows to the Supreme Being an existence separate from his works, although he appears to be without attributes. The astronomy of this Purāṇa presents the relative sizes and situations of the planets, with their cars and steeds and other appurtenances, revolving around the pole (to which they are attached by cords of air) as the wheel turns on its pivot. Little information concerning its exact age is to be derived from internal evidence, but it is supposed to be one of the oldest of the Purāṇas.

THE BHAVISHYA,

containing fourteen thousand five hundred stanzas, treats of the creation, repeating almost the very words of the first chapter of Manu, the rest of the work being purely a manual of religious rites and ceremonials, although a few legends enliven the series of precepts. It is not very properly called a Purāṇa, and was probably written prior to the Mohammedan conquest.

BRAHMA VAIVARTA.

This is decidedly a sectarian work, and appears to have no other reason for its existence than to induce faith in Kṛishṇa and Rādhā. It is of little value as collateral authority, and the most of its stories are too absurd for repetition. Kṛishṇa is here spoken of as "the sole existent and eternal being—the center of a luminous sphere of immeasurable extent and inconceivable splendor." Vishṇu is represented as coming from his right side and Śiva from his left. Brahmā, who is often spoken of as the Supreme God, is represented as springing from Kṛishṇa. All the gods and goddesses proceed from different parts of his person, and each of them at birth recites a short hymn or prayer in his honor. Brahmā is represented as saying:

"I adore Kṛishṇa, who is free from the three qualities, the one imperishable Govinda, who is invisible and void of form; who is visible and assumed the shape of a cowherd . . . . the lord of the mystic dance, and its performer, and the delighter in the graces of its evolutions." Rādhā, his favorite wife, proceeds from his heart; from the pores of her skin proceed three hundred million gopīs or nymphs, while a like number of gopas, the swains of the nymphs, proceed from the pores of Kṛishṇa's skin, and the cows which these swains are to attend also issue from the pores of Kṛishṇa's skin.

The twenty-eighth and twenty-ninth chapters are devoted to a description of Goloka, the heaven of Kṛishṇa. It is a sphere of light tenanted by gopīs, gopas and cows, the only human beings admitted being the votaries of Kṛishṇa. The author sometimes describes Goloka as being round, and again speaks of it as a square. In one passage he gives it a diameter of thirty millions of yojanas, and in another he extends its circumference to a thousand millions. Indeed, the compiler seems to have paid very little attention to the consistency of the narrative, assigning various origins to the same god or goddess. Thus, Sarasvatī, the goddess of speech, is said in one paragraph to come out of the mouth of Kṛishṇa, and in another is represented as one of the subdivisions of Prakṛiti, and again is spoken of as issuing from the tongue of Lakshmī. These incoherencies are quite characteristic of this Purāṇa, which is full of contradictory repetitions.

According to this work the original and only cause of Kṛishṇa's incarnation was his love for Rādhā, and he came down to the world to be her lover. The incidents of Kṛishṇa's birth, as the eighth child of Vasudeva and Devakī, are narrated in the usual manner; his infant exploits are also recited, and his marriage with Rādhā is said to have been celebrated by the distribution of viands and treasures in large quantities. The incompatibility of such profusion with the financial condition of his foster father Nanda, the cowherd, is apparently not noticed by the author, although the hero of the festivities is represented in the next chapter as stealing the curds, for which he is tied to a tree and whipped by his foster mother, Yaśodā. Kṛishṇa is also represented as carrying off and hiding the clothes of the nymphs while they were bathing in the river.

It is claimed in this Purāṇa that when Vishṇu boasted of being lord of all, he was swallowed by Kṛishṇa, all but his head, but was restored on recovering his senses. Kṛishṇa's marriage with other wives is also narrated. The circumstances of his death by a wound from a hunter, the destruction of his tribe, and the submersion of Dvārakā are also alluded to. This Purāṇa is said to be so sacred that the attentive hearing of one quarter of a verse is equal in merit to the gift of the heaven of Kṛishṇa. Although it is differently classified it appears to be one of the last of the Purāṇas from its own avowal that it was intended to "clear up the discrepancies observable in these works." That it was compiled after the Mohammedan invasion is evident from the allusion that it makes to the supremacy of the Mleććha rulers, and the particular branch of the Hindū system which it advocates makes it very probable that it emanated from a sect which originated about four centuries ago with the Gosains.

THE LINGA

consists of eleven thousand stanzas, and is said to have been originally composed by Brahmā. In the account of creation as given by this Purāṇa, Brahmā and Vishṇu are represented as fighting for the supremacy during the intervals of creation, but the great fiery Linga suddenly springs up and puts them both to shame, as after traveling upwards and downwards for a thousand years neither of them could find its beginning or ending. Upon the Linga the sacred syllable Om is visible, by which Brahmā and Vishṇu become enlightened and acknowledge and eulogize the superior glory of Śiva. Śiva repeats the story of his incarnations (twenty-eight in number), intended doubtless to exceed in number the incarnations of Vishṇu. The work is assigned to about the eighth or ninth century.

THE VARĀHA

is narrated by Vishṇu, as Varāha (the boar), to the personified earth. Like the Linga-purāṇa, this is a religious manual almost wholly occupied with forms of prayer and rules for devotional observances addressed to Vishṇu. There is no leaning to the particular adoration of Kṛishṇa, and there are other indications of its belonging to an earlier stage of Vishṇu worship.

THE SKANDA

is "that in which the six-faced deity (Skanda) has related the events of the Tatapursha Kalpa enlarged with many tales." It is said to contain eighty-one thousand and one hundred stanzas. This Purāṇa has no existence in a collected form, and the fragments in various parts of India which are affirmed to be portions of it aggregate a mass of stanzas even more formidable than has been enumerated. They contain minute descriptions of the temple of Śiva, and a vast number of legends illustrating the holiness of Kāśī. Other portions are devoted to the holiness of Urissa and other localities and temples. It is doubtful what proportion of these fragments properly belongs to the Skanda-purāṇa.

THE VĀMANA

contains an account of the dwarf incarnation of Vishṇu and includes about seven thousand stanzas. It is largely devoted to the worship of the Linga and to the illustration of the sanctity of certain holy places. In the words of a distinguished Orientalist (Wilson) "Its compilation may have amused the leisure of some Brāhman of Benares three or four centuries ago."

THE KŪRMA

is "that in which Jānarddana in the form of a tortoise in the regions under the earth explained the objects of life, duty, wealth, pleasure, and liberation." The greater part of it inculcates the worship of Śiva and Durgā, although it is represented as being given by one of the incarnations of Vishṇu. Its date cannot be very early, for it is avowedly posterior to the establishment of the Tāntrika, the Śātka and the Jain sects, and these were not known in the early centuries of our era.

THE MATSYA.

This Purāṇa, after the usual prologue, opens with the account of how the Matsya, or fish avatar of Vishṇu, preserved a king named Manu with the seeds of all things in an ark from the waters of the great inundation, the story of the flood which was told in one of the Brāhmaṇas, and later in the Mahā-bhārata, being substantially repeated here. The genealogical chapters are much the same as those of the Vishṇu-purāṇa. The work has drawn largely from the Mahā-bhārata; it also quotes the Padma-purāṇa, and is therefore subsequent to that work.

THE GARUḌA.

The greater part of this document is devoted to the description of Vratas, or vows of self-restraint, of holidays, of sacred places dedicated to the sun, and to prayers addressed to the sun, to Śiva, and to Vishṇu. It contains also treatises on astrology, palmistry, and precious stones, and one still more extensive on medicine. There is nothing in this work to justify the name. Garuḍa is the eagle bird (half man) on which Vishṇu rides, and it is possible that there is no genuine Garuḍa-purāṇa in existence.

THE BRAHMĀṆḌA.

"That which has declared in twelve thousand two hundred verses the magnificence of the egg of Brahmā, and in which an account of the future Kalpas is contained, is called the Brahmāṇḍa-purāṇa, and was revealed by Brahmā." This Purāṇa, like the Skanda, is no longer procurable in a collected form, but is represented by a variety of *Khandas* professed to be derived from it. The facility which this state of things affords for imposition is very great, and the Skanda and the Brahmāṇḍa have for this reason sometimes been called "the Purāṇas of thieves and impostors."

The mythology of the Purāṇas is much more developed than that of the Mahā-bhārata, in which Vishṇu and Śiva are apparently regarded merely as great heroes, not having as yet developed into rival gods. Kṛishṇa, who was afterward made so prominent, is not even the hero of the Mahā-bhārata, although he appears as a great chieftain; but as Prof. Lassen has shown, "The real worship of Kṛishṇa is not found before the fifth or sixth century." In mediæval times there was much sectarian feeling between the worshipers of Brahmā, Vishṇu, and Śiva, each sect being jealous of its favorite system and devoted to its favorite god. Hence, the Purānas which were compiled about this time were each of them devoted to the exaltation of the particular deity who happened to be the favorite of the compiler. In modern times Śiva is the most popular object of worship with Brāhmans, while Kṛishṇa is the favorite god of the lower classes. We have here given the briefest possible résumé of the contents and teachings of these productions of mediæval times, and will now consider the mythological hero of the Purāṇas—the god Kṛishṇa.

CHAPTER XXIII.

KṚISHṆA.

A MULTITUDE OF PERSONS NAMED KṚISHṆA—LIFE OF KṚISHṆA, THE SON OF VASU-DEVA—DEATH OF KṚISHṆA—RESEMBLANCES TO CHRISTIAN HISTORY VERY SLIGHT—WORSHIP OF THE "DARK GOD"—SUMMARY.

INTIMATELY connected with the Purāṇas is their hero, Kṛishṇa. The meaning of the word is "dark" or "black," and the frequency with which the name occurs in Hindū literature would seem to indicate that whenever a male child was born with a complexion unusually dark he was named Kṛishṇa, or that in later times he was named for the popular god of the Purāṇas.

The earliest mention of the name in the Ṛig-veda is where a hymn of adoration to Indra praịses that god for having slain the wives of Kṛishṇa.[1]

Afterward the same god is said to have slain fifty

[1] Wilson's trans. Rig-veda Sanhita, Vol. I, page 260.

Sanhita sometimes means collection, and the Rig-veda Sanhita containing one thousand and seventeen hymns, is the oldest and most important collection of the early prayers, invocations and hymns of the Hindus. Sanhita may also mean the words of the Veda euphonically combined instead of separated as in the Pada text. Prof. Wilson's translation is based upon the commentary of the native scholar Sayana. It represents the long line of Vaidic tradition which the Hindus have preserved, and shows the English reader what the natives suppose the Rig-veda to mean. See note to page 23.

thousand Kṛishṇas,[1] all of whom were Rākshasas or demons. Indra is represented as the great protector of his votaries in battle. He defended his Āryan worshipers in all their conflicts; he also punished for the benefit of man those who neglected religious rites. He (Indra) tore off the black skin of the aggressor as if burning with flame; he utterly consumes him who delights in cruelty.'

"Allusion," says the translator, "is here made to the legend that an Asura, named Kṛishṇa the black, advanced with ten thousand followers to the banks of the Amsumatị river, where he committed fearful devastation until he was defeated by Indra, who stripped him of his skin." "The swift moving Kṛishṇa with ten thousand demons stood on the Amsumati; by his might Indra caught him snorting in the water. He (Indra) smote his malicious bands. I have seen the swift moving demon lurking in an inaccessible place in the depths of the river. Indra with his ally smote the godless host as they drew near."[2]

Kṛishṇa, a Ṛishi of Angira, is also spoken of in the Ṛig-veda Saṇhitā. In the Mahā-bhārata the name Kṛishṇā[3] is an epithet applied to the princess Draupadī who married the five Pāṇḍavas. Kṛishṇa-dvaipāyana (the dark-colored, island-born man) was the grandfather of the Kauravas who bore so important a part in the great war, and he is also said to be the arranger or editor of the Mahā-bhārata and the compiler of the Purāṇas, the oldest of which are ascribed

[1] There is no mention in the Rig-veda of any *god* by this name.

[2] Vol. V, p. 192.

[3] The long mark on the final a, indicates the feminine form of the word.

to the sixth or seventh century of the Christian era. The Hindūs have an easy method, however, of disposing of little chronological difficulties of a few centuries by asserting that their heroes are born again as men whenever their services are needed upon the earth. In the Ćhāndogya Upanishad we find a Kṛishṇa who was the son of Devakīputra, but of him nothing is known except that he was a pupil of Ghara. The name was also borne by a son of Havird-hana and by one of the Andhra princes.

In the later forms of Hindū literature we find Kṛishṇa, the son of Vāsu-deva[1] and Devakī, who figured as a great chieftain in the Mahā-bhārata, and during a large part of the Christian era has had divine honors paid to him. Kṛishṇa was also one of the names of Arjuna. In the Mahā-bhārata where the son of Droṇa is said to have entered the camp of the Pāṇdavas at night to avenge his father's death, his progress was arrested at the gate by the gigantic form of Śiva. This god of destruction was robed in a tiger's skin, while his long arms were adorned with bracelets of serpents. His body glowed like the sun, and "hundreds and thousands of Kṛishṇas were manifested from the light issuing from his person." Kṛishṇa-tarkālaṅkāra, a commentator, flourished somewhat later, and Kṛishṇa-misra, the dramatic author, is supposed to have lived in the twelfth century of the Christian era. Kṛishṇa Bahadur was the name of a publisher in Calcutta in 1840. Thus we find that in Hindū literature, the name Kṛishṇa is applied to sixty thousand beings who were demons, "hundreds and thousands" more

[1] There are nine Vasu-devas in Indian literature.

who issued from the god of destruction, as well as to the wife of the five Pāṇḍu princes, and in later times to princes, sages, commentators, editors, publishers, and others too numerous to mention; indeed, it is now the custom to name children for popular gods. The native professor or pandit who lived for five years with Sir Monier Williams in India was named Kṛishṇa-varmā.

LIFE OF KṚISHṆA, THE SON OF VASU-DEVA.

Of this great multitude named "dark colored," the Kṛishṇa who commands the greatest attention is the eighth son of Vasu-deva and Devakī. Of his life there is little or no authentic history, but in later times a vast amount of myth and legend has been built around it.

He belonged to a tribe well known in Hindū history as the Yādavas. These nomadic descendants of Yadu migrated to different localities, grazing their cattle and raising butter for sale to the people around them. It is not known when they first entered Hindūstān, but at the time of Kṛishṇa's birth they appear to have settled near the city of Mathura (afterwards called Muttra) on the banks of the river Jumna, about one hundred and twenty miles south of the city of Hastināpur.

At one time during his early manhood, Kṛishṇa and his companions left their encampment at a rural village near by and paid a visit to the city of Mathura, where it appears that they conducted themselves in a manner entirely consistent with their rough characters, breaking through the royal gate and committing other depredations. It was during a great festival which was attended by raja Kaṉsa the usurper, who was bitterly hated by his subjects. During the festivities a wrestling match degenerated into a disgraceful fight, in which Kṛishṇa and his older brother, Bala-rāma, bore a prominent part. Many men were slain and at last the unpopular raja himself was killed by Kṛishṇa. The rude cowherd became popular from having relieved the city of a tyrant, and an effort was made to ennoble his birth by representing him to have been in reality the son of a chieftain of the tribe.[1]

He eventually became a chief, and is represented as a successful warrior, although rather unscrupulous as to the means employed for the attainment of his ends. For instance, the Great War of the Mahābhārata seems to have turned upon the death of Droṇa, the venerable commander-in-chief of the Kauravas. He had nearly vanquished the Pāṇḍavas by the slaughter of their troops, but Kṛishṇa, knowing of his great love for his gallant son, suggested that word be sent him that his son was slain. The cruel falsehood pierced the brave heart of the father, although the arrows of the foe had failed to reach it, and laying down his arms, he became an easy prey to the Pāṇḍavas. Again, in the desperate single combat between Arjuna and Karṇa, when Arjuna was badly wounded and nearly defeated, an accident to the wheel of his chariot compelled Karṇa to cease fighting, and laying down his arms, he called to his opponent saying, "Hold your hand for a moment, and give me a chance to recover my wheel, for it is no mark of

[1] Wheeler's Hist. of Ind., Vol. 1, p. 469.

manhood to strike at me whilst I am in this extremity." Arjuna temporarily stayed his hand, but being instigated by Kṛishṇa, he severed the head of Karṇa from his body, while the victim was engaged upon the wheel of his chariot.[1] The Mahā-bhārata records still another instance in which Kṛishṇa advised a blow so cowardly that it brought upon the man who gave it the bitter reproaches of his own brother. But the rude and amorous warrior was the Apollo of the cowherds. Handsome, dashing, and vain, this universal lover appealed to the admiration of feeble-minded women everywhere, and around the very slight framework which history furnishes, masses of myth and legend have grown. He is represented as the husband of sixteen thousand wives, and the father of one hundred and eighty thousand sons, while his military exploits have been repeated with wonderful exaggerations and mythical additions.

THE DEATH OF KṚISHṆA.

The incidents connected with the death of Kṛishṇa are as well attested as anything concerning which we are entirely dependent upon Hindū sources for information. The Mahā-bhārata relates the story in careful detail, and it is repeated and corroborated by the Vishṇu-purāṇa and also endorsed by the Brahma-vaivarta-purāṇa.

According to these and other Hindū authorities, Kṛishṇa and the people of his capital city Dvārakā, encamped at a place of pilgrimage upon the sea-shore,

[1] This chapter being somewhat of the nature of a summary necessarily includes a few incidents previously alluded to.

ostensibly for the purpose of paying their devotions to the deity of Dvārakā; but they carried an abundance of wine with their other stores, and feasting and drinking became their chief occupation. There were jugglers, musicians, dancers and actors to furnish entertainment, but the chief attractions were the great jars of wine, and the warriors of the tribe sat down in groups around them. Laughing and jesting being followed by taunts and bitter words, the scene of revelry became a drunken melee, in which the intoxicated men fought each other blindly until the whole tribe was exterminated except Kṛishṇa and one or two others who were not injured themselves, although they had slain their full share of victims. After the disgraceful fight was over, Kṛishṇa found his older brother dead beneath a banyan tree, and going into a thicket near by he sat down in troubled meditation upon the loss of his kindred and the destruction of his tribe. While thus absorbed in his own sad thoughts, he was seen by a passing hunter, who, mistaking him for a wild animal, discharged an arrow and slew him upon the spot.

The Mahā-bhārata gives a description of the funeral rites and pictures the grief of his sixteen thousand widows, five of whom were burned alive upon Kṛishṇa's funeral pile. The story of his death has been repeatedly endorsed by Hindū authorities, as late as the fifteenth century of the Christian era. It cannot, however, be received as history in our sense of the word, as there is really no authentic history in connection with this strange character. The idea that Kṛishṇa was crucified is an extravagant myth of exceedingly modern and quite untrustworthy manufacture.[1]

The Vishṇu-purāṇa, which dates from the eleventh century of the Christian era, states explicitly that "the arrow entered the sole of his foot, which was the only vulnerable part of his body."[2] Hence he was not even transfixed.

RESEMBLANCES TO CHRISTIAN HISTORY VERY SLIGHT.

Very early in the Christian era the story of the cross penetrated India, and Pantænus, who lived about A. D. 180, found there the gospel of Matthew, which had been left with the people by still earlier missionaries.[3]

The royal grants to early Christians, inscribed on copper plates and containing signatures in Pahlavī characters, are still in existence, showing that Christianity had attained a position of some importance there, even during the earlier centuries of the Christian era.

Not only was the story of the Christ carried into India by the early missionaries, but according to Prof. Weber's version of a paragraph in the Mahā-bhārata, it was brought home by the Brāhmans themselves. Both Weber and Lassen interpret a passage in the Mahā-bhārata to the effect that early in the Christian era three Brāhmans visited a community of Christians, and that on their return "they were enabled to intro-

[1] In his foot notes to this chapter Sir Monier Williams writes: "*I know nothing of this absurd myth*," showing that it has never reached the higher circles of scholarship. It is, however, freely circulated in America in the writings of Madame Blavatzky and others. See "Isis Unveiled," etc.

[2] Possibly this idea may have been borrowed from the vulnerable heel of Achilles.

[3] Eusebius, Book V, Chap. 9, p. 10.

duce improvements into the hereditary creed, and more especially to make the worship of Kṛishṇa Vāsu-deva the most prominent feature of their system."[1] In addition to the testimony of these celebrated Orientalists we have much internal evidence in the Mahā-bhārata that "improvements" have been introduced in favor of Kṛishṇa, for the primitive work has been incrusted and overlaid with legends and myths which have his glory for their sole object. It is so evident that these are interpolations of a later date that J. Talboys Wheeler says: "The compilers of the Mahābhārata have so frequently *tampered with the text* for the purpose of associating Kṛishṇa and his family with the Pāṇḍavas that it is difficult to accept statements that have this object in view."[2]

The Brāhmanical compilers, in their anxiety to connect him with the heroes of the Great War, have ignored even the geographical position, and represent the Pāṇḍavas as visiting the Yādava chieftain in his bed-chamber, while he takes a part in their councils as frequently as if he lived in the same city, whereas Kṛishṇa's residence at Dvārakā was on the western coast of the peninsula of Gujarāt, at least seven hundred miles in a direct line from the city of Hastinā-pur. But they could only interpolate incidents and overlay the primitive poem with stories of his marvelous power; they could not make him the hero of the Mahā-bhārata, but only an erratic chieftain who indeed poses sometimes as a god, but whose assumption of divinity is greatly at variance with his personal character.

After the history of Christ had been in the world

[1] Page 279, this volume. [2] Hist. of Ind., Vol. I, p. 68.

for hundreds of years, the Purāṇas, as the Hindūs now have them, made their appearance, and here we find the wildest growth of fancy combined with slight imitations of historical facts. Those which are especially devoted to the exaltation of Kṛishṇa are the Vishṇu, which dates from A. D. 1045, the Bhāgavata, supposed to have been written by Vopadeva, in the twelfth century, the Brahma-vaivarta, which appears to have emanated from a sect called Gosains, about four centuries ago, and the Padma-purāṇa of the fifteenth century.

In these works of the mediæval times, Kṛishṇa's birth is surrounded by wonderful phenomena. The sky is luminous above his head, and the nymphs of heaven sing with joy over the birth of the four-armed child. Raja Kaṉsa appears in the character of King Herod and slays the first six children of Devakī, the mother of Kṛishṇa; the seventh son, Bala-rāma, escapes his hand only by a miracle. Therefore the father takes the infant Kṛishṇa as soon as he is born and carries him away to a place of safety. He is followed by the many-headed serpent Śesha, and the snake protects the babe from the rain by spreading his hoods over him, until the child is exchanged for the daughter of Yaśodā, who is carried back and placed in the arms of Devakī. Kṛishṇa is afterwards represented as conquering the serpent, and in answer to his plea for mercy allows him to live, but commands him to depart with all of his followers into the sea.

The resemblances to Christian history in the life of Kṛishṇa are, however, very slight, even in the most recent forms of Hindū literature; but it must be confessed that others have been added in modern times by men who cannot read a word of Sanskṛit. His name has been spelled Chrishna, or even Christna, apparently for the purpose of confounding the two. He has also been called Yezeus, and sometimes Jezeus for the same reason. But the dishonesty of this course (provided always it is not the result of ignorance) is unpardonable.

The name of Yezeus as an appellation of Kṛishṇa was invented, according to Max Müller, by a fanciful Frenchman,[1] and Richard Collins, in his address before the Philosophical Society of Great Britain, says: "The addition of the name Jezeus to Kṛishṇa has no warrant from any Hindū book that I am acquainted with. It bears no resemblance to any of the many names by which Kṛishṇa is commonly denoted in India, and it is not possible for it to be a transliteration of any imaginable combination of letters, either in Sanskṛit or in any of the dialects of South India."[2]

The statement that Kṛishṇa was born in a cave, that his herald was a star and his presents gold and frankincense, etc., are all the productions of a vivid imagination in *very modern times*. The idea that he was born of a virgin cannot be entertained for a moment by any one who is at all acquainted with the subject, in view of the great prominence given to Kṛishṇa's older brother in Hindū literature.

[1] Prof. Müller writes: "The name Yezeus was invented, I believe, by Jacolliot, and is a mere corruption of Yadu. I answered Jacolliot once (Int. to Sci. of Rel. page 24), but these books hardly deserve notice." (Trans. Vic. Inst., Vol. xxi, page 179.) Sir Monier Williams and Prof. E. B. Cowell of Cambridge think that the name Jezeus may be a corruption of the word Isa, which properly belongs as a title to Siva.

[2] Trans. Vic. Inst., Vol. XXI, p. 174.

In their standard works the statement is repeatedly made, that Kṛishṇa was the eighth child of his mother, and the Vishṇu-purāṇa informs us that her first six children were the offspring of the demon, Hiraṇyakaśipu.[1]

Dr. Leitner, Vice-Chancellor of the University of Punjab, writes that "Kṛishṇa is a half historical character, and the coincidences of his life and that of Christ are too vague to justify the least connection with the narrative regarding Christ, or *vice versa.*"[2]

WORSHIP OF THE "DARK GOD."

In the later forms of Hindū literature, it is claimed that Kṛishṇa came down from heaven to be the lover of Rādhā, and it is in this form that he is most popular, unless we except his wayward childhood. According to the Vishnu-purāṇa, Vishṇu pulled two hairs out of his head, the one being white and the other black, and the white one developed into the son of Rohinā, while the black one entered into Devakī (also a woman of the Yādava tribe) and developed into Kṛishṇa. It is said in the Bhāgavata-purāṇa that "When Kṛishṇa and his elder brother Bala-rāma began to grow, they were dressed in frocks of blue and yellow, and their hair was trimmed like the wings of a crow, and wooden ornaments were hung from their necks, and they had playthings in their hands. One day Yaśodā (his foster mother) was very angry with Kṛishṇa because he would eat dirt, and she took a stick to beat him, but when she came to him he

1 Vish. Pur., p. 498. 2 Trans. Vic. Inst., Vol. XXI, p. 179.

opened his mouth, and she looked in and saw three worlds, and she marveled greatly for a while and then remembered it no more." The picture of Kṛishṇa as the boy thief stealing butter and curds from the cowherds, or carrying off the garments of the bathers, has an irresistible attraction for his worshipers.

Some of his later adventures are too gross for repetition, but they illustrate the low origin of the cowherd, and the disorder and violence which prevailed in his tribe. He is also connected with the horrible rites of Jagan-nāth, and in the festivities of this god the images of Kṛishṇa and his elder brother, Bala-rāma, and also of his sister, Subhadrā, are brought prominently forward.[1] The Padma-purāṇa gives a list of one hundred and eight names of Kṛishṇa to be repeated by the devotee every morning; and the reader will recall that in the Bhagavad-gītā he reveals himself in his glory to Arjuna, whereupon the frightened warrior exclaims, "O god, I see your body, I see you are of countless forms, possessed of many arms, stomachs, mouths, and eyes, on all sides. I see you void of beginning, middle, end. Of infinite power, of unnumbered arms, having the sun and moon for eyes, having a mouth like blazing fire, and heating the universe with your radiance. The three worlds are affrighted, for these groups of gods are entering into you; seeing your mighty form with many mouths and eyes, with many arms, thighs, and feet, with many

[1] Major General Cunningham, who so ably conducted the Archæological Survey of India, has demonstrated that the images of this god and his brother and sister in the Jagan-nath temple at Puri were derived from the three combined emblems of the Buddhist Trinatra.

stomachs and many jaws, all people are much alarmed. And all the bands of kings, together with our principal warriors, are rapidly entering your mouths, fearful and horrified by reason of your jaws. And some of their heads are seen stuck in the spaces between the teeth. As a river's waters run towards the sea, so do these heroes enter your mouths. As butterflies enter a blazing fire, so do these people enter your mouths only to their destruction. Swallowing all these people, you are licking them over and over again from all sides with your blazing mouths."[1]

It is impossible to imagine a greater contrast than that between this description and the simple story of the Christ; but the tedious and unmeaning ceremonies still performed in the presence of the idol are equally suggestive of this contrast. Sir Monier Williams, during a recent visit to India, was allowed to witness the early morning service in a Vaishṇava temple, at Poona, and we give his graphic description of the scene in his own words.

"The idol of the god Kṛishṇa first underwent a process of being aroused from its supposed nocturnal slumbers by the attendant priest, who invoked the deity by name. Then a respectful offering of water in a boat-shaped vessel was made to it. Next the whole idol was bathed in holy water poured over it from a small perforated metal lota. Then the attendant priest standing near, applied sandal paste with his finger to

[1] Bhagavad-gita, Telang's trans., pp 93-95.
In a previous chapter (page 60) attention has been called to the difference in the translations furnished by native and English scholars. The native scholars are inclined to use coarser language than that refined English which comes to us from the pens of such men as Prof. Williams, Max Müller, Dr. Muir, and others.

the idol's forehead and limbs, and taking a brush painted the face with a bright coloring substance, probably saffron. Next, the idol was dressed and decorated with costly clothes and ornaments. Then the priest burnt camphor and incense and moved the lights before the image, at the same time ringing a bell. Then flowers and the leaves of the sacred tulasī plant, were offered, followed by an oblation of food, consisting of cooked rice and sugar. Next, water was taken out of a small metal vessel with a spoon and presented for sipping. The god was supposed to consume the food or feast upon its aroma, receiving at the end of every meal an offering of betel for the supposed cleansing of his mouth, and a spoonful more of water for a second sipping.

"Finally the priest prostrated himself before the idol, and terminated the whole ceremony by putting the god to sleep for the day.

"While he was going through these ceremonial acts he appeared to be muttering texts, and during the whole service a Brāhman was seated on the ground not far off, who intoned portions of the tenth book of the Bhāgavata-purāṇa, descriptive of the life of Kṛishṇa, reading from a copy of the work placed before him. At the same time a band of musicians outside the temple played a discordant accompaniment with tom-toms, fifes, and drums.

"In the evening the process of waking, undressing and redressing the image was repeated, but without bathing. Flowers and food were again offered, prayers and texts were intoned, a musical service was performed and the idol was put to sleep once more."[1]

[1] Brah. and Hin., p. 144.

The fairest estimate of any book or religion is obtained by an examination of its influence upon the lives of men, and it is easy to see that this foolish round of ceremonies before the idol morning and evening can only have a degrading effect both upon priest and people. Indeed, this senseless adoration of the image of Kṛishṇa prevents all moral and intellectual development in his devotees. But far more injurious than idolatry is the worship of an immoral god, and the influence of the boy thief, the dishonorable warrior, or the licentious lover is far more degrading to the people of India than a lifetime spent in dressing and undressing, washing and painting an idol. "Among the Hindūs," says Wilson, "entire dependence upon Kṛishṇa or any other favorite deity, not only obviates the necessity of virtue, but it sanctifies vice. Conduct is wholly immaterial. It matters not how atrocious a sinner a man may be, if he paints his face, his arms, with certain sectarial marks; or if he die with the word Hari or Rāma or Kṛishṇa on his lips, he may have lived a monster of iniquity, he is certain of heaven."[1]

SUMMARY.

In looking over the facts here gathered together, we learn, 1st: That Kṛishṇa worship is nowhere found in the early Vedic writings; that, although sixty thousand Kṛishṇas are mentioned in Wilson's translation of the Ṛig-veda, they are all the names of black demons whose mission is depredation and devastation.

2d. That in the Mahā-bhārata we have the mention of "hundreds and thousands" more which issued

[1] Rel. of Hin., Vol. II, p. 75.

from Śiva, the god of destruction, and in the whole dark multitude of persons who bear this name, we find represented gods and demons, men and devils, warriors and princes, sages and commentators, editors and publishers.

3d. That the light thrown upon the real life of the warrior who was afterwards deified by his admirers, reveals a very unscrupulous character.

4th. That the resemblances to the facts of Christian history are very slight and evidently introduced into Hindū literature in later times.

5th. That the effort to show a similarity between two names of such entirely opposite signification as Christ and Kṛishṇa is of very modern origin, and repudiated by all scholars.

6th. That the revelation of Kṛishṇa's character which was made to Arjuna, is as far from divine symmetry as his conduct was from decent morality.

7th. That the idolatry of the boy thief, the dishonorable warrior, and the licentious lover is utterly degrading to the people of India.

8th. That the fairest estimate of any book or religion is an examination of its influence upon the lives of men, and the worship of this deity with his sixteen thousand wives has not elevated or improved the morals of his devotees. It is certain that much of the pollution and degradation attendant upon Kṛishṇa worship is utterly unfit for description.

And yet Kṛishṇa classes have been formed in prominent cities of the United States and the priests of Hindūism are trying to gain votaries even among civilized people. Certain it is, that if our clean hearted

American women were acquainted with the true character of the cult, they would flee from its contaminating touch. Let them consider the gross immoralities which are boastingly ascribed to Kṛishṇa in their own standard works—let them investigate the unspeakable obscenity which pertains even to the *worship* of the "dark god."

Let them read the Vishṇu-purāṇa (Wilson's translation), which is devoted to the exaltation of Kṛishṇa, and which may be found in our large libraries. Let them study these things from a scholarly and scientific standpoint, then all illusions concerning this cult will quickly vanish, and they can no longer be deceived by wilful misrepresentations made by interested parties.

CHAPTER XXIV.

CONCLUSION.

HINDŪ LITERATURE — HINDŪISM — TEACHING — THE EPIC POEMS — THE PURĀṆAS — VEDIC WORSHIP BETTER THAN IDOLATRY.

WE have now followed the principal line of Hindū literature from its earliest beginnings in the hymns of the Ṛig-veda down to the Purāṇas of the Middle Ages. Having examined the liturgy of the Brāhmaṇas, the mystical philosophy of the Upanishads and the legal code of the Hindūs; having wandered through the tropical luxuriance of their epic poetry and the fanciful cosmogonies of their Purāṇas; having studied the character of their gods from the beginning of their mythology down to Śiva and Kṛishṇa, their most modern deities, we are prepared to appreciate not only the beauties of their literature, but the relative value of their teachings.

HINDŪISM.

The term Hindūism is applied to the complex system of faith which characterizes the modern Hindū thought, and which appears to be a union of Brāhmanism and Buddhism; of theism and polytheism—a system which, although influenced to a certain extent by a purer principle, scruples not to worship still the serpent power, or to mingle the adoration of the fish or the boar with that of the living God.

Nearly two hundred millions of the people of India are bewildered with the strange tenets of a creed which combines the teachings of monotheism with the worship of a multitude of idols—which declares in one paragraph that there is but one god, and still inculcates on every page the veneration of some of the millions of deities in the Hindū pantheon.

The word Hindūism may also be used to indicate the ritualism of that people in its various phases of development from its birthplace in the highlands around the sources of the Oxus river down to the idol temples of to-day, where the modern deities, Śiva and Kṛishṇa, are supposed to hold their court.

Hindūism as the appellation of all their religious thought was born in the early hymns of the Ṛig-veda, those simple pastoral songs, reaching back nearly to the birth of Moses, and living still in the literature of men. The ages which have come and gone since their musical numbers were first breathed upon the still air have enhanced rather than diminished their beauty. The great heart of humanity has ever hungered for the loving touch of the Infinite. Away back in the ages, so near to the morning of time, the children of men saw the sun as he moved on his triumphal march through the heavens, or floated away at evening on a sea of gold and crimson splendor, and they sang the glories of Mitra, the god of day.

When the tropical sun poured down his noonday heat, and the flowers wilted beneath his touch; when the earth was parched and her sands were barren;

when her rivers were low and famine was abroad in the land; then the clouds were gathered in a dark canopy before the sun, and showers were poured upon the thirsting earth, while the sons of the Southland looked upward again and brought their offerings of praise to Indra, the rain god.

When the soft wind passed through the heated air and came laden with the fragrant breath of the orange and mango blossoms they praised the bright Maruts, the breezes with their "dappled steeds" that brought healing unto man.

When night came down and cooled the fevered landscape with her gentle touch, and kissed with her cool breath the burning brow of her worshiper, then he sang of Varuṇa, the sky god, whose countless eyes look down upon the deeds of men.

When the shadows of night fled away before the gray light of morning, the imaginative Hindū dreamed that the dawn was a beautiful woman wearing a robe of silvery cloud and a diadem of tinted pearl. When the crimson sunlight flushed the eastern sky he fancied that her pure face was blushing beneath the kisses of the god of day, and Ushas, the goddess of the morning, wearing her crown of golden light, received his homage.

Thus the early hymns of the Veda were chanted prayer and praise, and Hindūism was brightest and purest at its fountain head. But this simple nature worship multiplied itself in a thousand forms. It was burdened with the liturgy and priestcraft of the Brāhmaṇas, the mystical teachings of the Upanishads, and the cruelty of the Code of Manu. Altars were stained with human blood, and for two thousand years living women were burned upon the dead bodies of their husbands, while innocent babes were thrown to the sacred crocodiles of the Ganges. Beginning with the adoration of the sun and stars, Hindūism sank lower and lower until in the Purāṇas of mediæval times even the conduct of Kṛishṇa is eulogized, and licentiousness becomes a feature of public worship.

TEACHINGS.

We have seen that the earliest hymns of the Ṛig-veda are beautiful songs of praise to the forces and glories of nature, which, however, soon degenerate into the rambling, wearisome liturgy of the Brāhmaṇas with their burden of priestly rule and their cardinal doctrine of pantheism, which claims that God is everything and everything is God; that the gods are nourished by the food which is offered in sacrifice, and without which their deities would perish with hunger.

We have found the Upanishads to be the doctrinal portion of the Veda—a wilderness of mystical speculation with fanciful cosmogonies and theories concerning the origin of man. The main object of the Upanishads appears to be the discovery of some method of escaping from the endless round of transmigration and of resting in the arms of oblivion. To this end is inculcated the virtue of absolute inaction of body and mind. Man is taught that he must neither love nor hate, hope nor fear, for the most complete mental and physical idleness, the utmost freedom from all emotion, is the nearest approach to the heavenly state of complete and eternal unconsciousness, which is the highest spiritual ambition of Hindūism.

It is claimed that he who would attain this perfected state must go through six successive courses of penance, each course to be continued for twelve years, and that during these seventy-two years he must do absolutely nothing except to meditate upon Brahma. If he does not do this in the present life he may perform the necessary penance in some future condition induced by transmigration.

Sir Monier Williams speaks of two devotees whom he saw in India, the one at Gaya and the other at Benares. The arm of the first was entirely withered by inaction, while his motionless fist was so tightly clenched that the nails were growing through the back of his hand. The other "looked like a piece of sculpture, sitting in a niche of the Anna-purna temple, perfectly motionless and impassive, with naked body smeared all over with white ashes, matted hair, and the forefinger of the upraised hand pointing to the heaven to which in imagination he seemed to be already transporting himself."[1]

The epic poems of India, the Rāmāyaṇa and the Mahā-bhārata, also teach the philosophy of self-discipline and mortification until a condition of complete apathy is attained.

There is a constant round of ceremonies, sacrifices, and oblations. There is the worship of monkeys and serpents, of birds and tigers, of elephants and parrots, of the turtle, the crocodile, and a multitude of other animals, as well as trees, plants, and stones. Indeed,

[1] Brah. and Hin., p. 87.

the worship of the women of India at the present day consists largely in walking hundreds of times around a tulasi plant, which is supposed to represent the wife of Vishṇu, or Sītā, the devoted wife of Rāma. Yet, as compared with the endless round of ceremonies, a few years of austerities or enforced idleness is the work which of all others bestows the greatest merit. A condition of entire mental vacuity is represented as being the nearest to complete identification with the one universal spirit, which involves liberation from all personality and consciousness.[1]

The Purāṇas, which claim to be direct revelations from deity, constitute the bible of one of the most modern forms of Hindūism, viz., Vaishṇavism, or the worship of Vishṇu, and the form in which this sect now shows itself principally is in the worship of Kṛishṇa, one of the latest incarnations of Vishṇu. Vaishṇavism is perhaps the most composite of all the religions of India. It seems to teach all forms of Hindūism, regardless of their opposite characteristics: it advocates the claims of one god and also of a multitude; it teaches pantheism and penance, self-mortification and self-indulgence, virtue and licentiousness.

It often advocates monotheism, and at times sets aside all other gods than Vishṇu. The Hindū theist claims that there is but one god, one Being in millions of forms. To this universal spirit, devotion may be

[1] The universal testimony of Hinduism is that the spirit or soul is immortal, but says Prof. Williams, "It is generally better to translate the philosophical terms Atman, Brahman, and Purusha by 'spirit' rather than by soul, because the expression 'soul' is liable to convey the idea of thinking and feeling, whereas pure Atman, Brahman and Purusha neither 'think, nor feel, nor are conscious.'" (Brah. and Hin., note to page 27.)

rendered through thousands of inferior gods; through the ghosts of dead ancestors; through living heroes, animals, and plants; through mountains and stones; through the stars of heaven or the painted idols of earth. Hence, he asserts that whenever any one of the millions of gods in the Hindū pantheon is propitiated by sacrifice or oblations, the Supreme Lord is gratified. But instead of believing "that there is one mediator between God and man," he holds that there are thousands, nay, millions, of mediators, any one of which may be a tiger or a cow, a fish or a serpent, a crocodile or a baboon.

The early Vedic worshiper paid his homage to the sun and moon, but the modern Hindū adores the crocodile, which hides amidst the weeds of the Ganges.

How is the mind of the worshiper fallen, when, instead of offering his praises to the icy brow of the Himālaya, flushed with the rays of the setting sun, he brings his oblation to the serpents that infest the rocks at her feet?

Far better than modern idolatry was their primitive worship of mountain and storm; better than the confused medley of their creeds were the oblations down by the shores of the crested sea; better than warrior worship, their songs of praise to the stars that sweep around the midnight throne; better than the idol temples of to-day were the sacred groves on the foothills of the Himālayas, where the golden eagle circled above the highest crags, and the goddess of the morning, with tinted robe and crown of pearl, smiled down upon her worshiper.

INDEX.

T.